Wake Up and Smell the Coffee -

Lake States Edition

Laura Zahn

Down to Earth Publications
St. Paul, Minnesota

Other books by Laura Zahn:

WAKE UP & SMELL THE COFFEE - Southwest Edition
WAKE UP & SMELL THE COFFEE - Pacific Northwest Edition
WAKE UP & SMELL THE COFFEE - Upper Midwest Edition
Bringing Baby Home: An Owner's Manual for First-Time Parents
Room at the Inn/Minnesota - Guide to Minnesota's Historic B&Bs, Hotels and Country Inns
Room at the Inn/Wisconsin - Guide to Wisconsin's Historic B&Bs and Country Inns
Room at the Inn/Galena Area - Guide to Historic B&Bs and Inns Close to Galena and Dubuque
Ride Guide to the Alaska Railroad with Anita Williams

To Marj Bush

who was one of the first to legitimize
Dessert for Breakfast
and who buys heavy cream by the half-gallon
and doesn't apologize for it

Published by **Down to Earth Publications**
 1032 West Montana Avenue
 St. Paul, Minnesota 55117

Distributed to the book trade by **Voyageur Press**
 123 North Second Street
 Stillwater, Minnesota 55082
 1-800-888-9653 or 612-430-2210

ISBN 0-939301-94-6

Library of Congress Cataloging in Publication Data

Zahn, Laura C., 1957-
 Wake Up and Smell the Coffee - Lakes States Edition.

 Includes index.

1. Breakfasts 2. Cookery 3. Bed and Breakfast Accommodations - Midwest - Directories

TX 733.Z3

Dewey System - Ideas and Recipes for Breakfast and Brunch - 641.52

Cover Illustration by Lynn Fellman, Golden Valley, Minnesota

Maps by Jim Miller, St. Paul, Minnesota

Printed in the USA on partially-recycled, 100% acid-free paper

Printed on
recycled paper

Many thanks to
Kristina Ford, Ann Burckhardt, Tami Johnson, Kathy O'Neill, Mary Zahn,
Jan Kerr, Peg and Jim Stahlman, Denise Anderson and David Karpinski

Special thanks to the innkeepers
for sharing their best recipes and artwork,
for their cooking hints and ideas,
for their contacts and willingness to "spread the word"
and for their enthusiasm and encouragement.

I also thank them for the privilege
of being the "middleperson" in communicating their favorite recipes
to many hungry cooks and readers.

Introduction

How times change.

When I did the first edition of this cookbook in 1988, I needed to obtain recipes from Bed & Breakfast inns in five states to compile enough for the Upper Midwest Edition. Now, six years later, the number of B&Bs in this region has easily doubled, perhaps tripled. This book, the fourth regional U.S. edition and the second one in this neck of the woods, had enough diverse, quality submissions from B&Bs in only three states, and it's the biggest book to date. Not only were there more B&Bs to contact, there were three state associations through which to contact them. And the innkeepers have become more savvy, and, as competent business people, are willing to use an opportunity like this for promotion.

But the more things change, the more they stay the same.

I started these cookbooks because the recipes innkeepers were making for their guests begged to be shared. And there was a lot of information needed about what B&Bs were, how they operated, and who operated them. Those needs still exist today, and I'm still attempting to meet them.

Besides, I still love B&Bs. (And, judging by their phenomenal growth, so do plenty of other folks.) There are lots of ways to explain it, but perhaps it's best illustrated by the driving directions printed in the brochure of one of the B&Bs featured in this book: "In Standish, turn left onto Grove Road, which is on the curve next to the Twisty Freeze. Go north 9 miles to third stop sign, turn right, go 1 mile, turn left, go 2 miles, turn right, go 1 mile, turn left, go 4 miles to Ryan Rd., turn left, go 1 mile to the corner of Clark and Ryan roads." Not the type of thing you'd find on a hotel or motel brochure.

Turns out that particular B&B is within a few miles of where my grandparents had a summer cottage, and where I happily spent two weeks nearly every summer of my childhood. It's also close to a camp where I counseled, and not far from a river I canoed many times. Doing a book on these three states -- one where I grew up and two where I've spent a good deal of my adult life -- is particularly gratifying.

But it's more than that. Michigan, Wisconsin and Minnesota have many things in common. Such as towns named Prescott (one in Wisconsin, one in Michigan), Lake City (Michigan and Minnesota), Hastings (Michigan and Minnesota) and Alma (Wisconsin and Michigan). But most of all, we are the Lake States. Great lakes, inland lakes, *natural* lakes. Clear blue lakes for which people in other parts of the country would give their eyeteeth.

Many of these inns are on lakes or in towns that are "lake towns" (or rivertowns, for that matter). Others are in large towns, quiet neighborhoods or on farms. As is true to the very concept of B&Bs, each of the 125 in this book is different. But wherever they are, whatever accommodations they have, they have one thing in common: they offer an inviting place small enough so guests can lie in bed and "wake up and smell the coffee." Here you can awake to the aroma of Pumpkin Apple Streusel Muffins or Banana Cinnamon Pancakes wafting up the stairs. All the innkeepers herein cook from scratch because they are people who know that food is more than fuel for our bodies, that it can simply say, "welcome," or it can nourish the very soul.

If you can't get to a B&B right away, at least you can bring the pleasures of a B&B breakfast to your own breakfast table. Many of the innkeepers were generous enough to share their most treasured recipes, the ones they make over and over again. My hope is that you will find a few that you, too, will treasure and enjoy over the years. Yes, many things change, but the pleasure we take in eating good food, and in cooking it for those we love, never will. - LZ

Things You Should Know

- Before beginning to cook or bake, please read the entire recipe to find out how hot to preheat the oven, what size pan(s) to grease, or how many hours or days ahead of time the recipe must be started.

- Baking and cooking temperatures are listed in degrees Fahrenheit.

- Remember to preheat the oven to the temperature listed in the recipe before baking.

- Assume that white (granulated) sugar is called for in these recipes when the ingredient listed is "sugar." Powdered (confectioner's) or brown sugar are listed as such. Unbleached flour is listed simply as "flour;" hardly any innkeeper is using all-purpose white (bleached) flour these days.

- Brown sugar is "packed" into the measuring cup, not loose, unless otherwise specified.

- Oatmeal in these recipes means uncooked oatmeal (the terms "oats" or "rolled oats" aren't used because they may mean different things to different people). Usually either "quick-cooking" or "old-fashioned" oatmeal can be used.

- For yeast breads or for preserves and recipes which involve canning, read the package instructions on yeast or pectin thoroughly. You may wish to consult an all-purpose cookbook with detailed instructions for these processes.

- Recipes have been listed in chapters according to the way in which innkeepers serve them. For instance, you will find some fruit dishes in chapters other than "Fruits," and dishes that could be suitable as "Dessert for Breakfast" are included in other chapters because the innkeepers serve them as snacks, holiday fare or even entrees. The longer table of contents, therefore, also serves as an index so you can double-check other chapters at a glance. An index to major ingredients is in the back.

- While the format of the recipes has been standardized, the directions remain in the words of the innkeepers as much as possible.

- Innkeepers had the opportunity to double-check and re-test their recipes before printing. Not all recipes were tested by the author. While "tester's comments" appear on many recipes, some recipes were tested but no comment was made simply because none was necessary. Testing was done in a non-commercial home kitchen.

- "From-scratch" recipes were solicited. Recipes which were submitted but contained a number of pre-packaged ingredients, or which were tested and turned out really awful, were rejected. Also, only inns with guestrooms and kitchens in the same building -- places where guests literally can wake up and smell the coffee -- were included. Inns were members of their state B&B association when solicited. For information on the associations and their standards, see addresses on page 254.

- Most innkeepers encouraged experimentation with their recipes, such as substituting or adding ingredients for personal preferences or health reasons. Many of these recipes, they said, were devised through their experimentation with a basic recipe.

- Before eating the food being prepared, cooks are urged to make sure any dishes using egg yolks or egg whites are heated to at least 160 degrees Fahrenheit, which is necessary to kill salmonella virus that may be present in raw eggs, or to use pasteurized eggs, which may be purchased in small cartons in the dairy sections of many grocery stores.

Contents by Chapter

Contents

Fruits

Entrees

Eggs:

French Toast:

Pancakes:

Holiday Fare

Dessert for Breakfast

Other Favorites

Index

Contents by Inn

Travel Information

Order Form

About the Author

MICHIGAN

1. Union Pier - *The Inn at Union Pier*
2. Lakeside - *The Pebble House*
3. St. Joseph - *South Cliff Inn B&B*
4. Jackson - *Summit Place B&B*
5. Brooklyn - *Chicago Street Inn*
6. Ann Arbor - *The Urban Retreat B&B*
7. Fennville - *The Kingsley House*
8. Saugatuck - *Wickwood Country Inn*
9-10. Holland
    Dutch Colonial Inn
    The Parsonage 1908
11. Fruitport - *Village Park B&B*
12. Alma - *Candlelight Cottage B&B*
13. Frankenmuth - *Bed & Breakfast at The Pines*
14. Bay City - *Stonehedge Inn B&B*
15. Sebewaing - *Rummel's Tree Haven B&B*
16. Prescott - *Duncan's Country B&B*
17. Houghton Lake - *Stevens' White House on the Lake*
18. Pentwater - *The Pentwater Inn*
19. Ludington - *The Inn at Ludington*
20. Frankfort - *Morningside B&B*
21-23. Traverse City
    Cherry Knoll Farm B&B
    Linden Lea on Long Lake
    Victoriana 1898
24. Suttons Bay - *The Cottage B&B*
25. East Jordan - *Easterly Inn B&B*
26. Boyne City - *Duley's State Street Inn*
27. Mackinac Island - *Cloghaun B&B*
28. Champion (Lake Michigamme) - *Michigamme Lake Lodge*
29. Big Bay - *Big Bay Point Lighthouse B&B*

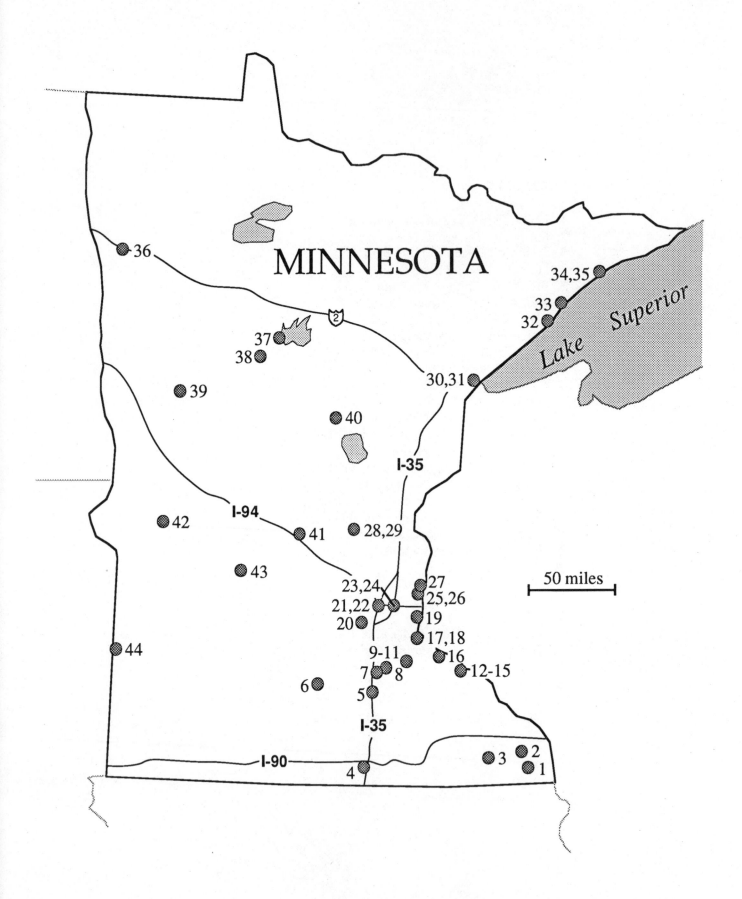

MINNESOTA

1. Caledonia - *The Inn on the Green*
2. Houston - *Addie's Attic B&B*
3. Lanesboro - *Cady Hayes House B&B*
4. Albert Lea - *The Victorian Rose Inn*
5. Faribault - *Cherub Hill B&B*
6. St. Peter - *Park Row B&B*
7. Dundas - *Martin Oaks B&B*
8. Northfield - *Dr. Joseph Moses House B&B*
9-11. Cannon Falls
 Candlewick Country Inn
 Country Quiet Inn B&B
 Quill & Quilt
12-15. Lake City
 Evergreen Knoll Acres
 The Pepin House
 Red Gables Inn
 The Victorian B&B
16. Red Wing - *Hungry Point Inn*
17-18. Hastings
 A Country Rose
 Thorwood and Rosewood Inns
19. Afton - *Afton Country B&B*
20. Chaska - *Bluff Creek Inn*
21-22. Minneapolis
 1900 Dupont
 Evelo's B&B
23-24. St. Paul
 Chatsworth B&B
 Prior's on Desoto

25-26. Stillwater
 Heirloom Inn B&B
 The Rivertown Inn
27. Marine on St. Croix - *Asa Parker House*
28-29. Princeton
 Oakhurst Inn B&B
 Rum River Country B&B
30-31. Duluth
 A. Charles Weiss Inn
 The Ellery House B&B
32. Silver Bay - *The Inn at Palisade*
33. Little Marais - *The Stone Hearth Inn*
34-35. Lutsen
 Caribou Lake B&B
 Lindgren's B&B
36. Crookston - *Elm Street Inn*
37. Walker - *Tianna Farms B&B*
38. Nevis - *The Park Street Inn*
39. Vergas - *The Log House on Spirit Lake*
40. Deerwood - *Walden Woods B&B*
41. Cold Spring - *Pillow, Pillar & Pine Guest House*
42. Morris - *The American House*
43. Spicer - *Spicer Castle B&B Inn*
44. Hendricks - *Triple L Farm*

Lake Superior

Lake

40,41

39

43 42
44
38
37
45
36

WISCONSIN

46
47
49-51 48
52

I-94

33,34
35

32
31 30
26-29
25
24

23

2 3,4
5
6 7 8 9
10

11,12
13
14
17 I-94
15
16 I-90 18 19
1

22
21
20

50 miles

WISCONSIN

1. Cassville - *The Geiger House*
2. West Salem - *Wolfway Farm B&B*
3-4. Sparta
    The Franklin Victorian
    Just-N-Trails
5. Ontario - *The Inn at Wildcat Mountain*
6. Viola - *The Inn at Elk Run*
7. Reedsburg - *Parkview B&B*
8. Wisconsin Dells - *Historic Bennett House*
9. Portage - *The Inn at Grady's Farm*
10. Baraboo - *Pinehaven B&B*
11-12. Plain
    The Bettinger House
    The Kraemer House
13. Spring Green - *Hill Street B&B*
14. Madison - *Annie's B&B*
15. Belleville - *Abendruh B&B Swisstyle*
16. Albany - *Oak Hill Manor B&B*
17. Fort Atkinson - *The Lamp Post Inn*
18. East Troy - *Greystone Farms B&B*
19. Kansasville (Racine County) - *The Linen & Lace B&B*
20. Mequon - *The Sonnenhof B&B Inn*
21. Cedarburg - *The Stagecoach Inn B&B*
22. Port Washington - *Port Washington Inn*
23. Plymouth - *Yankee Hill Inn B&B*
24. Two Rivers - *Red Forest B&B*
25. Algoma - *Amberwood Inn*
26-29. Sturgeon Bay
    The Inn at Cedar Crossing
    The Scofield House B&B
    White Lace Inn
    Whitefish Bay Farm B&B

30. Baileys Harbor - *The Potter's Door Inn*
31. Ephraim - *The French Country Inn of Ephraim*
32. Sister Bay - *The Wooden Heart Inn*
33-34. Stevens Point
    Dreams of Yesteryear
    The Victorian Swan on Water
35. Wisconsin Rapids - *The Nash House B&B*
36. Crandon - *Courthouse Square B&B*
37. Phillips - *East Highland B&B*
38. Lac du Flambeau - *Ty-Bach B&B*
39. Montreal - *The Inn*
40-41. Bayfield
    Cooper Hill House
    Old Rittenhouse Inn
42. Hayward - *The Mustard Seed B&B*
43. Springbrook - *The Stout Trout B&B*
44. Spooner - *Aunt Martha's Guest House*
45. Cumberland - *The Rectory B&B*
46. Osceola - *Pleasant Lake Inn*
47. Houlton - *Shady Ridge Farm B&B*
48. Hammond - *Summit Farm B&B*
49-51. Hudson
    The Grapevine Inn
    Jefferson-Day House
    Phipps Inn
52. Prescott - *The Oak Street Inn*

Why start the morning with the same old (boring) glass of orange juice? B&Bs break all the rules for the morning eye-opener. Many B&Bs serve a variety of unusual juices or stir a little almond-flavored liqueur into the morning coffee. Some even have a special house-blend of fresh-roasted coffee beans. Read on to see how some innkeepers add variety, as well as nourishment. Local ingredients -- tart cherries, apple cider, fresh vegetables and fruits, even rhubarb -- go into a number of their favorite concoctions. Whether it's an iced cappuccino on a sultry summer morning or a mug of hot spiced cranberry punch on a cold winter day, innkeepers do their best to make even beverages special.

Beverages

Cherry Delicious

Ingredients:

2 cups pitted, unsugared, frozen tart red cherries
About 2 cups milk
2 tablespoons sugar
Dash of nutmeg
3 scoops vanilla ice cream

- Place cherries in a food blender.

- Add enough milk to cover cherries (milk should be at the 2-cup level in the standard blender container).

- Add sugar and nutmeg.

- Cover container and blend at high speed until smooth, stopping to scrape down sides of container as needed.

- Add ice cream and blend again at high speed until thick and thoroughly combined.

- Pour into four goblets and serve immediately, or store blender container in freezer for up to 5 minutes, and then serve.

Tester's Comments: This is a good excuse to have your ice cream early in the day!

Makes 4 servings

from **Whitefish Bay Farm B&B**
3831 Clark Lake Road
Sturgeon Bay, WI 54235
414-743-1560

The Door County cherries for this eye-opener come from Gretchen and Dick Regnery's own cherry orchard. Before guests start their day, their all-you-can-eat farm breakfast includes some type of fruit, and this recipe is a favorite. Guests sip or spoon it from crystal goblets set at the dining room table.

Regnerys were not always cherry growers. They were not even farmers. They had administrative jobs in Milwaukee that kept them "tied to a desk," so they started a search for a small farm and art gallery. Their goal was to raise sheep and exhibit Dick's photography and Gretchen's parent's weaving. A B&B seemed a good possibility, too. "The perfect farm came with a newly planted cherry orchard, so we learned yet another skill." The 1908 American Foursquare farmhouse on the 80-acre farm took eight years to completely restore and turn into a B&B with four guestrooms.

Other Whitefish Bay Farm B&B recipes:
Heavenly Bananas, page 126
Oatmeal Surprise Pancakes, page 166

Cider Cream

Ingredients:

1 quart vanilla ice cream
1/2 gallon (4 cups) apple cider (not apple juice)

Also

Cinnamon

- Scoop about 2 cups of ice cream into a standard blender container.
- Cover with about 2 cups of cider.
- Put the top on the blender and blend until smooth.
- Pour into serving glasses and sprinkle top with cinnamon. Repeat with remaining ingredients.

Makes 4 large servings

from **Wolfway Farm B&B**
W2105 County Road B
West Salem, WI 54669
608-486-2686

"Cider Cream was suggested to me by the owners of a local orchard," said Dianne Wolf. Since she and Dave, her husband, run a dairy farm, it was the perfect cooperative promotion for dairy and apple products -- plus it's delicious and guests love it.

Wolfway Farm opened as a B&B in 1989, the same time the LaCrosse River State Bike Trail opened. The trail runs to within 100 feet of the farm, and the farm is located midpoint on the 21.5-mile trail. The LaCrosse River trail connects with two other bike trails, one in Sparta and one in LaCrosse, so the B&B is attractive for both serious and slow bikers.

But Dianne has found many guests come just to visit a working farm. "Many people no longer have any contact with a farm background," she said, and want to take a tour.

The 560-acre operation is a modern dairy farm, so perceptions of "Old MacDonald's Farm" quickly vanish. Modern milking equipment and farm machinery fascinate guests, she said. She enjoys helping to educate people about Holsteins and what farming in the '90s is really like.

Their farm was homesteaded by Dave's family in the 1850s. The large house was built in the 1920s. It was constructed with room for hired help, so two upstairs bedrooms and a basement apartment where employees once lived have been turned into guestrooms. Guests enjoy a "full country breakfast" with eggs, pancakes or French toast, meat and fruit breads or coffeecake. Guests are served in the large farm kitchen.

Iced Cappuccino

Ingredients:

    4 cups double- or triple-strength gourmet coffee
    1/4 cup sweetened condensed milk

- Brew coffee to the desired "strength."
- Cool coffee to room temperature in a covered quart jar.
- Refrigerate coffee.
- In a standard blender container, blend coffee and sweetened condensed milk until frothy. "It is a bit on the sweet side, so you can adjust the sweetened condensed milk to your taste."
- Pour into tall glasses filled with ice and serve.

Makes 4 servings

from **Summit Farm B&B**
1622 110 Avenue
Hammond, WI 54015
715-796-2617

Iced cappuccino is perfect on a hot summer day, say Innkeepers Laura and Grant Fritsche. They obtained the recipe from a friend who asked for it in a favorite Turkish restaurant in Washington, D.C., then the Fritsches modified it to fit their needs and tastes, Laura said.

Laura describes their inn as "a family-oriented B&B." The farmhouse was built in 1910, and Fritsches purchased it in 1985. It took six years of loving restoration before they opened their two guestrooms. "We tried to keep as much history in the house as possible," she said, noting that the plumbing and wiring systems are thoroughly modern.

Breakfast here often features some fresh fruit or vegetables from their garden or orchard. Even the fruit syrup might be homemade. Guests might be served a fresh fruit salad or fruit and cheese plate, French toast or an oven pancake, sausage or ham, and a fruit slush or gourmet coffee. In addition to the food, the country pastel and floral decor with family antiques in all the rooms helps guests relax and enjoy country living.

"Country living" includes visiting with the sheep, chickens, ducks "and a fine assortment of kittens," Laura said. The Fritsches have seven acres located down a quiet country road, and guests are welcome to enjoy the property. The B&B is 30 minutes from the Twin Cities area and close to Willow River State Park for fishing, swimming, hiking and cross-country skiing.

Another Summit Farm B&B recipe:
Crab Apple Butter, page 106

Orange Froth

Ingredients:

    1 cup milk
    1 cup water
    1 6-ounce can frozen orange juice concentrate
    1 teaspoon vanilla extract
    1/4 cup sugar
    10 ice cubes

Also:

    1 6-ounce can pure, unsweetened pineapple juice, optional
    Nutmeg

- In a standard blender container, combine milk, water, orange juice concentrate, vanilla, sugar and ice cubes.
- Blend at high speed for about 30 seconds or until the ice cubes are crushed.
- This serves five. If a little more is needed, add a little pineapple juice and a few ice cubes, then blend again.
- Pour into five (or six) goblets. Sprinkle or grate a little nutmeg on top for garnish and serve.

Makes 5 servings

from **The Kraemer House**
1190 Spruce Street
Plain, WI 53577
608-546-3161

Gwen Kraemer's icy eye-opener awaits guests at the dining room table, though hot coffee and freshly-baked cookies already greeted them in the upstairs hallway. Gwen makes sure the coffee is set near the four guestrooms for early-risers or those who need "a cup of Joe" right away.

Located just seven miles from Spring Green in the village of Plain, the Kraemer House has been open since 1982. Gwen was approached by local tourism officials about opening her home to accommodate overflow crowds attending the Shakespearean festival at Spring Green's American Players Theater or visiting the House on the Rock. Gwen and Duane, her husband, opened a couple of rooms on key weekends only.

But Gwen soon found she was cut out for innkeeping, and they now offer four guestrooms, decorated in Laura Ashley linens and family antiques. Gwen tries to offer something special to travelers, right down to terry robes and complimentary chocolates, made by a Haywood chocolatier.

Another Kraemer House recipe:
Soft Sugar Cookies, page 197

Rhubarb Juice

Ingredients:

Fresh rhubarb stalks
Water
Sugar
Apple, cranberry, pear, peach or orange juice

- Wash rhubarb and cut into 2-inch pieces.
- Place rhubarb pieces in a large kettle. Add enough water to just cover the stalks.
- Boil for approximately 15 to 20 minutes or until the stalks are mushy.
- Strain the juice through cheesecloth, then discard or compost the stalks.
- Add 1/2 cup sugar to each quart of strained juice. Stir well.
- Mix equal amounts of rhubarb juice with apple, cranberry, pear, peach or orange juice. Cover and refrigerate until serving time.

Tester's Comments: For sweet spring rhubarb, 1/4 cup sugar per quart is plenty. Orange juice was a good mixer.

from **The Geiger House**
401 Denniston Street
Cassville, WI 53806
608-725-5419

"We can't give our guests *rhubarb* to drink," Penny and Marcus Neal remember thinking when Penny's mother suggested Rhubarb Juice as a way to use up the prolific rhubarb they inherited when they bought the inn. "Nevertheless, my mother gave us some Rhubarb-Peach to try. We placed it on the table one morning, not telling guests what it was and secretly hoping that they would not ask," Penny said, admitting she and her husband are not rhubarb fans. "It was surprisingly delicious and very well received." Today it's a breakfast specialty about which they proudly tell others.

Rhubarb isn't the only thing Neals "inherited" when they bought this 1855 Greek Revival home in 1992. Cherry, apple and plum trees bloom in the backyard, and their fruit is often used in recipes. The front is just steps away from the Mississippi River, and a ferry boat crossing to Iowa operates nearby.

Neals offer four guestrooms to travelers who want to unwind in a sleepy river town -- Neals themselves stepped out of life in the fast lane to become innkeepers here. They found the Geiger House on one of their travels to the area, heard it was for sale and "couldn't let this opportunity slip by."

Other Geiger House recipes:
Black Olive Quiche, page 137
Hearty Sausage with Apples, page 230

Rhubarb Punch

Ingredients:

8 cups diced fresh rhubarb stalks
5 cups water
Sugar
1-1/2 cups orange juice
1/4 cup lemon juice

Also:

1 cup pineapple juice, optional
Red food coloring, optional
Clear soda pop, such as 7-Up
Vanilla ice cream, optional

- In a large kettle, simmer the rhubarb in water until it is quite mushy.
- Strain and measure the juice. Put the juice back in the large kettle and discard the stalks.
- Add up to 1/4 cup sugar for each cup of juice, depending on sweetness desired.
- Stir well and simmer until sugar is dissolved. Then remove from heat and cool.
- Mix in the orange, lemon and optional pineapple juices and a drop or two of red food coloring.
- The mixture can be frozen at this point. Or refrigerate until serving.
- To serve, fill a glass two-thirds full with rhubarb juice, one-third with soda pop. Add a scoop of vanilla ice cream, optional, for a rhubarb float.

Tester's Comments: Soda makes this light and spritzer-like. Be careful of adding too much sugar.

Makes about 12 one-cup servings

from **Parkview Bed & Breakfast**
211 North Park Street
Reedsburg, WI 53959
608-524-4333

"I got this recipe from my mother and made it for my family for years," said Innkeeper Donna Hofmann, who's changed the recipe somewhat. "When rhubarb is plentiful, I make several batches and freeze it to enjoy later."

Donna has risen to the challenge of running a B&B and restoring an 1895 Queen Anne house. Built by a family who owned a hardware store, the original woodwork and door knobs and other fine touches remain. But Donna, Tom, her husband, and their three teens have removed the shag carpet, suspended ceilings and florescent lights added later. Using 40 double rolls of wallpaper inside and more than 40 gallons of primer and paint outside, they opened their home as a four-guestroom inn in 1989.

Another Parkview B&B recipe:
Dorothy's Easy Kringle, page 38

Spiced Cranberry Punch

Ingredients:

    9 cups cranberry juice
    9 cups pineapple juice
    4-1/2 cups water
    Dash of salt
    5 cinnamon sticks, broken into pieces
    1 teaspoon cloves, ground

Also:

    Brandy, optional

- In a 30-cup "industrial" percolator coffee pot (or a large kettle), mix cranberry juice, pineapple juice and water.
- Place salt, cinnamon sticks and cloves in the basket of the coffee pot (or in cheesecloth, with the ends tied together to make a bag).
- Heat or "perc" thoroughly.
- Pour into mugs and serve piping hot. Brandy may be served "on the side."

Makes 22 one-cup servings

from **Cherub Hill B&B**
105 Northwest First Avenue
Faribault, MN 55021
507-332-2024

This recipe "not only tastes great, but the aroma as it brews makes the whole inn smell wonderful," said Innkeeper Kristi LeMieux.

Kristi and Keith, her husband, opened three guestrooms in this Queen Anne Victorian home after two years of restoration and research. They found that Cherub Hill was the retirement home of Jonathan Noyes, the first headmaster at Faribault's School for the Deaf, which is still operating today. It was designed for him by Olaf Hanson, believed to have been America's first hearing-impaired architect. The lovely parquet floors, oak woodwork and stained glass windows are original.

"Running the B&B has been a perfect way for us to share our love of this historic house and town with others," Kristi said. Guests will find a full cookie jar, locally made chocolates on their pillow and fresh fruit on the dining room table. In addition to the Sakatah Singing Hills State Bike Trail, Faribault is home to famous Faribo Blankets, Treasure Cave Blue Cheese and the Tilt-a-Whirl. Guests can shop for antiques or outlet mall bargains.

Another Cherub Hill recipe:
Strawberry Soup, page 133

Tomato Vegetable Juice

Ingredients:

1 peck (1/4 bushel) ripe tomatoes
1 large green pepper
1 large onion
4 tablespoons brown sugar, loosely packed
2 tablespoons salt
1 tablespoon celery salt
1 tablespoon paprika

Wash tomatoes and remove stems, then cut each in half. Wash, core, seed and chop pepper. Peel and chop onion.

In a large kettle over medium heat, stir and cook tomatoes, pepper and onion, smashing tomatoes with a potato masher. Cook until vegetables are very soft.

Put vegetables through a sieve or colander. Return juice to the kettle.

Mix brown sugar, salt, celery salt and paprika into the juice. Bring to a boil, stirring often, then simmer for 5 minutes.

Pour juice into quart bottles or fruit jars and freeze or process, following safe canning procedures.

Makes about 5 quarts

from **The Bettinger House**
855 Wachter Avenue
Plain, WI 53577
608-546-2951

This juice is a way to save the flavor of ripe summer tomatoes all year. Innkeepers Marie and Jim Neider might serve it to guests along with a fruit cup, homemade breads and rolls and applesauce and cheese.

"Jim and I and some friends thought this house would make a great B&B," said Marie. "It was my grandmother's house and it held such memories for me and my family." Her grandparents, Elizabeth and Philip Bettinger, hosted traveling entertainers and medicine peddlers in this brick Victorian farmhouse. Later, Elizabeth ran a boarding house, serving both breakfast and dinner, and Marie grew up next door.

But the 1904 structure needed major work. "It took us four solid months of night and day work to replace all the walls, ceilings, fixtures, electricity and plumbing," Marie said. They opened in May 1987 and have six guestrooms. The work agreed with them so well they restored a Queen Anne-style home in nearby Spring Green two years later. It's known as Hill Street B&B.

Very Berry Orange Juice

Ingredients:

1 6-ounce can frozen orange juice concentrate, thawed
1 10-ounce package frozen strawberries, thawed
Cold water to fill a standard food blender, about 3 cups

- Pour juice, berries and water into a standard blender container.
- Cover and blend until well-mixed and starting to get fluffy.
- Pour into six goblets or juice glasses and serve immediately.

Makes 6 servings

from **Park Row Bed & Breakfast**
525 West Park Row
St. Peter, MN 56082
507-931-2495

"This recipe comes from gourmet cook Karen Torp of Edina. It's a lovely color," said Innkeeper Ann Burckhardt. "Transform it into punch if you wish." She notes that the least expensive strawberries are OK since they'll be blended, but warns not to try this juice in a food processor.

Blended juice is always served in wine glasses as part of the large breakfast for Park Row guests. Ann knows many of her guests come to her B&B because of her distinguished career as a food writer at the Star Tribune of the Twin Cities, and she aims to make breakfasts memorable. Standard fare also includes a hot egg dish, a hot bread and a fruit dessert -- and that's a hot dessert in winter, or perhaps a fresh fruit parfait in summer.

But Park Row hospitality doesn't stop at the table. Guests are invited to browse through Ann's cookbook library. The four guestrooms all have thick comforters on queen-sized beds. The help-yourself cookie jar is always full.

Ann opened St. Peter's first B&B in early 1990 in this gingerbread-trimmed Carpenter Gothic home. "I got into innkeeping because I needed a new challenge after many years in food writing," a job she continues four days a week in the Twin Cities, 66 miles away.

"Visits to B&Bs all over Britain prompted the idea," which was encouraged by her daughter. Friends say combining her home economics background, food writing and innkeeping all made perfect sense, and "everything fell into place," Ann agrees.

Other Park Row B&B recipes:
June-Time Conserve, page 109
Cheese Omelette Oven-Style, page 140

Coffee is enjoying such popularity recently that an explosion in interest in coffeecakes can't be far behind. Many of these tantalizing coffeecakes fill the whole house with a comforting aroma of cinnamon or apples and rouse anyone with half a sweet-tooth straight out of bed. The best thing about coffeecakes may be that it's socially acceptable to eat them for a first or main course rather than holding off until dessert. Some of these recipes can be stirred up in no time at all. A few contain yeast or have dough that needs to be rolled out, taking a bit more time. Either way, the results are mouthwatering -- and they can do double duty for dessert or tea, as well as breakfast or brunch.

Coffeecakes

Apple Harvest Strudel

Ingredients:

Dough:
- 2-1/2 cups flour
- 1 cup sour cream
- 1 cup butter, softened

Filling:
- 2 Granny Smith apples, peeled, cored and chopped
- 1/2 cup raisins
- 1/2 cup sugar
- 1/2 teaspoon cinnamon
- 1/4 teaspoon nutmeg
- 1/2 cup chopped pecans or walnuts

Also:

Powdered sugar

🍂 For dough: With an electric mixer, beat flour, sour cream and butter. Remove from bowl and knead on a floured surface until smooth and elastic. Then wrap tightly in plastic wrap and refrigerate overnight.

🍂 For filling: Place apple slices, raisins, sugar, cinnamon, nutmeg and nuts in a saucepan. Stir and cook over medium low heat until apples soften.

🍂 Separate dough into 3 parts. On a lightly floured surface, roll the first third out until it is about 1/4-inch thick ("it should make a rectangle approximately 8 x 12 inches").

🍂 Divide filling into thirds. Lightly spread one third over the entire rectangle ("it will spread when cooking"). Roll up jelly-roll fashion, starting with the long side.

🍂 Move the strudel to a greased cookie sheet. Repeat with other two sections of dough. Bake in a preheated oven at 350 degrees for 20-30 minutes or until strudel is golden brown (or freeze the unbaked strudels at this point).

🍂 Remove from the oven, cool slightly and slice diagonally. Dust with powdered sugar.

Makes 36 slices, 12 per strudel

from **Cloghaun Bed & Breakfast**
On Market Street   P.O. Box 203
Mackinac Island, MI 49757
906-847-3885

Apple Harvest Strudel is always a favorite on the all-you-can-eat breakfast buffet at this B&B each morning. "Every day we have bagels and croissants as well as at least two fresh-baked items, fresh fruit" and beverages, said Innkeeper Dorothy Bond, who runs the inn seasonally with her husband, Jim.

Cloghaun, Gaelic for "Land of Little Stones," is an 1884 Victorian-style two-story home, built by Jim's great-grandparents to house their large family. Jim and Dorothy spent three years restoring the home and now offer 10 guest-rooms to travelers who want the peace of being one block from the ferry dock, yet close to the car-free island's many popular attractions.

🏠 *Another Cloghaun B&B recipe:*
Apple Raisin Oat Bran Muffins, page 50

Apple Walnut Coffeecake

Ingredients:

6 tablespoons butter, softened
3/4 cup sugar
1 egg
1 teaspoon vanilla extract
1 cup buttermilk, divided
2 cups flour
2 teaspoons baking powder
1/2 teaspoon salt
2 large apples, peeled, cored and sliced

Streusel Topping:
2 cups brown sugar, packed
1/2 cup flour
1/4 cup cinnamon
3/4 cup coarsely chopped walnuts
1/2 cup butter, melted

☛ With a mixer, cream butter and sugar. Beat in egg and vanilla. Beat in half of the buttermilk.

☛ In a separate bowl, mix the flour, baking powder and salt.

☛ Beat half of the flour mixture into the creamed mixture. Then beat in the rest of the buttermilk and the rest of the flour mixture.

☛ Stir in the apples by hand.

☛ Spread the batter in a greased and floured 9 x 13-inch pan.

☛ For Streusel Topping: Place brown sugar, flour, cinnamon and walnuts in a medium-sized bowl. Stir in melted butter until mixture is combined and crumbly. Sprinkle on top of the coffeecake batter.

☛ Bake in a preheated oven at 350 degrees for 25 to 30 minutes, until the coffeecake is golden brown or a toothpick inserted in the center comes out clean. Serve warm.

Makes 12 servings

from **The Inn at Cedar Crossing**
336 Louisiana Street
Sturgeon Bay, WI 54235
414-743-4200

The innkeepers here cut this cake into eight gigantic servings, but most folks will find they can get 12 or 16 servings from this fragrant cake. It's served in the guest lobby on the first floor, downstairs from the guestrooms.

Guests stay in one of nine country guestrooms in this historic mercantile building. Former banker Terry Wulf opened the inn in 1986. She gutted the upstairs apartment building and had guestrooms and a sitting area built and decorated to her specifications, using local craftspeople. Her restaurant on the first floor opened three years later. Door County regional specialties are on the menu for both restaurant patrons and inn guests.

🏠 *Other Inn at Cedar Crossing recipes:*
Blueberry Grand Marnier Preserves, page 105
Perfect Berry Chambord Preserves, page 113
Chilled Cherry Soup, page 123
Dried Fruit Relish, page 190

Blueberry Cake

Ingredients:

1/2 cup port wine
2 cups flour
2 tablespoons cornmeal
1-1/2 cups sugar
1-1/2 teaspoons baking powder
1-1/2 teaspoons baking soda
1 teaspoon cinnamon
1 teaspoon ground cloves
1/4 teaspoon salt
1 whole egg and 2 egg whites
2/3 cup buttermilk
1/4 cup canola oil
1 teaspoon vanilla extract
2 to 3 cups fresh or dry-pack frozen blueberries, dusted with flour

Also:

Powdered sugar

- In a small saucepan, reduce the port over medium heat to 1/4 cup. Cool.
- In a large bowl, combine flour, cornmeal, sugar, baking powder, baking soda, cinnamon, cloves and salt.
- Add the port, eggs, buttermilk, oil and vanilla. Stir until smooth. Gently fold in blueberries.
- Lightly spray a 7 x 11-inch glass baking pan with cooking spray. Pour batter into the pan.
- Bake in a preheated oven at 350 degrees for 40 to 45 minutes or until a toothpick comes out clean.
- Remove from oven. Sprinkle with powdered sugar and serve warm or at room temperature.

Makes 9 to 12 servings

from **Wickwood Country Inn**
510 Butler Street
P.O. Box 1019
Saugatuck, MI 49453
616-857-1465 or FAX 616-857-4168

If a port-flavored coffeecake seems creative, it's because the innkeeper in charge of the menus here is the former co-owner of the Silver Palate gourmet food shop in New York City and co-author of three bestselling Silver Palate cookbooks. Julee Rosso Miller and husband Bill Miller went into innkeeping at Wickwood in 1991. Julee's breakfasts might include this as one of the fresh baked goods, served in the Garden Room of this 11 guestroom inn.

Other Wickwood Inn recipes:
Sunday Pecan Coffeecake, page 45
Oatmeal Raisin Cookies, page 233
Spicy Artichoke Dip, page 238

Candy Bar Coffeecake

Ingredients:

1/4 cup butter or margarine, softened
2 cups flour
1/2 cup sugar
1 cup brown sugar, packed
1 cup buttermilk
1 egg
1 teaspoon baking soda
1 teaspoon vanilla extract
6 English toffee candy bars (like Heath) or peanut butter-based honeycomb bar (like Butterfinger)
1/2 cup chopped nuts, optional

- In a large bowl, cream butter, flour, and sugars. Reserve half a cup.

- Beat in buttermilk, egg, baking soda and vanilla, mixing well.

- Pour batter into a greased 7 x 11-inch pan.

- Crush candy bars by putting them in a plastic bag or between waxed paper and crushing with a hammer or rolling pin.

- Mix crushed candy with reserved crumbly mixture and optional nuts. Sprinkle mixture over batter.

- Bake in a preheated oven at 350 degrees for 30 minutes or until a toothpick inserted in center comes out clean.

Tester's Comments: Good as a dessert cake, too, especially with a dollop of whipped cream.

Makes 12 servings

from **The Jefferson-Day House**
1109 Third Street
Hudson, WI 54016
715-386-7111

"My mom made this for years," said Innkeeper Sharon Miller, who serves this coffeecake with a scoop of light whipped topping instead of calorie-laden ice cream. Sharon prefers the toffee candy, "but either is very good."

Sharon and Wally Miller might serve this as part of their generous three-course breakfasts, served up on Depression Glass with a liberal helping of humor. These former teachers turned the 1857 Italianate home on a quiet street in this St. Croix River town into a welcoming B&B with four large guestrooms, including a three-room suite where breakfast can be enjoyed on the sunporch. "We're 'people persons' who love old houses and furnishings," Sharon said. "We also love staying at B&Bs," and they've visited 60-some now -- giving them both the guest and owner perspective on innkeeping. Sharon and Wally love the St. Croix -- they're boaters, too -- and they cheerfully direct guests to all the "secrets" that the rivertowns have to offer in the St. Croix Valley.

Dorothy's Easy Kringle

Ingredients:

2 cups flour
1/2 cup margarine
1 cup sour cream

Also:

1 egg white, beaten slightly
Filling, such as fresh fruit (such as a mixture of 2 grated Granny Smith apples, 1/4 cup raisins, 1 tablespoon sugar, 1/4 teaspoon cinnamon, mixed)
Powdered sugar frosting, optional

- Cut flour and margarine together with a pastry cutter or forks. Stir in sour cream.

- Wrap the dough tightly in plastic wrap and refrigerate for 24 hours (or freeze for later use).

- A day later, divide dough into four parts. On a floured surface, roll out each cold dough quarter to a 9 x 16-inch rectangle. Trim off any rough edges.

- Carefully lift each rectangle to a cookie sheet. Divide the filling into quarters. Spread one quarter down the center of each rectangle, covering about one-third of the dough.

- Fold one-third of the dough from one side into the middle of the filling. Then fold the other third in to meet the first dough in the middle. A little of the filling can show or dough can overlap a bit.

- Brush pastry with egg white. Bake in a preheated oven at 350 degrees for at least 20 minutes, more for fresh fruit fillings.

- Drizzle with powdered sugar frosting while warm and serve.

Tester's Comments: This recipe is close to puff pastry. It's one of the few doughs I could roll really thin, plus pick up and move without "breaking" it. I tried several fillings and the favorite was grated apple with raisins, cinnamon and sugar. Frosting is very optional -- this is quite rich.

Makes 4 kringles, serving 4 each

from **Parkview Bed & Breakfast**
211 North Park Street
Reedsburg, WI 53959
608-524-4333

Innkeeper Donna Hofmann obtained this recipe years ago from a friend, Dorothy Johnson. Johnson lived in the Racine, Wis., area, where Kringle is famous. Donna made the recipe for years for her family before they opened their B&B in 1989. Now it's often part of a large breakfast served to guests.
Donna and Tom and their three teens restored this 1895 Queen Anne Victorian, located in Reedburg's historic district. Their B&B remains a family affair, where everyone pitches in to serve breakfast, stencil guestrooms, dry garden flowers or paint the house (no small job, soaking up 40 gallons).

Another Parkview B&B recipe:
Rhubarb Punch, page 29

Fruit Custard Coffeecake

Ingredients:

2 cups flour	**Topping:**
1 cup "lite" margarine	1/2 cup flour
4 tablespoons water	1/4 cup sugar
4 cups mixed fresh fruit, chopped, and/or berries, washed	1/4 cup brown sugar, packed
2 cups nonfat vanilla or plain yogurt	1/4 cup "lite" margarine
1-1/2 to 2 cups sugar	
2 eggs	
6 tablespoons flour	
2 teaspoons vanilla extract	
1 teaspoon salt	

- In a large bowl, mix 2 cups flour, margarine and water. Pat dough into bottom of 9 x 13-inch pan.

- Layer the fruit over the dough.

- In a separate bowl, beat yogurt, sugar, eggs, flour, vanilla and salt. "Adjust sugar amount for sweetness of the fruit. Rhubarb needs the full 2 cups." Berries, pears and peaches need 1/2 cup less.

- Pour this custard over the fruit layer.

- In a small bowl, mix topping ingredients with a fork or pastry cutter. Sprinkle over custard.

- Bake in a preheated oven at 350 degrees for 45 to 60 minutes, until top is golden brown and the custard layer is cakelike and firm in the middle ("watch closely after 45 minutes -- each oven is different"). Serve warm or cold.

Tester's Comments: The bottom layer is very rich using margarine -- butter would be too much so. Berries in part of the fruit layer are out of this world. Try it as a dessert cake, as well.

Makes 16 servings

from **The Sonnenhof B&B Inn**
13907 North Port Washington Road
Mequon, WI 53097
414-375-4294

"Any fruit can be used," says Innkeeper Georgia Houle about one of the beauties of this recipe. "One of the best I ever made was a combination of one apple, one peach, one pear and a pint of blueberries -- nothing but raves!" She modified an old recipe to cut back on the fat content. "Taste didn't suffer one bit." Guests enjoy this coffeecake as part of a full, homemade breakfast.

Georgia and husband Tom's inn is a restored three-story Dutch Colonial farmhouse, parts of which were built in 1845. Set on 21 acres, the three-guestroom inn is a short walk from their tennis court and fish pond, where guests can catch and release. Many guests are surprised that the country quiet here is only 17 miles north of Milwaukee. Historic Cedarburg and its restaurants and shops are only four miles away, close enough for a bike ride.

German Coffeecake

Ingredients:

Dough:
- 2 cups warm water
- 1/2 cup sugar
- 2 packets active dry yeast
- 1 tablespoon salt
- 6-1/2 cups flour
- 2 eggs
- 1/2 cup shortening

Also:
- Raspberries, apricots, raisins, other fruit, optional

Filling:
- 2 cups heavy or sour cream
- 2 eggs, beaten
- 1/2 cup sugar
- 1-1/2 tablespoons flour
- 1 teaspoon vanilla extract

Crumb Topping:
- 1 cup sugar
- 1 cup flour
- 1/2 cup butter or margarine
- Cinnamon, optional

- For dough: Mix water, sugar and yeast until dissolved.

- Add salt and 2 cups of the flour. Beat with a mixer for 2 minutes.

- Beat in eggs and shortening. Then add remaining flour, mixing well.

- Cover and let "rise" in a warm, draft-free place for 20 minutes. Meanwhile, prepare filling.

- For Filling: In a medium saucepan, heat cream. Mix in eggs, sugar, flour and vanilla, stirring constantly over medium heat until thick. Remove from heat and cool.

- Divide dough into 6 parts. Roll on a lightly floured surface to fit 6 greased cake pans or pie plates.

- Spread filling on top of dough. Top with fruit, if desired.

- For Topping: Mix sugar, flour, margarine and cinnamon to taste with a fork or pastry cutter. Sprinkle over filling.

- Let dough rise again, until about double, allowing 40 minutes or more. Bake in a preheated oven at 350 degrees for 15 to 20 minutes or until golden brown. Serve warm.

Makes 36 servings

from **Heirloom Inn B&B**
1103 South Third Street
Stillwater, MN 55082
612-430-2289

"This recipe is easier than it looks -- it is easily cut in half -- and the küchen is moist, yeasty and delicious," said Innkeeper Sandie Brown. "These can be made ahead and frozen to use later." Sandie uses this recipe, which was obtained years ago, as part of a full breakfast served in the dining room. Sandie and Mark, her husband, purchased this Italianate B&B that was built as a dentist's home right after the Civil War. Browns offer three antique-filled guestrooms just a half mile from downtown Stillwater, an historic St. Croix River town close to the Twin Cities.

Another Heirloom Inn recipe:
Pecan Crescent Cookies, page 235

Grandma Felke's Küchen

Ingredients:

1 cup milk
1/4 cup plus 2 tablespoons sugar
1/4 cup margarine
1/4 cup water
1/2 teaspoon salt
1 packet active dry yeast
3 to 4 cups flour
1 egg, beaten
1/2 cup raisins

Topping:
Margarine, melted
1/4 cup sugar
1 tablespoon cinnamon

Also:

Jam or jelly

- In a saucepan, heat milk, sugar, margarine, water and salt until margarine is melted and sugar dissolves (do not boil).

- In a large bowl, mix the yeast, 3 to 4 cups flour, egg and milk mixture with a wooden spoon. Add raisins and beat until a soft dough forms.

- Turn dough out onto a lightly floured surface and knead until smooth and elastic.

- Place dough in a greased bowl. Cover and let rise in a warm, draft-free place until double, 60 to 90 minutes.

- Place dough in a greased 9 x 13-inch pan and spread dough out. Cover and let rise again until double, about 60 minutes.

- Melt margarine. Brush it on top of the küchen. Sprinkle with cinnamon and sugar.

- Bake in a preheated oven at 350 degrees for 20 minutes. Serve warm with favorite preserves.

Makes about 20 slices

from **The Pentwater Inn**
180 East Lowell Street
P.O. Box 98
Pentwater, MI 49449
616-869-5909

"My Grandmother Felke taught me to make this when I was 12 years old," said Innkeeper Sue Hand. "She baked about eight of these every Saturday and would bring them to her children for their Sunday breakfast." Sue had to convert the recipe from an oral one with "six handfuls of flour, pinch of salt," and this recipe is reduced to half of the one her grandma gave her.

Sue and Dick, her husband, served this as part of their breakfasts for guests staying in the five guestrooms, but health problems forced them to sell the B&B in 1994. The 1880 home was built by a local merchant and is located two blocks from downtown, five blocks from the Lake Michigan sand dunes "and one of the most beautiful beaches in the country." Pentwater draws visitors year 'round and the Inn is open to welcome them.

Rhubarb Cake

Ingredients:

2 cups flour
1-1/4 cups sugar
1 teaspoon salt
1 teaspoon baking soda
1 teaspoon cinnamon
1/4 teaspoon cloves
1/2 cup shortening
2 eggs
1/3 cup milk
2 cups coarsely chopped rhubarb, fresh or "dry pack" frozen

Topping:
2/3 cup flour
1/2 cup brown sugar, packed
1 teaspoon cinnamon
4 tablespoons butter
1/2 cup chopped walnuts

✒ Sift flour, sugar, salt, baking soda, cinnamon and cloves into a large bowl.

✒ Mix in shortening, eggs and milk.

✒ Stir in rhubarb by hand, mixing until just combined.

✒ Spread batter into a greased 9 x 13-inch pan.

✒ For Topping: Mix flour, sugar and cinnamon. Then cut in the butter with a fork or pastry cutter, until mixture is crumbly. Stir in nuts.

✒ Sprinkle topping evenly over batter. You may pat it down into batter a bit.

✒ Bake in a preheated oven at 350 degrees for 35 minutes or until a toothpick inserted in the center comes out clean. Remove from oven and let sit a few minutes before cutting.

Tester's Comments: This is one of the few recipes that is equally good warm or cold. For a strawberry-rhubarb flavor, substitute a little strawberry yogurt for some of the milk.

Makes 20-24 servings

from **Dr. Joseph Moses House B&B**
1100 South Division Street
Northfield, MN 55057
507-663-1563

Innkeeper Kathleen Murphy remembers this coffeecake from her childhood, when her mom used their fresh spring rhubarb. She notes that apples can be substituted for the rhubarb, and that it can double as a snack or dessert cake.

Kathleen and Ron Halverson "stumbled onto the idea of innkeeping" when they fell in love with the Moses House, built in 1929 by a prominent doctor. They became only the fourth owners of this well-cared-for home, opening four guestrooms in 1990. Northfield is home to both Carleton and St. Olaf Colleges, and is known as the place where the Jesse James Gang was defeated.

🏠*Another Moses House recipe:*
Crispy Cinnamon French Toast, page 156

Snickerdoodle Coffeecake

Ingredients:

1/2 cup butter
2 cups sugar
2 eggs, separated
1/4 teaspoon salt
2 teaspoons baking powder
3 cups flour
1 cup milk
1 teaspoon cinnamon
3 teaspoons powdered sugar

- In a large bowl of an electric mixer, cream butter and sugar.
- Add egg yolks and salt. Beat thoroughly.
- Sift baking powder into the flour.
- Add flour and milk to egg mixture alternately, beating well after each addition.
- In a separate bowl, beat the egg whites until light and frothy. Then fold them into the batter.
- Spread batter in a greased 9 x 13-inch pan.
- Sift cinnamon and powdered sugar over the top.
- Bake in a preheated oven at 350 degrees for 30 minutes or until a toothpick inserted in the center comes out clean. Remove from oven and let sit a few minutes before cutting.

Makes 20-24 servings

from **The Franklin Victorian**
220 East Franklin Street
Sparta, WI 54656
608-269-3894 or 800-845-8767

"My mom made Snickerdoodle for special breakfasts," said Jane Larson. "We loved it, but over the years, she lost the recipe. Then several years ago, my great aunt gave me an old cookbook from my great-grandparents' home area in Vermont." The Snickerdoodle recipe found there was for cookies, but Jane improvised, and "out came the coffeecake of my childhood!"

Breakfast is served by Jane and Lloyd, her husband, in the formal dining room, which has a built-in buffet and parquet floor. The woodwork throughout the home is rich and varied. The home was built in the 1890s by banker W.G. Williams, who had ash, oak, maple and fir cut and dried over a 10-year period. The Larsons, both teachers, raised their family in this large home and turned it into a four-guestroom B&B in 1988, after Lloyd's retirement. Two popular state bike trails -- the Sparta-Elroy and the LaCrosse River trails -- run within a mile or so of their B&B.

Sour Cream Coffeecake

Excellent (handwritten)

Double for 9x13 55-60 min (handwritten)

Ingredients:

1 cup sugar
1/2 cup butter
3 eggs
2 cups flour
1 teaspoon baking powder
1 teaspoon baking soda
A pinch of salt
1 cup sour cream
1 teaspoon vanilla extract

Topping:
3/4 cup brown sugar, packed
4 tablespoons flour
3 tablespoons butter
1 teaspoon cinnamon
3/4 cup chopped walnuts

- In a large bowl, cream sugar and butter.

- Beat in eggs, one at a time.

- Slowly add flour, baking powder, baking soda and salt.

- Stir sour cream and vanilla together. Fold into the batter by hand.

- For Topping: Mix brown sugar, flour, butter and cinnamon with a fork or pastry cutter until crumbly. Stir in nuts.

- Grease a Bundt or tube pan. Sprinkle one-third of the topping on the bottom.

- Cover topping with half the batter. Sprinkle another third of topping on top of batter.

- Cover with the remaining batter. Sprinkle on the last third of topping.

- Bake in a preheated oven at 350 degrees for 55 to 60 minutes. Remove from the oven and cool for several minutes before inverting on a serving plate.

Makes 18 large slices

from **The Stagecoach Inn B&B**
W61 N520 Washington Avenue
Cedarburg, WI 53012
414-375-0208

Claudia Connor brought this old family recipe with her to work at this B&B, where she serves a continental breakfast in what is now the Stagecoach Pub/gathering room. Breakfast might include muffins and this coffeecake, enjoyed before a day of antiquing and other shopping in historic Cedarburg.

Owners Liz and Brook Brown restored this 1850s inn, built of stone on the main street as the Central House Hotel. They now have 13 guestrooms, including three in the Weber Haus, an 1847 home across the street. Cederburg is just northwest of Milwaukee, a popular getaway with many restored buildings and a quaint country feel.

Another Stagecoach Inn recipe:
Puff Danish, page 214

44

Sunday Pecan Coffeecake

Ingredients:

2 cups sugar
1/4 cup canola oil
1 tablespoon minced lemon zest
1 egg and 2 egg whites
1/2 cup nonfat plain yogurt
1/2 cup low-fat cottage cheese
2-1/2 teaspoons vanilla extract
2 teaspoons lemon juice
2 cups flour
1 teaspoon baking powder

"Filling:"
1/2 cup coarsely chopped pecans
1/4 cup brown sugar, packed
1-1/2 teaspoons cinnamon

- For "Filling:" In a small bowl, combine pecans, brown sugar and cinnamon. Set aside.

- In a large bowl, cream sugar, oil and lemon zest. Mix in egg and egg whites.

- In a blender, blend yogurt and cottage cheese. Add to egg mixture with vanilla and lemon juice.

- Slowly stir in the flour and baking powder until completely blended.

- Lightly spray a 10-inch Bundt pan with cooking spray, then lightly dust with flour. Pour in two-thirds of the batter. Sprinkle the "filling" evenly over the batter. Then top with remaining batter.

- Bake in a preheated oven at 350 degrees for 40 to 45 minutes. Cool slightly. Invert on serving plate.

Makes 18 large slices

from **Wickwood Country Inn**
510 Butler Street
P.O. Box 1019
Saugatuck, MI 49453
616-857-1465 or FAX 616-857-4168

"This is our most popular breakfast cake," said Alice Clark, an innkeeper at this award-winning inn. And guests here are served by innkeepers with some of the best repertoire of recipes anywhere -- owner Julee Rosso Miller is the co-author of the best-selling Silver Palate cookbooks.

Rosso Miller returned to Michigan after 25 years in New York City, where she co-founded the Silver Palate gourmet food shop. With husband Bill, a long-time Saugatuck resident, they purchased the elegant Wickwood from friends. The 1940 building has 11 guestrooms, four common rooms, a screened gazebo and a courtyard. The Wickwood recipe for being pampered is down comforters, flowers, antiques, robes and a bedtime snack in every room.

Other Wickwood Inn recipes:
Blueberry Cake, page 36
Oatmeal Raisin Cookies, page 233
Spicy Artichoke Dip, page 238

Most innkeepers love muffins because their guests do, and because muffins usually are easy to stir up, yet require only a short 20-minute-or-so baking time. So it's no surprise that many innkeepers wanted to share a favorite muffin recipe. This collection has several healthy recipes, with bran, oats or whole wheat flour, as well as some rich, exotic muffins or scones with sour cream, cream cheese or maple syrup. Many use locally-grown ingredients, such as apples, raspberries, blueberries, cherries, rhubarb or zucchini. One even features root beer. Another deliciously combines pumpkin and apples. Yet another contains sherry-plumped raisins. All of them will add variety to what otherwise might be ordinary "ho-hum" breakfasts.

Muffins, Biscuits & Scones

Amaretto Popovers

Ingredients:

 - 4 eggs, well beaten
 - 2 cups flour
 - 1/4 teaspoon salt
 - 1 cup water
 - 1 cup milk
 - 2 tablespoons Amaretto liqueur

Also:

 - Butter
 - Amaretto

- In a large bowl of an electric mixer, combine eggs, flour and salt.
- Add water slowly and beat vigorously.
- Mix in milk and Amaretto.
- Beat until smooth and bubbly.
- Meanwhile, heat a well-greased popover or muffin pan in oven as it preheats to 425 degrees.
- Pour batter into *very* hot popover pan until popover tins are half-full.
- Bake at 425 degrees for 40 minutes or until popovers are light brown. They should be crisp and brown on the outside, tender on the inside.
- Remove from the oven and place on serving plates immediately. Serve hot with softened butter that's been blended with a little Amaretto.

Makes 12 popovers

from **Amberwood Inn**
N7136 Highway 42
Algoma, WI 54201
414-487-3471

"When we were celebrating, Grandma would make her special popovers," said Innkeeper Jan Warren about this recipe. Now the popovers are on the breakfast table at this lakeside B&B, served with a large homemade breakfast.

Jan and George Davies came to Algoma for the summer and ended up staying permanently. They had been living and working in Arizona, but after 20 years, Jan's job was eliminated. "We came for the summer and the Chamber of Commerce talked to me about the B&B idea," Jan said.

They owned a 65-year-old Cape Cod home on 300 feet of Lake Michigan beach, located a mile south of Algoma. Algoma is considered the gateway to Door County and a trout and salmon fishing headquarters in its own right. They added on to the house, so the new section matches the old, and now have five guestrooms, each with a view of Lake Michigan. Guests can swim, fish in the surf, hike, ride the bikes and use the deck overlooking the lake.

Apple Buttermilk Muffins

Ingredients:

1-1/2 cups brown sugar, packed
2/3 cup vegetable oil
1 egg
1 cup buttermilk
1 teaspoon baking soda
1 teaspoon vanilla extract
1 teaspoon salt
2-1/2 cups flour, sifted
2 cups peeled, diced apple
1/2 cup chopped pecans

Topping:
1/4 cup brown sugar
3 tablespoons flour
4 tablespoons cold butter
1/2 teaspoon cinnamon

First, make Topping: Mix brown sugar, flour, butter and cinnamon with a fork or pastry cutter until crumbly.

In a large bowl, mix brown sugar, oil and egg.

In a separate bowl, mix buttermilk, baking soda, vanilla and salt.

Blend buttermilk mixture into sugar mixture alternately with flour.

Fold in the apples and pecans.

Pour batter into greased muffin tins until tins are two-thirds full. Sprinkle topping over batter.

Bake in a preheated oven at 350 degrees for 20 minutes or until the tops of muffins spring back when lightly touched.

Tester's Comments: Moist and delicious. I thought they might need cinnamon, but the topping "covers" it!

Makes 12-15 muffins

from **The Inn at Palisade**
384 Highway 61 East
Silver Bay, MN 55614
218-226-3505

These muffins often are on the breakfast table along with fruit and an egg dish at this inn on Lake Superior. Innkeepers Mary and Bob Barnett were on their way up Lake Superior's North Shore to the Gunflint Trail when they found a "for sale" sign on a 1950s motel adjacent to Tettagouche State Park near Silver Bay. That was in 1985 and two years later they bought it. In 1993, they completed a major renovation of the five guestrooms, the dining room and the exterior. A former brick fireplace in the dining room, for instance, has been redone with cobblestones, and the guestrooms have country decor and bay windows for a lake view. Named after nearby Palisade Head, where guests can hike and picnic with a view high above the lake, the inn has its own rocky beach for surf fishing or campfires. The Baptism River hiking trails at Tettagouche lead to Baptism Falls.

Apple Raisin Oat Bran Muffins

Ingredients:

1/2 cup raisins
1/4 cup water
2 cups oat bran
2 cups flour
1/2 cup sugar
3 teaspoons baking powder
1 teaspoon baking soda
1 teaspoon cinnamon
1/2 teaspoon nutmeg
1 whole egg and 2 egg whites
3/4 cup buttermilk
3/4 cup plain yogurt
1/4 cup molasses
1 tablespoon vegetable oil
1 cup grated apple

- "Plump" raisins by simmering them in the water, either in a saucepan or in the microwave. Cool.

- In a large bowl, mix oat bran, flour, sugar, baking powder, baking soda, cinnamon and nutmeg.

- In a separate bowl, stir together egg and egg whites, buttermilk, yogurt, molasses and oil.

- Make a "well" in the dry ingredients. Add the liquid ingredients and stir only until moistened.

- Fold in the apple and raisins.

- Fill greased or paper-lined muffin cups two-thirds full.

- Bake in a preheated oven at 375 degrees for 20 minutes.

Makes 48 muffins

from **Cloghaun Bed & Breakfast**
On Market Street P.O. Box 203
Mackinac Island, MI 49757
906-847-3885

Homemade baked goods are always a part of the continental breakfast buffet at this 10-guestroom inn. Guests get a good night's rest just a block from Mackinac Island's busy main street, then eat a hearty breakfast before exploring historic Ft. Mackinac, taking a bike or carriage ride, or enjoying the Grand Hotel's amenities, open to Cloghaun guests.

Or stick close to the recently-restored Cloghaun (well, everything's *close*), which Innkeeper Jim Bond's great-grandparents built for their large Irish family. Jim's late aunt had a large collection of island photographs, still displayed on original hooks, or guests can soak up island ambiance on the wicker veranda chairs. The island is reached by ferry -- no cars allowed.

Another Cloghaun B&B recipe:
Apple Harvest Strudel, page 34

Banana Macadamia Nut Muffins

Ingredients:

- 1-1/2 cups flour
- 1-1/2 teaspoons baking soda
- 1/4 teaspoon salt
- 1/8 teaspoon nutmeg
- 1-1/4 cups mashed ripe banana (2 or 3 bananas)
- 1/2 cup sugar
- 1/4 cup dark brown sugar, packed
- 1/2 cup butter, melted
- 1/4 cup milk
- 1 egg
- 1 cup unsalted macadamia nuts, toasted and chopped

- In a large bowl, combine flour, baking soda, salt and nutmeg.
- In a separate bowl, mix bananas, sugar, brown sugar, melted butter, milk and egg.
- Pour liquid ingredients into dry and mix.
- Fold in 1/2 cup macadamia nuts.
- Divide batter into 12 greased or paper-lined muffin cups. Sprinkle tops with remaining nuts.
- Bake in a preheated oven at 350 degrees for about 25 minutes, until golden brown.
- Remove from oven and transfer to wire rack to cool.

Tester's Comments: The addition of some flaked coconut makes these tropical and even more wonderful.

Makes 12 muffins

from **Yankee Hill Inn B&B**
405 Collins Street
Plymouth, WI 53073
414-892-2222

A basket of these muffins might be on the dining room table or in the breakfast room with French doors overlooking the yard and carriage house. Homemade muffins, breads or coffeecakes are always part of breakfast here.

Innkeepers Peg and Jim Stahlman opened a B&B in their Queen Anne in 1988, entering a new profession after Jim's job was eliminated and he was a mere 51. The energetic couple, who had real estate backgrounds, now own the home next door, and today they have 11 guestrooms between the two homes. The houses were built by the Huson brothers, Henry and Gilbert, who sold farm implements and dry goods downtown, a short walk down Yankee Hill.

Other Yankee Hill Inn recipes:
Rhubarb Bread, page 96
Aunt Josie's Lemon Butter, page 103

Bayfield Apple Raspberry Muffins

Ingredients:

2 egg whites
1/2 cup sugar
1/4 cup extra light pure olive oil
2 cups flour
2 teaspoons baking powder
1/4 teaspoon salt
3/4 cup Bayfield apple-raspberry juice (all apple juice or a mixture of raspberry and apple juice, made from frozen concentrates, may be substituted)
1 cup raspberries, fresh or "dry pack" frozen
2 cups chopped apples, preferably Bayfield Courtland or Macoun, peeled

Also:

Sugar

- In a large bowl, beat egg whites just until frothy. Stir in sugar and oil.
- Add flour, baking powder and salt.
- Mix in juice.
- Gently fold in raspberries and apples.
- Fill greased or paper-lined muffin tins three-quarters full. Sprinkle tops with a little sugar.
- Bake in a preheated oven at 400 degrees for 25 to 30 minutes. Serve warm.

Makes 12 muffins

from **Cooper Hill House**
33 South Sixth Street
P.O. Box 1288
Bayfield, WI 54814
715-779-5060

"This recipe won second place in the Bayfield Applefest Heart Healthy Contest in 1990," said Innkeeper Julie MacDonald. Apples and raspberries are to Bayfield what fudge is to Mackinac Island, so it's no wonder her recipe was a hit. She serves warm muffins along with fresh fruit to B&B guests.

Julie and husband Larry once led busy lives in the Twin Cities as a corporate travel agent and greeting card sales rep, respectively. They left that behind in 1989 after they bought a sailboat and simply didn't want to leave Bayfield. They bought the Cooper Hill House and three hours after signing the papers had their first guests. Restoration of the 1888 home was done by previous owners. MacDonalds redecorated the four guestrooms with family heirlooms.

They are here to stay -- they own a general store downtown and Larry was elected mayor in 1994. The B&B is a few blocks from downtown, where guests can catch the ferry to Madelaine Island or take an Apostle Islands excursion boat, shop or enjoy fresh Lake Superior trout at several restaurants.

Blueberry Buttermilk Muffins

Ingredients:

1 cup old-fashioned oatmeal
3/4 cup buttermilk
3/4 cup orange juice
3 cups flour
1 cup sugar
2 tablespoons baking powder
1 teaspoon salt
1/2 teaspoon baking soda
3 eggs, beaten
1/4 cup vegetable oil
1/4 cup butter, melted
1 tablespoon vanilla extract
1 teaspoon nutmeg
3 to 4 cups blueberries, fresh or "dry pack" frozen

- In a medium bowl, combine oatmeal, buttermilk and orange juice. Set aside.
- In a separate bowl, combine the flour, sugar, baking powder, salt and baking soda.
- In a third bowl, beat eggs, oil, butter, vanilla and nutmeg.
- Fold ingredients in all three bowls together in the largest bowl. Gently fold in blueberries.
- Fill greased or paper-lined muffin tins two-thirds full.
- Bake in a preheated oven at 400 degrees for 15 to 20 minutes. Serve warm.

Tester's Comments: Also great with 2/3 cup sugar, 1 egg and 2 egg whites, and 2 cups of large berries. The orange juice was an inspiration, a delicious addition.

Makes 18 muffins

from **The Stone Hearth Inn**
1118 Highway 61 East
Little Marais, MN 55614
218-226-3020

Wild blueberries picked along the North Shore of Lake Superior might find their way into this recipe, which Innkeeper Charlie Michels devised. He and wife Susan serve it with regional specialties at a dining table with a view of Lake Superior. They often bake 12 "Superior-sized" muffins instead of 18.

Lake Superior is what drew Charlie to this property, situated down a hill and among pines, just back from the lake. As a contractor and carpenter, he restored the 1893 homestead, which once served as an overnight stop along the shore. He converted 10 bedrooms into five and added a front porch and a large cobblestone fireplace. Susan was one of his first guests in 1990, and they were married on the lawn the next summer. In addition to the five guestrooms, two lakeside suites are in the converted boathouse.

Blueberry Oat Bran Muffins

Ingredients:

1 cup flour
2 teaspoons baking powder
1 teaspoon baking soda
1/2 cup brown sugar, packed
1/2 cup whole wheat flour
1/2 cup oat bran
1 cup plain or vanilla yogurt
1 egg, beaten
1/2 cup vegetable oil
1 teaspoon vanilla extract
1 cup blueberries, fresh or "dry-pack" frozen

- In a large bowl, stir together flour, baking powder and baking soda.
- Mix in brown sugar, whole wheat flour and oat bran.
- In a separate bowl, beat together yogurt, egg, oil and vanilla.
- Stir yogurt mixture into flour mixture.
- Fold in blueberries.
- Fill greased or paper-lined muffin tins two-thirds full.
- Bake in a preheated oven at 400 degrees for 15 to 20 minutes.

Makes 12 muffins

from **The Ellery House B&B**
28 South 21st Avenue East
Duluth, MN 55812
218-724-7639 or 800-355-3794

"This is a more nutritious muffin that we like to serve to guests who request a lower cholesterol breakfast or seem to be more health-conscious," said Innkeeper Joan Halquist. "We try to accommodate all special diets."

Cooking is enjoyable for the Halquists, as is working on old houses, being self-employed and offering a service people want -- all important pre-requisites for innkeeping. Also, "Joan and I wanted to work together in a small business" and be home for their children, Jim said. They opened their Queen Anne Victorian B&B in 1988, the second B&B in Duluth, home of the University of Minnesota-Duluth, many businesses and the gateway to Lake Superior's North Shore. Three of the four guestrooms have lake views. The B&B is close to restaurants, downtown Canal Park and the "lake walk" paved pathway that runs along the Lake Superior shoreline.

Another Ellery House recipe:
Orange Scones, page 64

Bonnie's Chocolate Zucchini Muffins

Ingredients:

3 cups flour
1 cup sugar
1 cup brown sugar, packed
1 teaspoon baking powder
1 teaspoon baking soda
1 teaspoon salt
1 teaspoon cinnamon
3 ounces grated milk chocolate bar
1 cup mini semi-sweet chocolate chips
1/2 cup chopped nuts, optional
3 eggs
3 teaspoons vanilla extract
1 cup vegetable oil
2-1/2 cups grated zucchini (about 3 medium zucchini)

- In a large bowl, combine the flour, sugar, brown sugar, baking powder, baking soda, salt, cinnamon, grated chocolate, chocolate chips and nuts.
- In a separate bowl, beat eggs. Mix in vanilla and oil. Fold in zucchini.
- Pour zucchini mixture into flour mixture. Stir only until all ingredients are moistened.
- Fill greased or paper-lined muffin tins three-quarters full.
- Bake in a preheated oven at 425 degrees for 18 to 20 minutes ("don't over-bake").

Tester's Comments: So good it's hard to believe there's a vegetable in here! Mini-chips definitely are best.

Makes 26 to 28 muffins

from **White Lace Inn**
16 North Fifth Avenue
Sturgeon Bay, WI 54235
414-743-1105

Chocolate and zucchini have been put together by many a muffin-maker, but only Innkeeper Bonnie Statz combines milk chocolate and semi-sweet for the breakfast table. Guests appreciate her creativity when they gather for breakfast at the main inn. Breakfast includes a variety of baked goods, and Bonnie tries to improve on old favorites and offer new treats for repeat guests. Guests might take off on the inn's bicycle-built-for-two, walk the few blocks downtown to explore Sturgeon Bay, or head further up the Door Peninsula before returning to a lavish room in one of three restored Victorian homes.

Other White Lace Inn recipe:
Pumpkin Apple Streusel Muffins, page 67
Lemon Herb Bread, page 89
Chilled Berry Soup, page 122

Cherry Chocolate Chip Muffins

Ingredients:

2 cups flour
3/4 cup sugar
4 teaspoons baking powder
1 teaspoon salt
1 cup fresh tart cherries
2 eggs
1 cup milk
1/2 cup butter or margarine, melted
3/4 cup semi-sweet chocolate chips

Topping:
1/4 cup sugar
1/2 teaspoon cinnamon

- In a large bowl, combine flour, sugar, baking powder and salt. Stir in cherries until blended.
- In a small bowl, beat eggs, milk and butter.
- Stir egg mixture into flour mixture just until all ingredients are combined.
- Fold in chocolate chips.
- Fill greased or paper-lined muffin tins almost to the top.
- For Topping: Mix sugar and cinnamon. Sprinkle on top of the batter.
- Bake in a preheated oven at 400 degrees for about 15 minutes. Serve warm.

Tester's Comments: Actually, these are good cold, too. Tart cherries and sweet chocolate are a nice mix.

Makes 12 muffins

from **The Potter's Door Inn**
9528 State Highway 57
Baileys Harbor, WI 54202
414-839-2003

"Of all the many muffin recipes I serve, this is everyone's favorite," said Innkeeper Shir Lee Wilson. She came up with the recipe to make use of the abundance of Door County cherries. Breakfast is served outdoors in the summer or inside in cooler weather, in the original 1860 log home portion of the inn. It's served on pottery made by Wes, an experienced potter who renovated a building on their 25 acres as a studio and gallery.

Wes and Shir Lee bought the farm in 1989 and opened the B&B as a side-business to the studio. The three-guestroom inn is in the main house, the original portion of which was built in 1860 by a young German immigrant. In 1898, the farmer added a stovewood log room, which remains a fine example of rare stovewood construction. The fireplace bricks, taken from the Clark Street Garage in Chicago, are believed to have bullet holes from the St. Valentine's Day Massacre of Al Capone. Guests at the inn, located between Baileys Harbor and Sister Bay, can ski on Wilsons' trails in the winter, enjoy the lilacs in the spring, and eat apples from the farmstead's trees in the fall.

Cherry Oatmeal Muffins

Ingredients:

2 cups oatmeal
2 cups flour
1 cup brown sugar, packed
3 teaspoons baking powder
3/4 teaspoon nutmeg
1/2 teaspoon salt
1-1/2 cups buttermilk
2 eggs, slightly beaten
1/2 cup vegetable oil
2-1/2 teaspoons almond extract
2 cups frozen or canned, drained tart cherries, coarsely chopped (in a food processor)

Also:

Extra oatmeal

- In a large bowl, combine oatmeal, flour, brown sugar, baking powder, nutmeg and salt.
- In a separate bowl, combine the buttermilk, eggs, oil and extract.
- Pour buttermilk mixture into oatmeal mixture and stir.
- Stir in cherries and let the batter sit for 10 minutes.
- Fill greased or paper-lined muffin cups almost full. Sprinkle additional oatmeal on top of the batter.
- Bake in a preheated oven at 375 degrees for 20-25 minutes or until the tops are lightly browned.

Makes 24 muffins

Big muffin tins - Bake 35 min. makes 8

from **Linden Lea on Long Lake**
279 South Long Lake Road
Traverse City, MI 49684
616-943-9182

Innkeeper Vicky McDonnell adapted this recipe to make use of the cherries produced in the Traverse City area. Vicky and husband Jim's two-guestroom B&B is 10 minutes from Traverse City and close to many "u-pick" farms.

The couple found this former summer cottage in 1979. It was built around the turn of the century, and it needed much work, but had a spectacular view of the 2,890-acre lake and sunsets over it. Jim, a former teacher, got to work, renovated the cottage and added an addition, and the contemporary B&B was born. They named it after England's lake district. Guests are welcome to take the rowboat to the islands, swim on the sandy beach or curl up by the fire (the mantel was handcarved from solid cherrywood in 1880).

Another Linden Lea recipe:
Applesauce Bread, page 76

Fresh Blueberry Muffins

Ingredients:

1 cup sugar
1/2 cup butter, softened
2 eggs
1 teaspoon vanilla extract
2 cups flour
2 teaspoons baking powder
1/2 teaspoon salt
1/2 cup milk
1 to 2 cups fresh blueberries
1 to 2 teaspoons freshly grated lemon peel

Also:

1 tablespoon butter, melted
Sugar

- In the large bowl of an electric mixer, cream sugar and butter until fluffy.

- Beat in the eggs, one at a time. Then mix in vanilla.

- In a separate bowl, mix flour, baking powder and salt. Add them to the egg mixture alternately with the milk.

- In a small bowl, mash 1/2 cup of the blueberries. Mix it into the batter, stirring just until blended.

- Toss the remaining blueberries with the lemon peel. Fold them into the batter.

- Fill greased or paper-lined muffin cups two-thirds full.

- Bake in a preheated oven at 375 degrees for 20 to 25 minutes. Remove from oven.

- Brush each warm muffin with melted butter and sprinkle with sugar. "Thoroughly cool in tins or muffins will crumble."

Tester's Comments: These are rich muffins that are good cold and without butter. Mashing the berries can be optional. Fresh raspberries are a wonderful substitute for blueberries.

Makes 12 to 15 muffins

from **Hungry Point Inn**
1 Olde Deerfield Road
Red Wing, MN 55089
612-388-7857

These muffins might be served at this B&B as part of Innkeeper Merriam Carroll Last's candlelight breakfast. She has set about to recreate a colonial New England settlement, set on a former working farm atop the Mississippi River bluffs. Circa 1750 decor is intended to be historic down to the candlesticks, and includes hand-woven baskets, a spinning wheel (guests can try it) and an Herb Drying Room. There are four "bed chambers" in the main house and a separate log cabin, all filled with antiques.

Excellent!!!!

Lemon Cream Cheese Muffins

Ingredients:

2/3 cup sugar
4 ounces cream cheese, softened
1 egg
1/3 cup oil
1/2 cup milk
1-1/2 tablespoons lemon juice
1-1/4 cups flour
1-1/2 teaspoons baking powder
1/2 teaspoon salt
1/4 cup chopped nuts

Glaze:
2 tablespoons lemon juice
2 tablespoons sugar
2 tablespoons butter, melted

If doubling recipe do not double glaze

- In a large bowl, cream sugar and cream cheese.
- Beat in egg and oil.
- In a measuring cup, mix milk and lemon juice, stirring to "sour" the milk.
- In a separate bowl, mix flour, baking powder and salt.
- Add the milk and flour to cream cheese mixture alternately, beating well after each addition.
- Stir in nuts.
- Fill greased or paper-lined muffin tins two-thirds full.
- Bake in a preheated oven at 350 degrees for about 20 minutes.
- For glaze, combine lemon juice, sugar and butter. Brush on hot muffins.

Tester's Comments: Don't use "low-fat" cream cheese -- it doesn't bake well. I preferred adding poppyseeds or blueberries instead of nuts, and adding a few drops of lemon extract for a more intense lemon flavor. Excellent!

Makes 9 muffins

from **A. Charles Weiss Inn**
1615 East Superior Street
Duluth, MN 55812
218-724-7016

These muffins are from Arlene Montgomery, a part-time cook at the inn. They might be part of the breakfast served in the formal dining room here, with its white oak built-in buffet, marble-topped sideboard and fireplace. This 1895 home, built for newspaper publisher A. Charles Weiss, is full of birdseye maple, cherry, dark oak and other touches typical of a home of its stature. But when Peg Kirsch Lee and Dave Lee bought it in 1989, it had fallen into "extreme disrepair," cut into nine small apartments that warranted a three-page, single-spaced work order from the city building inspector. By 1992, however, their work had earned an award from the Duluth Preservation Alliance, and their four-guestroom inn opened in 1993. The B&B is three blocks from Duluth's new Lakewalk, a walking path along Lake Superior.

Lemon Poppyseed Muffins

Ingredients:

1-3/4 cups flour
3/4 cup sugar
1 tablespoon baking powder
1 tablespoon poppyseeds
1 teaspoon grated lemon peel, dried or freshly grated
1 egg
About 3/4 cup milk
1/4 cup butter or margarine, melted
1 teaspoon lemon extract

- Mix flour, sugar, baking powder, poppyseeds and dried lemon peel (if dried is used).
- Break the egg into a measuring cup. Add milk to make 1 cup.
- In a separate bowl, beat milk/egg, butter, extract and fresh lemon peel (if fresh is used).
- Combine milk and flour mixtures.
- Fill greased or paper-lined muffin tins two-thirds full.
- Bake in a preheated oven at 350 degrees for 20 to 25 minutes or until tops turn golden brown.

Tester's Comments: These are delicious, so double the recipe and freeze any leftovers.

Makes 9 muffins

19 tins - Bake 30 min

from **Martin Oaks B&B**
107 First Street
P.O. Box 207
Dundas, MN 55019
507-645-4644

Guests at this home, listed on the National Register of Historic Places, dine on fine china by candlelight, and breakfast always comes with homebaked breads or muffins, an entree and dessert.

Innkeepers Marie Vogl Gery and Frank Gery have spent years restoring this 1869 home, which became a B&B in 1991 and has three guestrooms. It was built by the Martin family, whose most famous ties come from Sara Etta Archibald Martin's brothers. The Archibald brothers founded Dundas and began milling there, the first mill in the country to produce a patented flour. The patents were sold to what became General Mills. Today, visitors can see the mill ruins, just across the Cannon River from the B&B. Most guests come to relax in this small town where, "when everybody is home, we boast a population of 422," Marie said. The restored veranda and the grand piano in the parlor are always available for guests' use.

Another Martin Oaks recipe:
Great Pie Crust, page 229

Maple Muffins with Maple Butter Glaze

Ingredients:

2 eggs
1 cup sour cream
1 cup maple syrup
1 cup flour
1 cup bran flakes cereal
1 teaspoon baking soda
3/4 cup chopped hazelnuts, optional

Glaze:
2/3 cup maple syrup
6 tablespoons butter

- In a large bowl, beat eggs with sour cream and maple syrup.
- Mix in flour, bran flakes and baking soda. Stir only until all ingredients are moistened.
- Mix in optional hazelnuts.
- Fill greased muffin tins two-thirds full.
- Bake in a preheated oven at 400 degrees for 15 minutes or until a toothpick inserted in the center comes out clean.
- For Glaze: Mix maple syrup with butter in a small saucepan over medium heat, or heat in a microwave-proof bowl, until mixture is well-blended.
- Remove warm muffins from muffin tins. Place 1 teaspoon glaze into the bottom of each cup. Dip the top of each muffin to the glaze, then return muffins to cups. Let stand about 15 minutes so bottoms absorb glaze. Serve warm.

Tester's Comments: These are as good as they sound. I used too much glaze, though, and I might as well have opened my mouth and poured in the buttery syrup.

Makes 16-18 muffins

from **Walden Woods B&B**
16070 Highway 18 Southeast
Deerwood, MN 56444
612-692-4379 or 800-892-5336

"I've had this recipe for eons -- my father adores real maple syrup and I knew these would be perfect for him," said Innkeeper Anne Manly. "They can be prepared ahead. Let them cool completely, wrap tightly and freeze."

Maple syrup seems appropriate to serve in this log cabin B&B, built by Richard Manly after working in New York City. Anne met him when she stopped in to buy his wood carvings, up north on vacation from the Twin Cities. When they married, they decided the home in the Brainerd lakes region would make a perfect B&B. They have four guestrooms.

Other Walden Woods recipes:
Mother's Blueberry Bread, page 93
Three Cheese Casserole, page 152

Marjorie's English Country Scones

Ingredients:

1 cup butter, very cold or frozen
4 cups flour
2 tablespoons sugar
1 tablespoon baking powder
1 teaspoon baking soda
1/2 teaspoon salt
1-1/4 cups buttermilk
4 eggs

Modified American Devonshire Cream:
Sour cream
Whipped cream
Powdered sugar

Also:

Strawberry jam
Devonshire cream

- Grate 1 cup butter and place it in the freezer.
- In a large bowl, mix flour, sugar, baking powder, baking soda and salt.
- In a separate bowl, beat the buttermilk and eggs thoroughly.
- Cut frozen butter into the flour mixture with a food processor or pastry cutter.
- Mix in buttermilk and eggs.
- Fill greased muffin tins full. Place the muffin tin on a cookie sheet.
- Bake in a preheated oven at 375 degrees for 15 minutes. Serve scones warm with jam and Devonshire cream. For Devonshire Cream: Whip cream until very stiff. Mix equal parts sour and whipped cream, then sweeten to taste with powdered sugar.

Makes 16-18 scones

from **Asa Parker House B&B**
17500 St. Croix Trail North
Marine on St. Croix, MN 54047
612-433-5248

"The trick in this recipe is to prevent the butter from breaking down. Until you place it in the oven, keep the mixture cold," said Innkeeper Marjorie Bush. "If you can't bake the scones all at one time, place the batter in the refrigerator." This recipe is from her great aunt, who lives in England. "She gave me the recipe verbally, and this is the best I can remember it -- it works!"

Guests at this four-guestroom inn may not eat lunch after Marge's breakfast. She is a veteran innkeeper, and all her recipes are decadent. Breakfast is served in the dining room of this 1856 lumberman's home.

Other Asa Parker House recipes:
Poached Apples in Vanilla Creme Sauce, page 129
Blueberry Grunt, page 208
Cheese Lace Crackers, page 227

Northern Raised Biscuits

Ingredients:

2 packets actve dry yeast
1/4 cup warm water
2 cups buttermilk
5 cups flour
1/3 cup sugar
1 tablespoon baking powder
1 teaspoon baking soda
1-1/2 teaspoons salt
1 cup butter-flavored shortening or unsalted butter

- Stir yeast into warm water. Let stand 5 minutes or until bubbly.
- Add buttermilk and set aside.
- In a large bowl, mix flour, sugar, baking powder, baking soda and salt.
- Cut in shortening with a pastry cutter or fork until crumbly.
- Gradually stir in the buttermilk mixture, stirring gently with a fork.
- Turn dough out onto a floured surface. Knead lightly four or five times.
- Divide dough in half. Roll or pat out each half to 1/2-inch thickness. Cut into biscuits and place on greased cookie sheets. Cover with a clean kitchen towel. Let rise in a warm place for 60 minutes.
- Bake in a preheated oven at 400 degrees for 10 to 12 minutes or until lightly browned. To freeze, bake for half as long, cool, wrap tightly and freeze. Reheat for 6 minutes at 400 degrees. Serve hot.

Tester's Comments: These are just wonderful -- yeasty and buttery (due to butter-flavored shortening). Make the whole batch and freeze part.

Makes about 30 biscuits

from **The Victorian Bed & Breakfast**
620 South High Street
Lake City, MN 55041
612-345-2167

Innkeeper Joel Grettenberg adapted a southern biscuit recipe to get this one, and he serves them hot with homemade strawberry-rhubarb jam. Fruit, specifically apples, is what brought Joel and Sandy, his wife, to Lake City in the first place. But during that fall day-trip to buy apples, they saw this home, overlooking the Mississippi's Lake Pepin, with a "for sale" sign, and the two teachers from Rochester were love-struck. The 1896 home has lake views from all three guestrooms and every other window. They opened in the fall of 1986, two years after making the fated trek for apples.

Another Victorian B&B recipe:
Pineapple Carrot Bread, page 94

Orange Scones

Ingredients:

2 cups flour
1/4 cup sugar
2 teaspoons baking powder
1 teaspoon baking soda
1/4 teaspoon salt
1/2 cup butter
3/4 cup sour cream
1 egg
6 tablespoons (3 ounces) undiluted frozen orange juice concentrate, thawed

Also:

Powdered sugar

- In a large bowl, stir together flour, sugar, baking powder, baking soda and salt.

- Cut in butter with a pastry cutter or fork until mixture resembles coarse cornmeal.

- In a small bowl, beat sour cream, egg and 4 tablespoons juice concentrate.

- Stir liquid ingredients into dry until a soft dough forms.

- Turn dough out onto a lightly-floured surface. Knead several times. Divide dough in half.

- Pat each half into a 6-inch circle. Cut each circle into 6 wedges. Place wedges on a greased cookie sheet.

- Brush tops with remaining 2 tablespoons juice concentrate.

- Bake in a preheated oven at 425 degrees for 10 to 12 minutes, or until lightly browned and a toothpick inserted in the center comes out clean.

- Remove from the oven, dust with powdered sugar and serve hot.

Makes 12 scones

from **The Ellery House B&B**
28 South 21st Avenue East
Duluth, MN 55812
218-724-7639 or 800-355-3794

"Our orange scones are usually served warm out of the oven with orange marmalade or peach jam," said Innkeeper Joan Halquist. They even passed muster from a British guest, and Joan suggests them for tea. Joan and husband Jim's 1890 Queen Anne Victorian was built four blocks from Lake Superior for Ellery Holliday, a local real estate tycoon. The four guestrooms and common areas are full of original stained glass windows and antiques, and three have views of the lake. The Halquists' B&B opened in 1988. They welcomed the idea of going into business for themselves in scenic Duluth.

Another Ellery House recipe:
Blueberry Oat Bran Muffins, page 54

excellent

Peaches and Cream Muffins

Ingredients:

2 cups canned peaches, drained (save "juice")
4 cups flour
2 cups sugar
2 teaspoons baking powder
1/2 teaspoon salt
3 eggs
3/4 cup oil
2 cups milk

Filling:
8 ounces cream cheese, softened
3/4 cup sugar
1 tablespoon reserved peach "juice"
1 teaspoon almond extract
Topping:
1/2 cup sugar
1 teaspoon cinnamon

- Dice drained peaches to the size of peas. Set aside.
- In a large bowl, mix flour, sugar, baking powder and salt.
- In a separate bowl, combine eggs and oil. Then whisk in milk.
- Combine egg and flour mixtures. Then fold in diced peaches.
- For Filling: Beat cream cheese, sugar, peach "juice" and almond extract.
- Fill greased muffin tins half full of batter. Drop 1 teaspoon of the filling into each muffin cup of the batter. Top with 1-1/2 tablespoons more batter.
- For Topping: Mix cinnamon and sugar. Sprinkle over muffins
- Bake in a preheated oven at 350 degrees for 20 minutes. Serve warm.

Tester's Comments: I refuse to publicly admit how many of these my sister and nephew ate at one sitting.

Makes 24 muffins

from **Spicer Castle**
11600 Indian Beach Road
Spicer, MN 56288
800-821-6675 or FAX 612-796-4076

Hot muffins such as these are served with special butters while guests are seated at the table overlooking Green Lake or fireside in the dining room of this 1893 home. Marti and Allen Latham's country home really looks like a castle -- the turret, in which one of the guestrooms is set, was the reason fishermen started calling it "Spicer Castle" when they used it for a landmark.

Built by Allen's grandfather, John Spicer, founder of the city, the summer lake home was used by friends, family and business associates visiting Spicer's farm to look over his innovative farming practices. Allen spent his boyhood summers here. His mother would not allow major alterations and it is listed on the National Register of Historic Places. Lathams opened the Castle as a B&B in 1988. It now is winterized and has eight guestrooms plus two separate guest cottages on the five wooded acres.

Another Spicer Castle recipe:
Frances Spicer's Candied Citrus Peels, page 191

Pineapple Tradewind Muffins

Ingredients:

3 ounces non-fat ricotta cheese
1 cup sugar
2 egg whites
2 teaspoons vanilla extract
2 cups flour
1 teaspoon baking soda
1 teaspoon salt
1/2 cup non-fat sour cream
1 10-ounce can crushed pineapple, drained

- In a large bowl, beat ricotta, sugar, egg whites and vanilla.
- In a separate bowl, mix flour, baking soda and salt.
- Add flour mixture to egg mixture alternately with sour cream.
- Fold in pineapple by hand.
- Spray muffin tins with cooking oil spray. Fill tins nearly full.
- Bake in a preheated oven at 350 degrees for 15 to 25 minutes "or until lightly browned and the top of the muffin springs back to the touch."

Tester's Comments: I know these are low-fat and they are delicious, but I couldn't resist adding chopped macadamia nuts to half the recipe -- fabulous!

Makes 8-12 muffins

from **Dutch Colonial Inn**
560 Central Avenue
Holland, MI 49423
616-396-3664

These low-fat homemade muffins are among the repertoire of Innkeeper Diana Klungel, who makes sure muffins are part of breakfast here every day. Breakfast time is also when hosts Pat and Bob Elenbaas might assist guests finding their way around Holland (there's more to it than tulips!).

The Elenbaases' 1928 home was built for the original owner as a wedding gift, using the finest materials. But by 1983, when the Elenbaases bought it, it needed an overhaul. They restored the residence and moved in, but when their sons married and left they decided to use the home as a B&B. Work continued after the B&B opened in 1988, adding bathrooms, a front porch and an addition. Today they offer five guestrooms for business travelers, honeymooners or visitors to Holland's Hope College or other attractions.

Another Dutch Colonial Inn recipe:
Sausage Ring, page 181

Pumpkin Apple Streusel Muffins

Ingredients:

2-1/2 cups flour
2 cups sugar
1 teaspoon pumpkin pie spice
1/2 teaspoon salt
1 teaspoon baking soda
2 eggs, beaten
1 cup solid-pack canned pumpkin
1/2 cup vegetable oil
3 ounces cream cheese
2 cups peeled and chopped apples

Streusel Topping:
1/2 cup flour
1/2 cup sugar
3 tablespoons butter, melted
1/2 teaspoon cinnamon

- First, make the Streusel Topping: Mix flour, sugar, butter and cinnamon with a pastry cutter or fork until streusel is in pea-sized crumbles.
- In a large bowl, combine the flour, sugar, pumpkin pie spice, salt. and baking soda
- In a medium bowl, combine the eggs, pumpkin and oil.
- Combine the flour mixture and egg mixture, mixing just until blended.
- Microwave the cream cheese twice, for about 20 seconds each time, until soft. Blend it in.
- Fold in the apples. Batter will be thick.
- Fill greased or paper-lined muffin tins three-quarters full. Sprinkle with Streusel Topping.
- Bake in a preheated oven at 375 degrees for 20 to 25 minutes.

Tester's Comments: These are dense and rich. Raisins are a nice addition, but these are good as they are!

Makes 18 muffins

from **White Lace Inn**
16 North Fifth Avenue
Sturgeon Bay, WI 54235
414-743-1105

Innkeeper Bonnie Statz credits Mary Wauters, an innkeeper since 1987 at the White Lace Inn, with this and many other recipes. "We always feature a variety of at least three baked goods," Bonnie said, and this is a fall favorite, using pumpkin and Door County apples. In 1982, Bonnie and husband Dennis opened the first of what is now three houses on adjoining properties. It was a 1902 Queen Anne, followed by moving the Garden House to the property and restoring the adjacent Washburn House. The homes have 15 guestrooms with Laura Ashley prints and (what else?) white lace trimmings.

Other White Lace Inn recipes:
Bonnie's Chocolate Zucchini Muffins, page 55
Lemon Herb Bread, page 89
Chilled Berry Soup, page 122

Raspberry Sour Cream Muffins

Ingredients:

2 eggs
1 cup sugar
1/2 cup vegetable oil
1 teaspoon almond extract
2 cups flour
1 teaspoon baking powder
1/2 teaspoon salt
1/2 teaspoon baking soda
1 cup sour cream
About 3 ounces almond paste
1 cup fresh or frozen "dry pack" raspberries

Streusel Topping:
1/4 cup chopped pecans
1/3 cup brown sugar, packed
1/4 cup flour
2 tablespoons butter, melted

- First, make Streusel Topping: Mix pecans, brown sugar, flour and butter with a fork until crumbly.
- In a large bowl of an electric mixer, beat eggs. Gradually add sugar. While the mixer is running, slowly pour in vegetable oil and almond extract.
- In a separate bowl, mix flour, baking powder, salt and baking soda.
- Add flour mixture to egg mixture alternately with the sour cream.
- Cut almond paste into 12 pieces. Pat each piece into a disk the size of a quarter.
- Grease muffin tins or line with paper muffin cups. Spoon about 1 tablespoon batter into each.
- Divide half the raspberries among the cups. Then top each with an almond paste disk.
- Put remaining batter on top of almond paste. Top with remaining raspberries and streusel.
- Bake in a preheated oven at 375 degrees for 20 to 25 minutes.

Tester's Comments: Not an almond-lover, I substituted vanilla for almond extract and a disk of cream cheese for the almond-paste. Mighty tasty.

Makes 12 muffins

from **Addie's Attic Bed & Breakfast**
117 South Jackson Street
P.O. Box 677
Houston, MN 55943
507-896-3010

"With an abundance of raspberries from our own patch in the backyard, I'm always looking for ways to include them in my breakfasts," said Innkeeper Marilyn Huhn. She and Fred, her husband, bought this home, built in 1903. It had once served as the Houston Public School. The Huhns turned it into a B&B in 1991, completing nearly all of the restoration work themselves. They named their B&B after a former owner and offer four guestrooms, decorated with attic heirlooms. Many guests come to bike the Root River Trail and enjoy the bluff country and quiet, slower-paced life in southeastern Minnesota.

Root Beer Muffins

Ingredients:

- 1-1/2 cups flour
- 1/4 cup sugar
- 4-1/2 teaspoons baking powder
- 3/4 teaspoons salt
- 1/3 cup raisins
- 2 eggs, slightly beaten
- 1/4 cup butter or margarine, melted
- 12 ounces root beer soda pop
- 1-1/2 cups quick-cooking oatmeal

Also:

- Cinnamon-Sugar mixture

- In a medium bowl, combine flour, sugar, baking powder and salt.

- Remove 2 tablespoons and mix it with the raisins in a separate bowl. Set aside.

- In a separate bowl, combine eggs, butter, root beer and oatmeal.

- Mix root beer combination into flour. Fold in raisins.

- Fill greased or paper-lined muffin tins two-thirds full. Sprinkle lightly with cinnamon-sugar mixture.

- Bake in a preheated oven at 400 degrees for 20 to 25 minutes. Serve warm.

Makes 12-14 muffins

from **Morningside Bed & Breakfast**
219 Leelanau Avenue
P.O. Box 411
Frankfort, MI 49635
616-352-4008

"I created this recipe for a soda pop cooking contest, and it took second prize," said Innkeeper Shirley Choss. A food management major in college, Shirley enjoys experimenting with recipes and baking for B&B guests. Her full breakfasts include homebaked muffins and use local fruit, when possible.

Shirley and husband Gus opened this four-guestroom inn after searching for the right location for nearly three years, then spending another 15 months restoring the Queen Anne home. Having just stayed at a B&B out East, they decided to try innkeeping. The combination of a B&B, which would use her food skills, located in northwestern Michigan, where he could fish after retiring from Ford, met both their needs. The home overlooks Frankfort.

Other Morningside B&B recipes:
Benzie Medley Conserve, page 104
Bedeviled Ham and Eggs, page 136

Six Week Bran Muffin Mix

Ingredients:

6 cups flour
2 cups sugar
1-1/2 cups raisin bran cereal
5 teaspoons baking soda
2 teaspoons salt
4 eggs, beaten
1 cup vegetable oil
4 cups (1 quart) buttermilk

- In a large bowl, mix flour, sugar, cereal, baking soda and salt.

- In a separate bowl, beat eggs, oil and buttermilk.

- Pour buttermilk mixture into cereal mixture and mix well.

- Use some batter now or pour into a container with a cover and refrigerate for up to 6 weeks.

- When ready to use, fill greased or paper-lined muffin tins two-thirds full.

- Bake in a preheated oven at 350 degrees for 15 to 20 minutes or until a toothpick inserted in the middle comes out clean.

Makes up to 45 muffins

from **Tianna Farms B&B**
Highway 371
P.O. Box 968
Walker, MN 56484
800-842-6620 or FAX 218-547-2255

Muffins at the B&B are served with Tianna Farms Jelly, well-known for its wild-berry preserves which are made on the grounds of this estate in Tianna Farms Kitchens. Guests can visit the jam and jelly shop.

Tianna Farms began in the late 1920s as a dairy farm, built by Liza Vogt's grandfather on the shores of Leech Lake. John Emory Andrus Jr. had two sites of the farm, one here and one near Tianna Country Club, the golf course he later purchased and redesigned. Kept in the family, the large home was opened as a B&B in 1991. "We've always had people driving down the driveway to look at the gardens and grounds," Liza said, "so opening the house to the public seemed to be the natural course of events." In addition to the gardens, guests can enjoy the greenhouse, swimming area, dock and private harbor on Leech Lake, tennis court and 55 acres of grounds.

Liza has five guestrooms with lake or garden views. Since she doesn't live in the home, groups or families can rent the entire house by the weekend or week for reunions, weddings or other special events. Walker is a northcentral Minnesota resort town with many attractions.

Strawberry Rhubarb Muffins

Ingredients:

1-3/4 cups flour
1/2 cup sugar
2-1/2 teaspoons baking powder
3/4 teaspoon salt
1 egg, slightly beaten
3/4 cup milk
1/3 cup vegetable oil
3/4 cup diced fresh rhubarb
1/2 cup sliced fresh strawberries, plus 8 halves for the tops

Also:

Sugar

- In a large bowl, mix flour, sugar, baking powder and salt.
- In a small bowl, combine egg, milk and oil.
- Stir egg mixture into flour mixture just until all ingredients are moistened.
- Fold rhubarb and sliced strawberries into batter.
- Fill greased or paper-lined muffin this two-thirds full with batter.
- Press a strawberry half gently into the top of each muffin. Sprinkle tops generously with sugar.
- Bake in a preheated oven at 400 degrees for 20 to 25 minutes or until golden brown.

Tester's Comments: No need for butter on these -- the fresh rhubarb and berries make them moist.

Makes 8 large muffins

from **Chicago Street Inn**
219 Chicago Street
Brooklyn, MI 49230
517-592-3888 or FAX 517-592-9025

Karen and Bill Kerr got hooked on B&Bs when they stayed in one by accident, sort of. "We were visiting a resort area without reservations," Karen said. There was room at a local B&B and "we loved it." They returned to the village of Brooklyn, located just southeast of Jackson, and bought an 1886 Queen Anne Victorian that had been for sale for some time. They quickly sold their own home and opened the seven-guestroom inn four months later.

"Our inn had been a family home for 100 years and very well-cared for," Karen said. It was built as part of a farm, and its owners ran the mercantile store. The home's oak and cherry woodwork was cut from the farm's trees.

🏠*Other Chicago Street Inn recipes:*
Potato Hot Dish, page 180
Sour Cream Ripple Coffee Cake, page 217

Three Muffins to the Wind

Ingredients:

1/2 cup raisins
Sherry to cover (about 1/2 cup)
1-3/4 cups flour
1/4 cup sugar
2-1/4 teaspoons baking powder
1/2 teaspoon salt
1/2 teaspoon baking soda
1 heaping tablespoon oat bran
1 heaping tablespoon wheat germ
1 egg
3/4 cup buttermilk
1/2 cup vegetable oil
1/2 medium apple, grated

🐟 The night before, place raisins in a glass measuring cup. Cover with sherry and leave overnight.

🐟 In the morning, drain raisins ("saving liquid for fruit dishes or whatever. Drink it if it's that kind of morning.")

🐟 In a large bowl, combine flour, sugar, baking powder, salt, baking soda, oat bran and wheat germ.

🐟 In a separate bowl, mix egg, buttermilk and oil. Then grate in half an apple and stir.

🐟 Stir drained raisins into the flour mixture. Add buttermilk mixture. Stir only until combined.

🐟 Fill greased or paper-lined muffin tins two-thirds full.

🐟 Bake in a preheated oven at 400 degrees for about 20 minutes. Serve hot.

Makes 12 muffins

from **The Stout Trout B&B**
Rt. 1, Box 1630
Springbrook, WI 54875
715-466-2790

"My uncle always received a bottle of sherry for Christmas, and neither he nor my aunt cared for it, straight up. She used it to soak raisins which were used for everything, including these muffins," said Innkeeper Kathleen Fredericks. "She let us use them for decorating gingerbread men, but kept a close watch for snitching!" Kathy serves the muffins with wild plum jam.

Her B&B is a former fishing resort on Gull Lake, between Hayward and Spooner. She took the run-down lodge, complete with Elvis paint-on-velvet decor, and gutted it. A year later, only the original plank floors remained, and four "English-Country-meets-Shaker-style" guestrooms were opened.

🏠*Another Stout Trout recipe:*
Poached Pears and Craisins, page 130

Zucchini Muffins

Ingredients:

3 eggs
1 cup vegetable oil
1-1/2 teaspoons vanilla extract
3/4 cup sugar
1 cup brown sugar, packed
3 cups flour
2 teaspoons cinnamon
2 teaspoons cloves
2 teaspoons nutmeg
1 teaspoon baking powder
1 teaspoon baking soda
1 teaspoon salt
3 cups grated zucchini

- In a large bowl, beat eggs and oil. Add vanilla, sugar and brown sugar and mix well.
- Beat in flour, cinnamon, cloves, nutmeg, baking powder, baking soda and salt.
- Fold in zucchini.
- Fill greased or paper-lined muffin cups three-quarters full.
- Bake in a preheated oven at 350 degrees for 30 minutes.

Makes 24 muffins

from **The Inn at Grady's Farm**
W10928 Highway 33
Portage, WI 53901
608-742-3627

"As any gardener knows, once zucchinis start to ripen, they are abundant," understated Carol Moeller. "We've developed many recipes using the wonderful zucchini." This vegetable is but one grown organically in the garden, and apples, pears, cherries, raspberries, strawberries and mulberries also are cultivated on the farm of Carol and Donna Obright.

Carol and Donna opened The Inn at Grady's Farm after surviving 10 stressful years as restaurateurs. "This is a very pleasant alternative," Carol said. "Our culinary skills can still be put to use, as well as our love of people."

The inn is in a 1903 farmhouse that was a weekend retreat for Portage attorney Danial Grady. He raised Morgan show horses here and enjoyed relaxing in the country. The new owners found the home had been converted to a duplex but was structurally sound, so they added bathrooms to the four guestrooms and redecorated, opening in 1992. The home is filled with many different antique collections, many of which are family heirlooms.

Any way you slice it, absolutely *nothing* beats the smell of bread baking on a chilly morning. Well, perhaps the smell of cinnamon rolls baking. In this chapter, some recipes for rolls and breads with yeast, requiring time to "rise," are included. Several recipes are for sweet breads that can be whipped up in a few minutes, and which would do justice served as dessert. (And many of those are so moist and flavorful they require no buttering.) No matter what side you butter your bread on, there's sure to be a recipe to please you. These creations run the gamut of traditional to creative, from fruit breads to beer bread and ice cream caramel rolls, and back again to old-fashioned cinnamon rolls.

Breads

Applesauce Bread

Ingredients:

2 cups brown sugar, packed
1 cup butter, softened
2-1/2 cups applesauce
1 tablespoon molasses
1 teaspoon cloves
1 teaspoon nutmeg
2 cups raisins
4 cups flour
4 teaspoons baking soda

- Cream brown sugar and butter.
- Beat in applesauce, molasses, cloves and nutmeg.
- Mix the raisins with about 2 teaspoons of flour. Stir the raisins into the applesauce mixture.
- Mix the remaining flour and baking soda together. Add to raisin mixture.
- Pour batter into two greased and floured 9 x 5-inch loaf pans.
- Bake at 300 degrees for 65 to 70 minutes or until a toothpick inserted in the center comes out clean.
- Remove from oven and allow to cool a few minutes before removing from pan. Serve warm.

Tester's Comments: I thought this would need cinnamon, but it doesn't. It's moist and got very good reviews.

Makes 2 loaves

from **Linden Lea on Long Lake**
279 South Long Lake Road
Traverse City, MI 49684
616-943-9182

"My mother used to bake this in the fall and winter when there were extra apples to use up," recalled Innkeeper Vicky McDonnell. "With a family of nine, nothing went to waste. I never knew that it could be frozen until years later because growing up, there were never any leftovers!" The aroma from this bread baking takes her back to those autumn days.

Guests at this lakeside B&B can work up quite an appetite. They are welcome to swim on Vicky and Jim's sandy Long Lake beach, fish or take the rowboat over to one of the islands. McDonnells took a deteriorating summer cottage and turned it into a contemporary, multi-level B&B with two guestrooms, both with window seats from which to watch the sunset. The B&B is located minutes from Traverse City, Interlochen Center for the Arts, the Sleeping Bear Dunes National Lakeshore and other area attractions.

Another Linden Lea recipe:
Cherry Oatmeal Muffins, page 57

Aunt Lessie's Cinnamon Bread

Ingredients:

2 cups dark brown sugar, packed
1/2 cup butter
1 tablespoon cinnamon
1/4 teaspoon cloves
2-1/2 cups sifted flour
3/4 cup buttermilk
2 teaspoons baking powder
1 egg, beaten

- In a large bowl, cream sugar and butter.

- Add spices. Work in the flour until the mixture is crumbly. Remove 3/4 cup for topping.

- Measure buttermilk and stir the baking powder into it.

- Beat buttermilk mixture and egg into the flour mixture.

- Spread batter into a greased and floured 9 x 5-inch loaf pan. Sprinkle reserved crumbs on top.

- Bake in an oven preheated to 350 degrees for about 1 hour or until a knife inserted in the center comes out clean. Serve immediately with butter.

Tester's Comments: This dense, dark bread was sweet enough for me using light brown sugar.

Makes 1 loaf

from **The Lamp Post Inn**
408 South Main Street
Fort Atkinson, WI 53538
414-563-6561

Debbie and Mike Rusch take particular pride in not letting overnight guests go away hungry. Breakfasts at this Victorian home are so "full" that one guest remarked, "you should be called 'Breakfast & Bed!'" The meal might include this bread or muffins, fresh fruit, Canadian bacon and an egg dish.

Rusches moved into this home in 1988 after it had stood vacant for nine months. Major work -- including replastering, updating plumbing and electrical systems and refinishing floors -- was needed. Outside, a buried cobblestone sidewalk was uncovered and gardens planted. Less than a year later, the B&B opened with two guestrooms. Rusches now have three.

An antique phonograph is available in each guestroom, and guests are encouraged to use them. The parlor has Victorian furniture and drapes and a phonograph of its own. Mike and Debbie had a large collection of family heirlooms, so the entire inn is furnished in antiques. Breakfast is served on Depression glass in the newly-wallpapered formal dining room.

Dry

Banana and Wild Blueberry Bread

Ingredients:

2/3 cup sugar
1-1/2 cups flour
2 teaspoons baking powder
1/4 teaspoon salt
3/4 cup quick-cooking oatmeal
1/3 cup corn or canola oil
2 eggs, slightly beaten
2 large bananas, mashed
3/4 cup wild blueberries, fresh or frozen "dry pack"

- In a large bowl, sift together sugar, flour, baking powder and salt. Stir in oatmeal.
- Mix in oil, eggs and mashed bananas, stirring only until all ingredients are moist.
- Fold in blueberries.
- Pour batter into a greased and lightly floured 9 x 5-inch loaf pan.
- Bake in a preheated oven for 60 to 65 minutes or until a toothpick inserted in the middle comes out clean.
- Remove from oven. Cool in the pan 15 minutes, then remove from pan and place on a wire rack.

Tester's Comments: A surprisingly good flavor combination, even with "domestic" berries. Moist, too.

Makes 1 loaf

from **Lindgren's Bed & Breakfast**
County Road 35
P.O. Box 56
Lutsen, MN 55612
218-663-7450

Innkeeper Shirley Lindgren uses her mother's recipe to make this bread and serves it to her B&B guests as part of a full breakfast. In addition to enjoying the meal, guests can enjoy the view of Lake Superior from the great room.

Shirley and husband Bob bought this log home on Lake Superior's North Shore in 1967. But when they sold their Twin Cities' nursery businesses in 1987, they had major restoration done on the home and moved north for good (Bob bought a boat and Shirley headed for the trout streams). The B&B allows them to share their home and landscaped grounds with people, and their policy is, "When you are away from home, our home is your home."

Another remodeling project was done in 1992, and they now have four log or pine-paneled guestrooms. Guests are close to Lutsen skiing, golf and the Superior Hiking Trail, and they can toast marshmallows at the water's edge.

Cherry Cheesecake Nut Bread

Ingredients:

8-ounces cream cheese
1 cup margarine
1-1/2 cups sugar
1 -1/2 teaspoons vanilla extract
4 eggs
2-1/4 cups flour
1-1/2 teaspoons baking powder
1 cup chopped nuts
1 10-ounce jar maraschino cherries, drained and chopped

Icing:
1-1/2 cups powdered sugar
2 tablespoons milk

- In a large bowl, cream the cream cheese, margarine, sugar and vanilla.
- Beat in the eggs, one at a time.
- Sift flour with the baking powder. Add it to the creamed mixture.
- Fold in almost all the nuts and cherries, reserving a few for decoration.
- Pour batter into two greased and floured 9 x 5-inch loaf pans.
- Bake at 325 degrees for 45 to 60 minutes, or until a knife inserted in center comes out clean.
- For Icing: Combine powdered sugar and milk. Remove bread from pans to a wire rack. Drizzle on icing, then decorate with reserved nuts and cherries.

Makes 2 loaves

from **Stonehedge Inn B&B**
924 Center Avenue (M-25)
Bay City, MI 48708
517-894-4342

Guests at Ruth Koerber's inn enjoy this bread on the breakfast buffet, served with softened cream cheese (or straight up). Homemade breads, muffins or waffles and fresh fruit are always part of the buffet.

This seven-guestroom inn was built in 1889 for a lumber baron. Many of the original features -- speaking tubes, large fireplaces, gas and electric light fixtures, a warming oven and antiques -- will make guests feel that they've entered the late 19th century.

The distinctive English Tudor home is located on M-25 near downtown Bay City. Both business and pleasure guests enjoy its proximity to Bay City's best antique shops and restaurants.

Another Stonehedge Inn recipe:
Lemon Blueberry Nut Bread, page 88

Chopped Apple Bread

Ingredients:

1-1/2 cups raisins
Warm water to cover
3/4 cup shortening or vegetable oil
1-1/2 cups sugar
3 eggs
1/2 teaspoon salt
3/4 cup cold coffee
2-1/2 cups flour
1-1/2 teaspoons baking soda
1-1/2 teaspoons cinnamon
1 teaspoon cloves
1 teaspoon allspice
1-1/2 cups peeled, chopped apples
1 cup chopped walnuts

- Soak raisins in warm water to cover for 1 hour.
- In a large bowl, cream shortening and sugar. Beat in eggs.
- Slowly mix in salt and coffee.
- Add flour, baking soda, cinnamon, cloves and allspice.
- Fold in apples and walnuts. Drain raisins and fold them in.
- Pour batter into two greased 9 x 5-inch loaf pans.
- Bake in a preheated oven at 350 degrees for 1 hour.

Makes 2 loaves

from **The Kingsley House**
626 West Main Street
Fennville, MI 49408
616-561-6425

Apples aren't just on the menu at this 1886 Queen Anne Victorian B&B. The eight guestrooms all are named after varieties of Michigan apples in honor of Harvey J. Kingsley. He introduced apple trees to the area around Fennville, Saugatuck and Holland.

Innkeepers Shirley and Dave Witt restored Kingsley's turreted home after selling a B&B they operated in Holland. They wanted an historic home, and they found it. Using the original blueprints, these former teachers returned this home to its former glory, complete with the 150 spindles around the porch. Sandy Lake Michigan beaches are only a seven-minute drive.

Another Kingsley House recipe:
Apple Bars, page 222

Cinnamon Rolls

Ingredients:

3/4 cup butter-flavored shortening
1 cup milk
2 packets active dry yeast
1/2 cup very warm water
1 cup cold water
3/4 cup sugar
2 teaspoons salt
2 eggs
7 cups flour

Filling:
Butter, softened
1/2 cup sugar
1/2 to 1 teaspoon cinnamon

Also:

Raisins, optional
Powdered sugar frosting, optional

- Melt shortening in the milk by heating together in the microwave, then stirring.

- When the shortening is melted and milk is no longer hot, dissolve yeast in warm water. Then pour yeast into shortening and milk.

- In a separate bowl, combine the cold water, sugar, salt and eggs. Mix into yeast mixture.

- Stir in flour. Cover dough tightly and refrigerate at least overnight (will keep a week).

- In the morning, divide dough in half. Turn out onto a floured board and knead well. Add raisins.

- Roll out to approximately a 9 x 15-inch rectangle. Spread with butter. Mix sugar and cinnamon and sprinkle over dough, all the way to the edges.

- Roll rectangle up from the long side. Make about 12 slices. Place rolls about 1/2-inch from each other in greased baking pans. Repeat with other half of dough.

- Cover with a clean towel. Let rise in a warm draft-free place 1 hour or until rolls have doubled.

- Bake in a preheated oven at 350 degrees for 30 minutes.

Tester's Comments: These are as good as Mom made without having to get up at 5 a.m. to make them!

Makes about 24 rolls

from **Candlelight Cottage B&B**
910 Vassar Street
Alma, MI 48801
517-463-3961

"The dough is best after two or three days in the refrigerator," said Innkeeper Yvonne Wolfgang, who prefers to use Crisco shortening. "It's so nice to get it made ahead. The rolls smell great, too!" Homemade rolls, muffins and breads are always part of her breakfasts. Yvonne loves to bake and entertain. Located within view of Alma College, Yvonne and husband Ron's two guestrooms attract visitors to the college and town. They totally redecorated their Cape Cod home before opening as a B&B in 1987. Guests are treated to afternoon tea and evening snacks, as well.

Cinnamon Twists

Ingredients:

1 packet active dry yeast
1 cup heavy cream, warmed
1/2 cup butter, melted
1/2 cup margarine, melted
1 teaspoon salt
1 tablespoon sugar
1 egg
3-1/2 cups flour

Also:

Sugar
Cinnamon
Powdered sugar frosting, optional

- Dissolve yeast in warm cream.

- In a large bowl, mix butter, margarine, salt, sugar and egg. Stir in yeast mixture, then flour.

- Cover dough and chill for 2 hours. Then divide dough in three portions and refrigerate two portions. On a floured board, roll the other portion out to a rectangle or square 1/3 to 1/4-inch thick.

- Sprinkle sugar and cinnamon down the middle. Fold one outer third over the center, then sprinkle the top of it with sugar and cinnamon. Fold last third over. Cut into 1-inch strips the short way.

- Twist strips one time and place on a cookie sheet 1 inch apart. Push down ends with finger so twists don't unroll. Repeat for rest of dough. Let rise in a warm, draft-free place for 20 to 30 minutes.

- Bake in a preheated oven at 350 degrees for 10 to 15 minutes. Cool and frost, optional.

Tester's Comments: I had better luck cutting strips 1/2-inch wide. These are rich pastries -- don't grease the cookie sheets! And don't let the length of the recipe scare you -- these aren't difficult.

Makes about 36 twists

from **Pillow, Pillar & Pine Guest House**
419 Main Street
Cold Spring, MN 56320
612-685-3828

When businessman Marcus Maurin wanted to give his daughter a wedding gift, he gave no small token. It was this three-story Greek Revival mansion, measuring 8,000 square feet. In 1989, Linda and Mike Carlson opened the home as a B&B with three guestrooms. Guests will find original stained glass windows, oak and maple woodwork, antique light fixtures and a wrap-around porch. The Carlsons, who first stayed in a B&B in Maine, filled the house with heirloom antiques and serve family recipes, like this. Guests come to Cold Spring, an hour northwest of the Twin Cities, to enjoy area lakes, bike the Red River Trail, see the blue heron rookery, golf or ski. It's also home to Cold Spring Brewery, and colleges are close by.

Dill Casserole Bread

Ingredients:

    1 packet active dry yeast
    1/4 cup warm water
    1 cup cottage cheese
    2 tablespoons sugar
    1 teaspoon minced onion
    1 tablespoon butter, melted
    2 teaspoons dried dill
    2 teaspoons salt
    1/4 teaspoon baking soda
    1 egg
    2-1/4 to 2-1/2 cups flour

Also:

    Butter, melted

- Dissolve yeast in very warm water.

- Heat cottage cheese to lukewarm in microwave. Mix with yeast.

- In a large bowl, stir cheese mixture, sugar, onion, butter, dill, salt, soda and egg.

- Mix in flour to form a soft dough.

- Cover and let rise in a warm, draft-free place until dough doubles, about 90 minutes.

- Stir dough down. Turn into a greased 1-1/2 or 2-quart casserole dish. Cover and let rise again 30 to 40 minutes.

- Bake in a preheated oven at 350 degrees for 30 to 40 minutes or until deep golden brown and loaf sounds hollow when tapped. Remove from oven and brush with melted butter. Serve hot.

Makes 1 loaf, 18 slices

from **Aunt Martha's Guest House**
2602 County Road A, HCR 59
Spooner, WI 54801
715-635-6857

This might be one of the homemade breads that Mary Caskov serves to her guests on the breakfast buffet. She also serves homemade jellies.

Mary and her son, Robert Johnson, are partners in this country B&B. They turned their 1927 home into a three-guestroom B&B in 1990, named in memory of Mary's sister. It is located 15 miles from Spooner on a country road, surrounded by pines. "My son and I love to decorate and create -- I love to do crafts and anything creative. Together we've worked three years on this project," Mary said. "We like people and are enjoying the many new people we are meeting." Guests come to the area for the variety of outdoor recreation found in the sandy lake region of western Wisconsin.

Excellent

Dutch Apple Bread

Ingredients:

1/4 cup butter, softened
1/4 cup vegetable oil
1 cup sugar
2 tablespoons orange juice *much*
1 teaspoon vanilla extract
2 eggs
2 cups flour, sifted
1 teaspoon baking soda
1/4 teaspoon salt
1 cup apples, coarsely chopped
1/2 cup chopped nuts

Topping:
2 teaspoons sugar
1 teaspoon cinnamon
2 tablespoons finely chopped nuts

- In a large bowl, cream butter, oil and sugar. Beat in orange juice, vanilla and eggs.
- Sift together flour, baking soda and salt. Stir into egg mixture. Fold in apples and nuts.
- Butter two small (7-1/2 x 3-1/2 inch) bread tins or one 9 x 5-inch loaf pan. Spoon in batter.
- For Topping: Mix sugar, cinnamon and nuts and sprinkle on top.
- Bake in a preheated oven at 350 degrees for 50 minutes.

Makes 1 loaf

from **Pinehaven Bed & Breakfast**
E13083 Highway 33
Baraboo, WI 53913
608-356-3489

This homemade nut bread is often on the breakfast table, along with a large tray of fresh fruit and a hot main dish. Innkeepers Marge and Lyle Getschman enjoy breakfast time with their guests from all over the country.

Getschmans have found lots of folks are interested in their place since they opened in 1990. They rebuilt their chalet-style home in the pines so the four guestrooms would have views of the Baraboo Bluffs or their small private lake. (Yes, a paddleboat and rowboat are available for guests' use.)

But in addition to the setting, visitors come to see the Getschman's Belgian draft horses. Lyle's dad raised draft horses, and Lyle learned early to love them. Time permitting, Lyle will hitch a horse or team up for a wagon or sleigh ride. The horses are kept on the farm side of the highway, a pleasant walk from the main house.

Families with older children enjoy not just the B&B and its horses, but the Circus World Museum and North Freedom Steam Train in Baraboo. Pinehaven also is close to Devils Lake State Park.

Golden Squash Raisin Bread

Ingredients:

1 cup milk
1 cup cooked, mashed winter squash (Hubbard or Buttercup)
1/4 cup vegetable oil
1/4 cup honey
2 teaspoons salt
1 teaspoon cinnamon
1 teaspoon nutmeg or other spices
2 packets active dry yeast
1/2 cup warm water
2 eggs, beaten
1-1/2 cups raisins
6 to 6-1/2 cups flour, divided

Also:

Margarine, melted

- Scald milk. Stir in squash, oil, honey, salt, cinnamon and nutmeg. Stir to cool.
- Dissolve yeast in warm water. When all yeast is dissolved, add to squash mixture.
- Mix in eggs, raisins and half of the flour.
- Add remaining flour gradually, until dough leaves the sides of the bowl. Turn onto a floured board and knead until dough is elastic.
- Place in a greased bowl. Cover and let rise in a warm, draft-free place until double, about 1 hour.
- Punch dough down. Divide in half. Shape into two loaves and place in two greased 9 x 5-inch loaf pans. Brush tops of loaves with melted margarine. Cover and let rise in again until double.
- Bake in a preheated oven at 375 degrees for 40 minutes or until golden. Remove from pans to cool.

Makes 2 loaves

from **Bed & Breakfast at The Pines**
327 Ardussi Street
Frankenmuth, MI 48734
517-652-9019

Innkeeper Donna Hodge loves this bread sliced and toasted or for sandwiches. She often doubles the recipe for her family-style breakfasts. Donna and husband Richard opened their ranch-style home as a B&B in 1986. After their three children were grown and married, the Hodges had extra bedrooms. Since they'd enjoyed B&Bs themselves, they opted to open their own home. Frankenmuth's famous chicken dinners at the Bavarian Inn and Zehnder's, Bronner's Christmas shop and other shopping are year 'round attractions, and their home is within walking distance.

Another Bed & Breakfast at The Pines recipe:
Leonard Date Cookies, page 232

Gramma's Beer Bread

Ingredients:

3 cups self-rising flour (OR 3 cups flour, 4-1/2 teaspoons baking powder, 1-1/2 teaspoons salt)
3 tablespoons sugar
1 12-ounce can of beer, at room temperature

Also:

Milk

- In a large bowl, mix flour, sugar and beer.
- Place dough in a greased 9 x 5-inch loaf pan.
- Bake in a preheated oven at 400 degrees for 50 to 65 minutes, until golden brown.
- Brush the top with milk after baking to moisten crust.

Tester's Comments: This is a delicious, crusty bread. For a softer crust, bake at 375 for 60 to 70 minutes. A friend suggests using 1/2 cup wheat germ in place of 1/2 cup flour and adding 1/3 cup chopped pecans.

Makes 1 loaf

from **Dreams of Yesteryear**
1100 Brawley Street
Stevens Point, WI 54481
715-341-4525 or FAX 715-344-3047

"This bread conjures up memories of Gramma, a Polish cook who could feed 40-50 guests who crowded around the kitchen every Sunday," said Innkeeper Bonnie Maher. "I serve it with egg dishes for breakfast, or it's especially good with soups." It was Bonnie's grandparents and other relatives who gave her heirlooms that sparked her interest in things historic.

After Bonnie married Bill and had two children, they bought their first historic home: the Jensen house, a three-story Queen Anne Victorian located three blocks from downtown and two blocks from the Wisconsin River. In 1901, when construction was started, the newspaper reported "the building will be a modern one with all improvements, and will cost $3,000 or $4,000." John L. Jensen was a Danish immigrant who owned a thriving general store with a partner. Two of his sons, Gerald and Charles, also owned the home and it was Charles' widow, Janet, who sold it to Bonnie and Bill in 1987.

The Mahers became interested in B&Bs through another Stevens Point innkeeper, Joan Ouellette of the Victorian Swan on Water. Joan and her mom toured the home and suggested it for a B&B. "We fell in love with the whole concept," Bonnie said. They opened in 1990 and have four guestrooms.

Other Dreams of Yesteryear recipes:
Mom's Carrot Cake, page 211
Rhubarb Cobbler, page 216

Ice Cream Caramel Rolls

Ingredients:

Dough:
- 1/2 cup warm water
- 2 teaspoons active dry yeast (less than 1 packet)
- 2-1/4 cups flour
- 1/4 cup sugar
- 3 tablespoons non-fat dry milk
- 1/2 teaspoon ground cardamom
- 1 teaspoon salt
- 1/3 cup butter, melted
- 1 egg

Caramel Topping:
- 1/2 cup butter, melted
- 1/2 cup sugar
- 1/2 cup brown sugar, packed
- 1 cup vanilla ice cream, melted

🍂 In a measuring cup or bowl, mix water and yeast until yeast dissolves.

🍂 In a separate bowl, mix flour, sugar, dry milk, cardamom and salt.

🍂 Mix in butter, egg and dissolved yeast.

🍂 Turn dough out onto a floured surface. Cover with a clean towel and let "rest" for 20 minutes.

🍂 Knead for at least 10 minutes, preferably 15 (otherwise dough won't rise). Cover and let rise in a warm, draft-free place until dough doubles in size, about 1 hour.

🍂 Punch dough down and cut into 24 small pieces. Place in a greased 9 x 13-inch pan. (Dough can be covered and refrigerated overnight at this point. In the morning, let it sit out while making topping.)

🍂 Cover and let rise again. While dough is rising, make topping.

🍂 For Caramel Topping: Mix butter, sugars and ice cream. Pour mixture over risen dough.

🍂 Bake in a preheated oven at 325 degrees for 25 to 30 minutes. Remove from oven and cool for 5 minutes. Then invert pan onto a serving plate. Serve immediately.

Tester's Comments: This rich topping kept us reaching for more.

Makes about 2 dozen rolls

from **The Inn on the Green**
Route 1, Box 205
Caledonia, MN 55921
507-724-2818

"These sweet rolls are the most-asked-for recipe at the inn," said Shelley Jilek. "They look different every time but they are always good." Frozen sweet roll dough or dough from a bread machine can be used, and this busy innkeeper uses the latter. Shelley, a teacher, and husband Brad, an electrical contractor, became innkeepers after buying this large colonial home on a golf course. They remodeled the garden level to make two guestrooms and an atrium with whirlpool and sauna. They now have four guestrooms done in country decor. Guests can enjoy the 10 acres with gardens and an orchard, golf, cross-country ski or take in the fall colors in southeastern Minnesota's bluff country.

Lemon Blueberry Nut Bread

Ingredients:

1/2 1/4 cup margarine, softened
2 1 cup sugar
6 3 tablespoons fresh lemon juice
4 2 eggs
3 1-1/2 cups flour
2 1 teaspoon baking powder
2 1 teaspoon salt
1 1/2 cup milk
2 1 cup fresh or frozen "dry-pack" blueberries
   2 tablespoons grated lemon rind
1 1/2 cup chopped walnuts

- In a large bowl, cream margarine, sugar and fresh lemon juice. Then beat in the eggs.
- In a separate bowl, stir together flour, baking powder and salt.
- Add flour mixture to the egg mixture alternately with milk. Stir only enough to blend.
- Fold in blueberries, grated lemon rind and walnuts.
- Pour batter into a greased and floured 9 x 5-inch loaf pan.
- Bake at 350 degrees for 70 minutes, or until a knife inserted in center comes out clean.
- Remove from oven and cool. Store bread in the refrigerator.

Tester's Comments: A moist bread that won't crumble. I prefer it without nuts, but with a little lemon extract (1/2 teaspoon or so). Mix 2 tablespoons sugar with 2 teaspoons lemon juice for a glaze added after baking.

Makes 1 loaf

from **Stonehedge Inn B&B**
924 Center Avenue (M-25)
Bay City, MI 48708
517-894-4342

Repeat guests ask Innkeeper Ruth Koerber if this bread will be served during their stay. It's one of her most popular recipes, and she has a collection that spans 45 years. This and other homemade breads and muffins are served on the breakfast buffet, along with fresh fruit.

When guests sit down to breakfast, they have just spent the night as a lumber baron's family would at the turn-of-the-century -- but with more creature comforts. Bay City's heyday was during the lumbering era, when logs clogged the nearby Saginaw River. This English Tudor home was built in 1889 for a man who had made his fortune in lumber. Ruth turned it into a B&B in 1988, with seven guestrooms. Many original features remain.

🏠 *Another Stonehedge Inn recipe:*
Cherry Cheesecake Nut Bread, page 79

Lemon Herb Bread

Ingredients:

1 cup milk
2 tablespoons grated zest of lemon (peel)
1 tablespoon chopped fresh lemon balm
1 tablespoon chopped fresh lemon thyme
7 tablespoons butter, softened
1-1/4 cups sugar
2 eggs
2-3/4 cups flour
2 teaspoons baking powder
A pinch of salt
2 tablespoons fresh lemon juice

Glaze:
2 tablespoons fresh lemon juice
Powdered sugar
1-1/2 teaspoons grated zest of lemon

- Heat the milk (but do not boil). Remove from heat and mix in zest, lemon balm and thyme. Cool.
- In a large bowl, whip the butter, adding sugar gradually, beating until creamy. Beat in eggs.
- In a separate bowl, mix flour, baking powder and salt. Set aside.
- Pour the cooled milk-herb mixture into the butter mixture. Add lemon juice and mix well.
- Slowly add the flour mixture, stirring just until blended.
- Pour batter into two 9 x 5-inch greased loaf pans, filling each about one-third full.
- Bake in a preheated oven at 350 degrees for about 50 minutes, but don't let bread get brown.
- For Glaze: In a medium bowl, whisk lemon juice and powdered sugar together. "Keep adding powdered sugar until the glaze is the consistency of thick gravy." Stir in lemon zest.
- Remove bread from oven. Poke holes in tops with toothpicks, then pour glaze over both loaves.

Makes 2 loaves

from **White Lace Inn**
16 North Fifth Avenue
Sturgeon Bay, WI 54235
414-743-1105

How did Innkeeper Bonnie Statz come up with this one? "Experiment, experiment, experiment. I really wanted a moist lemon bread using herbs from our garden," she said. The extensive gardens tie together three historic homes-turned-inn, all on adjacent properties and connected by brick walkways through the garden. Bonnie and husband Dennis started in 1982 with one inn and five guestrooms and by 1986 had tripled that number and earned a solid reputation. Guests enjoy homebaked breads, Chilled Berry Soup or Norwegian fruit soup or fresh fruit before a day in Door County.

Other White Lace Inn recipes:
Bonnie's Chocolate Zucchini Muffins, page 55
Pumpkin Apple Streusel Muffins, page 67
Chilled Berry Soup, page 122

Low-Fat Banana Prune Bread

Ingredients:

4 cups mashed bananas
1 cup sugar, plus 2 tablespoons
1/2 cup applesauce
2 eggs
1 teaspoon vanilla extract
1/2 cup chopped "orange essence" prunes
1/2 cup chopped nuts
2 cups flour
1 tablespoon baking powder
1 teaspoon salt
1 teaspoon baking soda

- In a medium bowl, combine bananas and 1 cup sugar. Let stand for 15 minutes.

- Beat in the applesauce, eggs and vanilla. Stir in prunes and nuts.

- Sift together flour, baking powder, salt and baking soda. Stir into banana mixture.

- Grease two 9 x 5-inch loaf pans, then sprinkle the pans with 2 tablespoons sugar. Pour in batter.

- Bake in a preheated oven at 350 degrees for 45 to 50 minutes or until top springs back to touch.

- Cool in pan for 10 minutes. Then turn out on a wire rack.

Tester's Comments: A really moist bread for which the toothpick test won't work - bake for at least 45 minutes.

Makes 2 loaves

from **Greystone Farms B&B**
N9391 Adams Road
East Troy, WI 53120
414-495-8485

This bread "is better the second day, but it's usually gone by then!" Innkeeper Ruth Leibner got the recipe from a friend, then added the nuts and prunes. She might serve it as one bread enjoyed with a full country breakfast.

Ruth and daughter Alane operate this four-guestroom B&B on the family farm. Ruth jokes that she got into the B&B business after sprucing up the place. "Alane and I were painting the barn. Afterward, the darn thing looked so good we thought we ought to do something with it!" Truth is, the six kids were grown, and the farmhouse was perfect for it. They added an addition for their own living quarters and opened in 1986, having a farmhouse that dates back to the 1880s. Guests can act like kids again on the tree swing or hiking or biking quiet country roads.

Another Greystone Farms recipe:
Bread Pudding Cake, page 185

Mabel's Cranberry Bread

Excellent

Also used f3 raspberry

Ingredients:

2 cups flour (combination white/whole wheat, if desired)
3/4 to 1 cup sugar
1-1/2 teaspoons baking powder
1/2 teaspoon salt
1/2 teaspoon baking soda
1 egg, beaten
1/2 cup orange juice
2 tablespoons butter, melted
2 tablespoons hot water
1/2 cup chopped nuts
1 cup fresh cranberries, halved
Grated peel of 1 orange

- In a large bowl, sift together flour, sugar, baking powder, salt and baking soda.
- In a separate bowl, mix egg, orange juice, butter and hot water. Stir into the flour mixture.
- Mix in nuts, cranberries and orange peel, stirring well.
- Pour batter into a greased 9 x 5-inch loaf pan. Bake in a preheated oven at 350 degrees for 70 minutes.
- While the bread is still hot, wrap in waxed paper and refrigerate for 24 hours before serving.

Tester's Comments: Frozen cranberries, washed and chopped in the food processor, worked fine.

Makes 1 loaf

from Chatsworth Bed & Breakfast
984 Ashland Avenue
St. Paul, MN 55104
612-227-4288

Innkeeper Donna Gustafson got this recipe from her mother-in-law more than 40 years ago. "It's always a favorite at holiday time -- a loaf is a great gift." Donna serves it with butter, arranged on a pretty plate with a lace doily.

Donna and Earl, her husband, transformed their three-story family home into a B&B in 1986. "Our eight children grew up here and moved on out. We loved the house, the double tree-filled lot and convenient location," Donna said. The home is just a few blocks from the Governor's Mansion on Summit Avenue and the shops and restaurants on popular Grand Avenue. Since Donna wanted to start her own business, a B&B was her choice. The Gustafsons redecorated, added bathrooms and opened five guestrooms with international themes. They welcome a mix of business and pleasure travelers and those celebrating honeymoons and anniversaries or other occasions.

Molasses Bread

Ingredients:

1 cup flour
1-1/2 cups whole wheat flour
1 teaspoon baking soda
1 cup sour milk (to "sour" milk, stir 1 tablespoon vinegar into 1 cup milk)
1/4 cup molasses
3/4 cup honey

- In a large bowl, sift together the flours and baking soda.

- Add milk, molasses and honey and beat thoroughly.

- Pour into 3 or 4 small (3-1/2 x 6-inch) loaf pans or one 9x5 pan. Bake in a preheated oven at 325 degrees, 30 to 35 minutes for small pans, 50 to 60 minutes for large pan, or until a toothpick inserted in the center comes out clean. "It's best served the next day." Serve plain or warmed with butter.

Tester's Comments: Moist and sweet. Raisins or chopped dried apricots might be good additions.

Makes 1 loaf or 3 to 4 small loaves

from **The French Country Inn of Ephraim**
3052 Spruce Lane
P.O. Box 129
Ephraim, WI 54211
414-854-4001

At the French Country Inn, guests might enjoy this bread as an afternoon or evening snack with tea, or spread with cream cheese at breakfast. "Joan wanted a tea bread that could use honey instead of sugar. This also has no oil, so it's good for cutting down on fat," said Innkeeper Walt Fisher. He and his spouse/co-innkeeper Joan Fitzpatrick limit their intake of refined sugar.

Breakfast is served on blue Depression glassware in front of the beachstone fireplace. If this place has the feel of a northwoods lodge, it's by design. It was originally built as a comfortable summer home for a Chicago family who had 10 children. Walt and Joan now offer seven guestrooms (plus a separate guest cottage, formerly the summer kitchen and ice house).

Walt first traveled in B&Bs in Wales, when he worked there as an architect. He thought he'd like to return someday to operate a pub there. But years later, when he and Joan planned to leave Kansas City, Missouri, he researched inns. Ephraim not only had the inn for sale, but it was a picturesque, historic village with a European feel. Joan agreed to take the plunge; they bought the inn in 1988. Lake Michigan is only a block away. The inn is on a quiet street.

Another French Country Inn recipe:
Baked Apple Slices, page 120

Mother's Blueberry Bread

— not so much butter

Ingredients:

2 cups fresh or frozen blueberries, drained
4 cups flour
2 cups sugar
1/2 cup water
4 tablespoons butter
1 cup fresh-squeezed orange juice
2 eggs, beaten
2 teaspoons baking powder
1/2 teaspoon baking soda
1/2 teaspoon salt

Topping:
4 tablespoons butter
4 tablespoons sugar
4 tablespoons flour
2 teaspoons cinnamon

- Drain blueberries and sprinkle with a few tablespoons of the flour. Set aside.
- Boil water. Add butter, orange juice, eggs and sugar. Mix well.
- In a separate bowl, mix remaining flour, baking powder and baking soda.
- Combine flour and orange juice mixture. Fold in blueberries.
- For Topping: Mix butter, sugar, flour and cinnamon with a fork or pastry cutter.
- Pour bread batter into two greased and lightly-floured 9 x 5-inch loaf pans. Sprinkle on topping.
- Bake in a preheated oven at 325 degrees for 60 minutes or until a knife inserted in the center comes out clean.

Tester's Comments: A wonderful bread that's still wonderful using unthawed berries.

Makes 2 loaves

from **Walden Woods B&B**
16070 Highway 18 Southeast
Deerwood, MN 56444
612-692-4379 or 800-892-5336

Innkeeper Anne Manly serves this versatile bread at room temperature, warm or toasted, and says it "freezes beautifully." She includes it as part of a large breakfast at the log home her husband, Richard, built from scratch.

Richard has owned this property on a 40-acre lake in the Brainerd lakes region for years. After working for the National Audubon Society in New York City, he returned here to build his home and carve. Anne, a consulting forensic scientist, met him when she bought one of his carvings. Both had traveled internationally, staying in B&Bs, and opening their own was a natural decision after they married. Guests can enjoy the lake and trails.

Other Walden Woods recipes:
Maple Muffins with Maple Butter Glaze, page 61
Three Cheese Casserole, page 152

Pineapple Carrot Bread

Ingredients:

3 eggs
1/2 cup vegetable oil
1/2 cup butter, melted
1-1/2 cups sugar
2 teaspoons vanilla extract
2 cups shredded fresh carrots
1 8-ounce can crushed pineapple, undrained
3 cups flour
2 teaspoons baking soda
1-1/2 teaspoons cinnamon
1 teaspoon salt
3/4 teaspoon nutmeg
1/2 teaspoon baking powder
1 cup chopped nuts
1/2 cup raisins

- Beat eggs, oil, butter, sugar and vanilla until foamy.
- Stir in carrots and pineapple.
- Mix in flour, baking soda, cinnamon, salt, nutmeg and baking powder.
- Stir in nuts and raisins.
- Pour into two greased and floured 9 x 5-inch loaf pans.
- Bake in a preheated oven at 325 degrees for 1 hour. Serve warm or cold.

Tester's Comments: This bread is a lot like carrot cake -- try toasting it and spreading with cream cheese!

Makes 2 loaves

from **The Victorian Bed & Breakfast**
620 South High Street
Lake City, MN 55041
612-345-2167

This bread might be on the breakfast tray in the formal dining room. Guests dine by the room's bay window which overlooks Lake Pepin on the Mississippi River. The stained glass bay window was one of the treasures Innkeepers Sandy and Joel Grettenberg found in this 1896 home, built by a local bank director who appreciated the lake. Nine-foot ceilings, butternut woodwork and a lake view from every room are other attributes. Sandy and Joel opened their B&B in 1986 and offer three guestrooms.

Another Victorian B&B recipe:
Northern Raised Biscuits, page 63

Raspberry Bread

Ingredients:

1 cup butter, softened
1-1/2 cups brown sugar, packed
3 eggs, beaten
1/2 cup plain yogurt
Juice of 1 lemon (2 to 3 tablespoons)
2-1/2 cups flour
1 cup whole wheat flour
1-1/2 teaspoon baking soda
1/2 teaspoon cinnamon
3 to 4 cups fresh raspberries

- In a large bowl, cream butter and brown sugar. Beat in eggs.
- Beat in yogurt and lemon juice.
- Add flour, whole wheat flour, baking soda and cinnamon, beating until smooth.
- Carefully fold in raspberries so they are are broken as little as possible.
- Turn batter into two greased 9 x 5-inch loaf pans.
- Bake in a preheated oven at 325 degrees for 55 to 60 minutes or until a knife inserted in the center comes out clean. Cool bread in pans for 15 minutes before removing to a wire rack.

Makes 2 loaves

from **Shady Ridge Farm B&B**
410 Highland View
Houlton, WI 54082
715-549-6258

"We grow a lot of raspberries on the farm and I couldn't find anything but dessert recipes using them," Innkeeper Sheila Fugina said. "So I looked at several of my bread recipes, experimented and came up with this." She serves it with butter or honey butter, but guests often prefer it plain.

Guests who just can't wait to head for the barn to see the Fuginas' llama herd can share a picnic breakfast with the llamas. Some of the eight or so long-lashed llamas will accompany guests on walks, as well. The Fuginas have found the combination of a B&B and llama ranch to be perfect. Love or leave the llamas, guests enjoy the restored 1890 brick farmhouse with three guestrooms. Rooms have views of the farm, set in the scenic St. Croix Valley.

Other Shady Ridge Farm recipes:
Mulberry Jam, page 110
Rose Hip Syrup, page 115

Rhubarb Bread

Ingredients:

1-1/2 cups diced fresh or frozen rhubarb
1 cup sugar
1 cup brown sugar, packed
2/3 cup vegetable oil
1 egg
1 cup sour milk (to "sour" milk, mix 1 tablespoon vinegar into 1 cup milk)
1 teaspoon vanilla extract
1-1/2 cups flour
1 teaspoon baking soda
1 teaspoon salt
1/2 cup chopped nuts, such as walnuts or pecans

Topping:
1/2 cup sugar
1 teaspoon cinnamon
1 tablespoon butter

- In a medium bowl, stir rhubarb and sugar together. Set aside.
- In a large bowl, beat brown sugar, oil, egg, milk and vanilla together.
- Add flour, baking soda and salt. Mix well.
- Stir in rhubarb and nuts by hand.
- Pour batter into two greased and floured 9 x 5-inch loaf pans.
- For Topping: Mix sugar, cinnamon and butter with a fork or pastry cutter until crumbly. Sprinkle on top of batter.
- Bake in a preheated oven at 350 degrees for 55 to 60 minutes.

Tester's Comments: With fresh rhubarb, this is so moist there's no need to add butter.

Makes 2 loaves

from **Yankee Hill Inn B&B**
405 Collins Street
Plymouth, WI 53073
414-892-2222

"This bread freezes well, but it disappears *fast* when served," so Innkeeper Peg Stahlman rarely has any leftover to freeze. Besides, when all 11 guestrooms in two neighboring homes are full, she has quite a crowd to feed. Peg and spouse Jim began innkeeping in 1988 when they opened the Gilbert Huson house. The 1891 Queen Anne had been converted to apartments, so Jim and Peg's restoration uncovered many treasures, like gingerbread trim and wood staircase. Stahlmans later acquired the home next door of Gilbert's brother, Henry, listed on the National Register of Historic Places. Its square turret is one distinctive feature, and it has four guestrooms.

Other Yankee Hill Inn recipes:
Banana Macadamia Nut Muffins, page 51
Aunt Josie's Lemon Butter, page 103

Swiss Cheese Bread

Ingredients:

1 cup milk
1-1/2 tablespoons sugar
2-1/2 teaspoons salt
1 tablespoon butter
1 packet active dry yeast
1 cup warm water
5 cups sifted flour
2 cups grated Swiss cheese

Also:

Shortening or vegetable oil

- In a saucepan, scald milk, sugar, salt and butter. Remove from heat and cool until warm.

- In the large bowl, sprinkle yeast into warm water. Stir by hand to dissolve.

- Stir in cooled milk mixture. Then beat in 2 cups of flour.

- Mix cheese into the soft dough. Mix in remaining flour to make a stiff dough.

- Turn out onto a floured board and knead until smooth and elastic, adding just enough flour to keep the dough from sticking to the board.

- Place in a greased bowl, cover with a towel and let rise in a warm, draft-free place until double, about 1 hour.

- Punch dough down. Divide in half. Knead a few times, then place in a greased 9 x 5-inch pan.

- Repeat with other half of dough. Cover. Let rise until double. Coat top with shortening or oil.

- Bake in a preheated oven at 350 degrees for 45 minutes. Remove from pans and cool on wire rack.

Makes 2 loaves

from **Abendruh B&B Swisstyle**
7019 Gehin Road
Belleville, WI 53508
608-424-3808

Breakfasts at Mathilde Jaggi's B&B are "regional specialties, from a light fruit bake (French) to a hearty cheese and ham dish, common in the Bernese section of Switzerland," she said. As a certified French chef, she serves a breakfast with a European flair, one of things that makes her inn different.

Another is her home. Natives of Switzerland, she and husband Franz, a master mason, and their six children designed and built Abendruh, which means "evening peace" in Swiss. When the children grew up and moved out, Mathilde opened a B&B in the large stone and stucco home on two country acres, 18 miles south of Madison. Guests are treated like family, with use of the fireplaces, TV, piano and spacious lawn.

Tart Cherry Nut Bread

Ingredients:

2 cups flour
1 cup plus 2 tablespoons sugar
1-1/2 teaspoons baking powder
1/3 cup shortening
1 egg
1/2 cup orange juice
1 tablespoon grated orange peel
2 tablespoons warm water or warmed cherry juice
1 cup fresh, canned or frozen tart cherries, well drained, coarsely chopped
1/2 cup chopped nuts

- In a large bowl, sift together flour, sugar and baking powder.
- Cut in shortening with a pastry cutter or fork.
- In a separate bowl, mix egg, orange juice, orange peel and water or juice. Add to flour mixture.
- Fold in cherries and nuts.
- Pour batter into a greased 9 x 5 -inch loaf pan.
- Bake in a preheated oven at 350 degrees for 50 to 60 minutes or when a toothpick or knife inserted in the middle comes out clean.

Tester's Comments: Good without the nuts, too. This is another bread that's so moist butter isn't necessary.

Makes 1 loaf

from **Cherry Knoll Farm B&B**
2856 Hammond Road East
Traverse City, MI 49684
616-947-9806 or 800-847-9806

Guests think life is just a bowl of cherries after staying at this cherry orchard B&B. Innkeeper Dorothy Cump serves up cherries just about any way she can from the 1,200 trees husband Percy tends -- and from which guests are free to pick during July, the cherry "season."

The Cumps have owned this circa 1865 farmhouse since 1968. But when they retired from real estate in the Chicago suburbs in 1988, they hardly "retired." They set to work almost immediately to convert the home to a three-guestroom B&B, and added a gingerbread-trimmed front porch where guests like to rock and read. Many guests are content to hunt for morels in the spring on the 115 acres or "leaf peep" in the fall. Traverse City and Grand Traverse Bay beaches are 10 minutes away for those who want more "action."

Another Cherry Knoll Farm recipe:
Peachy Cherry Sauce, page 112

Whole Wheat Oatmeal Bread

Ingredients:

1 cup unbleached flour
1 cup whole wheat flour
1 cup old-fashioned oatmeal
1 teaspoon baking powder
1 teaspoon salt
1 teaspoon baking soda
1/4 cup molasses
1-1/4 cups plain yogurt
1/2 cup raisins or currants

- In a large bowl, mix flours, oatmeal, baking powder, salt and baking soda.

- In a separate bowl, beat molasses and yogurt.

- Combine yogurt mixture with dry ingredients.

- Mix in raisins or currants. "Mixture will be very stiff and you may have to mix it with your hands."

- Place dough in a greased 9 x 5-inch loaf pan. Set aside for 20 minutes.

- Bake in a preheated oven at 350 degrees for 50 to 60 minutes or until a knife inserted in the middle comes out clean.

Makes 1 loaf

from **The Inn at Ludington**
701 East Ludington Avenue
Ludington, MI 49431
616-845-7055

Innkeeper Diane Shields developed this recipe when she led a Cadette Girl Scout Troop and they were working on cooking badges. Little did she know then that she'd be serving it to B&B guests at an 1889 Queen Anne Victorian mansion-turned-inn. She might serve this bread with some of her homemade jams and jellies, using the best of the many locally grown fruits.

Diane knew many innkeepers and their inns well before she entered the profession herself. She owned and operated a reservation service, and she first saw this inn when she came to visit innkeepers in Ludington.

"When I found out it was for sale, I decided to pursue my dream of full-time innkeeping, and within three months had moved in, lock, stock and barrel." The three-story home has six guestrooms, to which Diane added bathrooms and redecorated after purchasing the inn in 1990.

🏠*Another Inn at Ludington recipe:*
Strawberry Shortcake Muffins, page 218

Whole Wheat Wild Rice Bread

Ingredients:

3 cups whole wheat flour
1 cup sugar
1 tablespoon salt
2 packets active dry yeast
2-1/2 cups milk
1/4 cup oil
1 egg, beaten
1 cup wild rice, cooked
3 to 4 cups "best for bread" flour

- In a large bowl, combine 2 cups of the whole wheat flour, sugar, salt and yeast. Mix for 30 seconds.
- In a saucepan, heat milk and oil until very warm.
- Mix milk mixture into flour mixture. Mix in egg. Beat with a heavy duty mixer for 3 minutes.
- Turn dough out onto a floured board. Knead in remaining cup of whole wheat flour, wild rice and bread flour until the dough is smooth and elastic.
- Cover with a clean towel, set in a warm, draft-free place and let rise until double, about 1 hour.
- Shape dough into four loaves and place into four greased 9 x 5-inch loaf pans.
- Cover and let rise again, about 30 to 40 minutes.
- Bake in a preheated oven at 350 degrees for 40 to 45 minutes.

Makes 4 loaves

from **The Rivertown Inn**
306 West Olive Street
Stillwater, MN 55082
612-430-2955

This bread, adapted from a family recipe of Chuck Dougherty's, is often served on the breakfast buffet at the Rivertown Inn, along with other homemade breads, muffins and pastries. Chuck also shapes this dough into baguettes and uses the loaf for evening hors d'oeuvres, served in the parlor.

Chuck, a former restaurateur, and spouse Judy, a former teacher, bought this nine-guestroom inn in 1987. The inn is a three-story 1882 Queen Anne Victorian, with a wrap-around porch, iron fence and gazebo. John O'Brien, a prominent lumberman, had the home built for his family on a hill high above the St. Croix River. Stillwater, the birthplace of Minnesota, was the scene of the logging boom, and the St. Croix had many sawmills and log rafts. Today, the historic town located about 30 miles east of the Twin Cities is a popular getaway. Guests come to Stillwater for antiquing, a dinner train and paddlewheel boat rides, plus a number of good restaurants and country shops, all located in the historic downtown.

There's nothing like homemade, and this chapter proves it. Innkeepers, highly regarded as a resourceful bunch, show how to make the most from what's at hand in the local fruit stand or even the backyard: crab apples, blackberries, cherries, strawberries, mulberries, rose hips and blueberries all were inspiration for these recipes. A few recipes for butters and spreads can transform an otherwise ordinary piece of toast or English muffin into a memorable breakfast treat. Try the jams, jellies, conserve and spreads on the Northern Raised Biscuits in the Bread chapter, and enjoy the sauces and syrups on pancakes from the Entrees chapter. In times of true desperation, enjoy Aunt Josie's Lemon Butter by the spoonful!

Preserves, Butters, Spreads & Sauces

Amaretto Sour Cream Sauce

Ingredients:

    3 cups sour cream
    3/4 cup brown sugar
    1/8 cup Amaretto liqueur (or more to taste)

Mix ingredients well. Serve over fresh fruit. Store covered in the refrigerator.

Tester's Comments: This recipe is easily adaptable by substituting the liqueur of your choice. For family-size amounts, try 1 cup sour cream, 1/4 cup brown sugar, 1 tablespoon liqueur.

Makes 3-1/2 cups

from **The Inn at Union Pier**
9708 Berrien Street
P.O. Box 222
Union Pier, MI 49129
616-469-4700 or FAX 616-469-4720

This sauce is served over Michigan berries, such as blueberries and raspberries, in the dining room. During the summer, guests appreciate the view of the garden and landscaped grounds. In the cooler months, they appreciate the warmth of the Kakelugn -- Swedish ceramic fireplace.

The fireplaces are present in most of the 15 guestrooms Innkeepers Joyce Erickson Pitts and Mark Pitts offer in three buildings. The buildings were originally built as a hotel in the early 1920s. They were operated as the popular Karonsky's Hotel, the only kosher hotel in Union Pier, Joyce said.

In 1983, new owners purchased the buildings and started extensive renovation that took two years. Originally 39 small rooms shared a total of six bathrooms -- and the shower was outdoors.

Today, the Great House (main house), Pier House, across the courtyard, and Cottage of the Four Seasons next door have rooms with private baths, large beds and comfortable antique or reproduction furnishings. The decor is more "cottage style" than lacey and frilly, Joyce said.

Joyce and Mark became the new owners in 1993, leaving high-stress careers in Chicago. "We looked at inns all over the country but found the perfect one close to home," Joyce said. They have the best of both worlds to offer guests, being 75 minutes from Chicago and 200 steps from the Lake Michigan beach.

Other Inn at Union Pier recipes:
Mexican Mini Frittatas, page 145
Oven-Roasted New Potatoes, page 234

Aunt Josie's Lemon Butter

Ingredients:

2 lemons
2 eggs
1 cup sugar
2 tablespoons butter

- Roll the lemons on their sides to make them more juicy. Cut them in half, squeeze or use a reamer to completely remove juice. Strain the juice to remove seeds and pulp. Set aside.
- Thoroughly beat eggs. Stir in lemon juice, sugar and butter.
- Pour mixture into a microwave-safe bowl. Microwave on "high" for 2 minutes, then stir. Microwave for 2 more minutes, stir, and then repeat for a third or fourth time until thickened.
- Stovetop method: Cook ingredients in a saucepan (or the top of a double boiler) over medium heat, stirring constantly until thickened. "Be very careful not to scorch."
- Cool. Place in a covered container and refrigerate. Serve as a spread or topping.

Tester's Comments: This is just great on Gingerbread Waffles, page 173. (Why didn't my family have an Aunt Josie?)

Makes about 2 cups

from **Yankee Hill Inn B&B**
405 Collins Street
Plymouth, WI 53073
414-892-2222

"Back in the dark ages, when I was a young girl," Peg Stahlman begins, "my father's Aunt Josie came to our home every September for the Buffington Family Reunion. Aunt Josie *always* brought Lemon Butter for the reunion picnic. It was her specialty and was always a hit!" Today, Aunt Josie's recipe finds its way to English muffins, toast or bagels on the dining room table here, and Peg also uses it as a topping for gingerbread or applesauce cake.

Celebrating heritage is something at which Peg and husband Jim work hard. They restored the Yankee Hill homes of two brothers who owned a dry goods store and a farm implement dealership. The inn now offers 11 guestrooms.

Hard work is not in the plans for most of their guests, who come to Plymouth, 50 miles north of Milwaukee, to relax. Downtown Plymouth, just over the footbridge, has an antique mall, shopping and restaurants. The Ice Age hiking/biking trail, Northern Kettle Moraine State Forest, Lake Michigan beaches, Kohler Design Center and Road America racing track are all nearby.

Other Yankee Hill Inn recipes:
Banana Macadamia Nut Muffins, page 51
Rhubarb Bread, page 96

Benzie Medley Conserve

Ingredients:

1-1/2 pounds fully ripe pears
1 orange
1 cup crushed pineapple, drained
1/2 cup dried tart cherries
Other fresh fruit as desired (peaches, apricots, berries, apples)
1 box powdered fruit pectin
5 cups sugar

- Peel and core pears. Grind them together with orange, or chop finely.

- Stir in pineapple. Chop dried cherries and mix in. If necessary, add other prepared fruit as desired to make 4-1/2 cups.

- In a saucepan, combine fruit and pectin, mixing well. Measure sugar and set aside.

- Over high heat, stirring constantly, bring fruit to a full rolling boil. Then stir in sugar all at once.

- Boil hard for 1 minute, stirring constantly. Then remove from heat and skim off foam.

- Stir and skim frequently over 6 minutes (cooling slightly prevents "floating" fruit in the conserve).

- Ladle quickly into hot, sterilized jelly or jam jars, leaving 1/2-inch space at top. Cover with sterilized, tight-fitting lids. Process according to directions on pectin box for jam.

Makes about 9 8-ounce jars

from **Morningside Bed & Breakfast**
219 Leelanau Avenue
P.O. Box 411
Frankfort, MI 49635
616-352-4008

"Benzie is fruit country," said Innkeeper Shirley Choss. Located on Lake Michigan south of Traverse City, the region produces cherries, apples, pears, peaches, apricots and berries. "It's a great place to live if you like to cook!" Or eat. Shirley serves this conserve with homemade biscuits or scones.

Guests here stay in what was built as a grand, hillside summer home, built in the 1890s. Nearly every room has a bay window, which looks out over Frankfort and the neighborhood of other Victorian homes. Shirley and Gus, her husband, took 15 months to restore the home, which had been apartments and a rooming house. They tried to restore the home to its original design, but added bathrooms to each of the four guestrooms. Guests have a short walk down the hill to town or a great Lake Michigan beach. Also, Frankfort is the southern entrance to Sleeping Bear Dunes National Lakeshore.

Other Morningside B&B recipes:
Root Beer Muffins, page 69
Bedeviled Ham and Eggs, page 136

Blueberry Grand Marnier Preserves

Ingredients:

4-1/2 cups frozen "dry pack" blueberries, chopped
1/2 cup (1-1/2 boxes) powdered fruit pectin
1/2 cup Grand Marnier liqueur
4 cups sugar

- Chop frozen berries in a food processor.
- Place berries in a large saucepan. Stir in pectin.
- Bring berries to a boil and boil for 1 minute, stirring constantly.
- Stir in Grand Marnier and sugar. Bring back to a rolling boil for 3 minutes, stirring constantly.
- Ladle into hot, sterilized jelly jars, leaving 1/2-inch space at the top. Immediately cover with sterilized, tight-fitting lids and bands (for more detailed directions, read the pectin package).
- Let jam sit for 24 hours before tasting. "For best results, do not change the recipe or make in larger quantities."

Makes 6 6-ounce jars

from **The Inn at Cedar Crossing**
336 Louisiana Street
Sturgeon Bay, WI 54235
414-743-4200

These preserves are some of the many produced by the kitchen at this inn, which guests can sample at breakfast and then take home a jar.

The kitchen is part of the restaurant, which opened in 1989 in the storefront on one of downtown Sturgeon Bay's main streets. It's the location that has, since 1884, housed a pharmacy, a boutique and a clothing store. The clothing store was owned by Gerhard Miller, a well-known Door County artist who worked in the store as a youngster.

When Terry Wulf bought the building in 1985, she concentrated her efforts on the upstairs, which was apartments. Armed with a vision of a quaint downtown inn like those found in Europe, she gutted the upstairs and constructed nine guestrooms and a common room with a fireplace. After seven months of working more than full-time, the inn opened. Each guestroom is decorated in different country decor, some with stenciling by a local artist or poster or canopy beds handcarved by a local woodworker.

🏠 *Other Inn at Cedar Crossing recipes:*
Apple Walnut Coffeecake, page 35
Perfect Berry Chambord Preserves, page 113
Chilled Cherry Soup, page 123
Dried Fruit Relish, page 190

Crab Apple Butter

Ingredients:

3 pounds crab apples, enough to make 9 cups when quartered
2-1/2 cups apple juice
1/2 cup cider vinegar
2 cups sugar
1 teaspoon cinnamon
1/4 teaspoon nutmeg
1/8 teaspoon mace

- Rinse the crab apples and cut into quarters to make 9 cups.
- In a large kettle, combine crab apples, apple juice and cider vinegar.
- Bring the mixture to boiling, then reduce heat. Cover and simmer about 30 minutes, stirring occasionally.
- Press the mixture through a food mill or sieve, until 5 cups of "butter" is obtained.
- Rinse the kettle and return butter to it. Stir in the sugar, cinnamon, nutmeg and mace.
- Bring mixture to boiling, then reduce heat to low. Simmer, uncovered, 60 to 90 minutes, stirring often, until the apple butter is very thick.
- Meanwhile, prepare five half-pint jars for canning. Sterilize jars and lids.
- Spoon crab apple butter into the hot, sterilized jars, leaving 1/2-inch space at the top. Wipe the jar rims, place lids and bands on the jars and adjust.
- Process the jars in a boiling water bath for 10 minutes (start timing when water boils). Then remove and cool jars on a rack.

Makes 5 half-pint jars

from **Summit Farm B&B**
1622 110 Avenue
Hammond, WI 54015
715-796-2617

"We serve this on fresh baking powder biscuits or crunchy croissants," said Innkeeper Laura Fritsche. "It smells like an apple orchard on a fall day."

Her B&B smells wonderful, too, when she cooks up a batch of this crab apple butter. "My son loves to help with this one — from picking those little apples to the first taste. He can hardly wait for it to cool." The apples come from their own trees. Much of their fruit and vegetables come from their garden and orchard, too. Laura and Grant, her husband, opened two guestrooms in 1992, after spending six years restoring their 1910 farmhouse.

Another Summit Farm B&B recipe:
Iced Cappuccino, page 26

Dolly's Blackberry Rhubarb Jam

Ingredients:

   5 to 6 cups boiling water
   4 cups sliced rhubarb
   4 cups sugar, divided
   2 cups blackberries

- In a large bowl, pour boiling water over rhubarb. Let it stand until cool. Then pour off water.
- Stir in 2 cups of sugar and the blackberries.
- In a large saucepan or kettle, bring mixture to a rolling boil over medium heat, stirring often.
- Boil for 3 minutes, stirring frequently.
- Mix in remaining 2 cups sugar. Boil 4 minutes, stirring frequently.
- Remove from heat. Pour into sterilized, hot jelly jars, leaving 1/2-inch space at the top. Immediately cover with sterilized, tight-fitting lids and bands. Store in the refrigerator (for up to a month) or in the freezer.
- Serve as jam or warm it slightly and serve as a sauce.

Makes about 6 8-ounce jars

from **The Victorian Swan on Water**
1716 Water Street
Stevens Point, WI 54481
715-345-0595

"A couple years ago a delightful Minnesota couple stayed and volunteered this recipe," said Innkeeper Joan Ouellette. "It is truly delicious and easy." Joan serves it warm over pancakes or French toast. Breakfast at her 1889 home is served in the cheerful breakfast room. Fresh fruit is followed by an entree, meat and breads "and, of course, dessert," Joan said. She is a creative cook who is always improving recipes.

Joan's four-guestroom B&B started as a home in another part of town. It was moved in 1938 by removing the third story and cutting the house in half. It resumed life as a duplex, which she and brother/partner Chuck Egle "undid" when they restored it. They used original blueprints and uncovered walnut parquet floors and a black cherry fireplace, among other original fixtures. The yard has been featured in a nursery catalog (Chuck is a landscape architect).

Chuck, a Stevens Point resident, actually found the house for Joan, who lived in Milwaukee. He wasn't sure she was serious at first. But indeed she was, and it turned out to be the right decision. "After eight years, I still love being an innkeeper and taking care of a beautiful old house," Joan said.

Another Victorian Swan recipe:
Peach Rum Sauce, page 111

Honey Spread

Ingredients:

1/2 cup honey
1 cup peanut butter, chunky or creamy ("I like to use chunky")
1/2 cup applesauce
1/2 cup raisins

☛ Mix ingredients in a medium bowl. Spoon into a pretty dish for serving. Serve on toast, English muffins and bagels.

☛ Cover and refrigerate leftovers.

Tester's Comments: The color is not real attractive, but the taste is. This is a good way to cut the stickiness of natural peanut butter. Best when served cold. Try it in celery sticks, too.

Makes about 2 cups

from **Rummel's Tree Haven B&B**
41 North Beck Street (M-25)
Sebewaing, MI 48759
517-883-2450

"Everyone likes it, especially children," said Innkeeper Erma Rummel about this recipe. "When they return they usually tell me that they hope I have it for them at breakfast." Special spreads, fruit in season, homemade granola and generous servings of a full breakfast make Erma's morning meal memorable.

Breakfast is also memorable because of its atmosphere -- relaxed and informal, like the rest of the stay at the home of Erma and her husband, Carl. "Guests smell breakfast cooking and invariably they come down earlier than planned, have a cup of coffee and visit as I cook," Erma said. The Rummels tell guests they offer more of a small homestay than a romantic Victorian B&B.

Erma and Carl opened their B&B in 1986, converting two upstairs bedrooms formerly used by their children to guestrooms. Many of their guests come to hunt or fish -- Sebewaing is only two hours from Detroit and 30 minutes from Bay City. Saginaw Bay holds perch, walleye, pike and catfish, and hunters find good goose, duck, deer and pheasant hunting. Some guests come just to walk in the country, take a bike ride or watch birds.

Erma, a teacher, and Carl, a building contractor, wanted to open a B&B after they both retired. Their home was built in 1878 as the original farm house on the Beck farm, a large farm with two barns. Becks then raised cows and chickens. Two generations of the Beck family farmed from this home. Guests are welcome to use the outdoor grill, watch the Rummel's collection of video tapes, or shoot the breeze. Carl is a fisherman and a duck decoy collector who can offer hunting and fishing tips to guests.

June-Time Conserve

Ingredients:

3-1/2 cups (1 pound) fresh rhubarb, cut in 1/2-inch pieces
4 cups (1-1/4 pounds) fresh strawberries
1/2 cup dried currants
1 cup water (part fruit wine may be used)
2 cinnamon sticks
5 cups sugar
1 cup almonds or walnuts, chopped

- Measure rhubarb, strawberries, currants, water and cinnamon sticks into a heavy 6- to 8-quart preserving kettle.

- Stir in sugar, stirring until sugar dissolves.

- Bring mixture to a boil over high heat, stirring constantly. Continue to boil and stir until mixture is very thick and sheets off the spoon, 45 to 60 minutes. Add nuts during the last 5 minutes of cooking.

- Remove from heat. Stir gently and skim off foam. Remove cinnamon sticks.

- Ladle conserve into hot, sterilized half-pint jars, leaving 1/4-inch space at the top. Wipe the jar rims and seal with sterilized canning lids.

- Process jars for 5 minutes in a boiling water bath. Then remove and cool jars on a rack.

Makes 5 half-pint jars

from **Park Row Bed & Breakfast**
525 West Park Row
St. Peter, MN 56082
507-931-2495

Innkeeper Ann Burckhardt may serve this colorful strawberry-rhubarb combination on hot homemade bread, a favorite part of her generous breakfasts. Breakfast guests may linger until late morning, feasting and talking at the dining room table.

Coming up with great breakfast recipes is no problem for Ann, whose two decades of food writing and home economics serve her well. Coming up with the perfect B&B took her nearly two years, however, after a search of five towns within an hour of the Twin Cities. The St. Peter home she opened, a lemon yellow Carpenter Gothic with gingerbread trim, was built in the early 1870s. The judge who owned it added a Queen Anne wing, complete with a turret and porches. Today, the winding carved oak staircase inside the turret is the entrance to a romantic guestroom that was the former master bedroom.

🏠 *Other Park Row B&B recipes:*
Very Berry Orange Juice, page 32
Cheese Omelette Oven-Style, page 140

Mulberry Jam

Ingredients:

2 pounds mulberries
5/8 cup water
Juice of 2 lemons
4 cups sugar

- In a large saucepan or kettle, mix mulberries, water and lemon juice.

- Heat slowly until simmering. Continue simmering until fruit is soft.

- Stir in sugar until it is dissolved. Bring mixture to a boil. Boil rapidly until the jam drops cleanly off a spoon (in clots or flakes), or when the temperature reaches about 220 degrees Fahrenheit.

- Remove from heat and skim off foam. Pour into hot, sterilized jelly jars, leaving 1/2-inch space at the top. Immediately cover with sterilized tight-fitting lids and bands.

Makes 7 or 8 8-ounce jars

from **Shady Ridge Farm B&B**
410 Highland View
Houlton, WI 54082
715-549-6258

"This is an old-fashioned recipe and a special favorite of our guests. They love picking mulberries off our trees, too," said Innkeeper Sheila Fugina. "People used to plant mulberries when they grew other fruit because the birds would be attracted to them and leave the other fruit alone."

Sheila and husband Britt's mulberries, raspberries, elderberries, gooseberries and other fruit are organically grown. Breakfast includes fruit, homemade breads and muffins with homemade preserves, and a main dish, served with homemade syrups. But those aren't the most appealing features. It's llamas.

Britt and Sheila have a herd of their own, plus some they are boarding or who are "on consignment," usually numbering 16 or more. The llamas and the B&B have proved to be a great combination – guests can take a llama for a walk or just watch them in the barn or barnyard. The Fuginas have started packing picnic lunches for guests who want to take a llama-assisted hike.

Some guests have gone so far as to buy their own llamas. But most come to venture into the Fuginas' country lifestyle, if only overnight. The 1890 brick farmhouse took 18 months to restore, and now the three guestrooms have views of the acreage. The farm is located in the St. Croix Valley.

Another Shady Ridge Farm recipe:
Raspberry Bread, page 95
Rose Hip Syrup, page 115

Peach Rum Sauce

Ingredients:

7 medium ripe peaches, washed and peeled
1 cup plus 2 tablespoons sugar
1/3 cup light rum

- In a large saucepan, crush peaches with a potato masher.
- Stir in sugar. Simmer over medium low heat, stirring often, for 15 to 20 minutes or until sauce is thick.
- Remove from heat and stir in rum. Serve hot. To store, cover and refrigerate or freeze.

Makes 4 cups sauce

from **The Victorian Swan on Water**
1716 Water Street
Stevens Point, WI 54481
715-345-0595

"I usually serve this with my Pecan Stuffed French Toast," said Innkeeper Joan Ouellette. "But it is wonderful on angel food or sponge cake or layered in parfait glasses with frozen custard, which is a great dessert for a Chinese dinner." Joan eats frozen custard every time she visits Milwaukee.

She used to live there. Back in 1986, she told her brother, who lived in Stevens Point, she wanted to open a B&B. He thought she was kidding. When he realized she was serious, he suggested this house. "It took one day to find the house," she said. Zoning and restoration took much, much longer.

Started in 1888, the home took three years to build. It was designed by a Boston architect for the owner of local dry goods stores. It was built in another part of Stevens Point. Fifty years later, it needed to be moved. Off came the third story and the house was cut in half. The home was slowly trucked across town, with electrical wires being lifted along the way. Set on this site near the Wisconsin River, it was put back together as a duplex.

Joan and her brother, Chuck Egle, restored the home as a B&B, and it's now on the Stevens Point Historical Homes Registry. Joan opened four guestrooms in 1986 after she and Chuck put in months of work, including adding bathrooms and redoing electrical systems. "Chuck is a landscape architect, so the yard got special attention," she says, complete with heirloom flowers, a circular brick entrance area and a rock garden waterfall.

Another Victorian Swan recipe:
Dolly's Blackberry Rhubarb Jam, page 107

Peachy Cherry Sauce

Ingredients:

1/4 cup sugar
2 tablespoons cornstarch
A dash of salt
1/2 cup water
1 10- or 12-ounce package frozen "dry pack" sliced peaches
1 cup frozen tart cherries or 1 can dark sweet cherries, drained
1 tablespoon butter
2 tablespoons Cointreau or apricot brandy

Also:

Whipped or sour cream

- In a saucepan, combine sugar, cornstarch and salt.
- Stir in water. Cook over low heat, stirring constantly, until sauce thickens and clears.
- Stir in frozen peaches and cherries, cooking until peaches are soft.
- Stir in butter and liqueur.
- Serve hot over waffles or pancakes with a dollop of whipped or sour cream on top.

Tester's Comments: This was really good using frozen peaches, so it must be wonderful with fresh ones.

Makes about 2 cups

from **Cherry Knoll Farm B&B**
2856 Hammond Road East
Traverse City, MI 49684
616-947-9806 or 800-847-9806

"I am constantly searching for cherry recipes and I developed this as an alternative to my cherry sauce," said Innkeeper Dorothy Cump. If she seems a little over-concerned with cherry recipes, forgive her: Percy, her husband, operates an orchard of 1,200 cherry trees. She puts the fruit to good use in their B&B. Dorothy's hearty breakfasts are served on cross-stitched placemats with a cherry design and with cherry napkin rings.

Guests can even pick-their-own during the height of cherry season, early July to early August. But if they miss it, they might be there for spring morel mushroom hunting or fall color season. With 115 acres, there's always something worth stopping in for. The B&B is an attraction in its own right, with three guestrooms filled with country decor and handmade quilts. It is Dorothy's "retirement" profession, after she and Percy spent 30 years in real estate. They've owned the house since 1968, but turned it to a B&B in 1988.

Another Cherry Knoll Farm recipe:
Tart Cherry Nut Bread, page 98

Perfect Berry Chambord Preserves

Ingredients:

1-1/4 cups strawberries
1-1/4 cups blueberries
1-1/4 cups blackberries
1-1/4 cups raspberries
1/2 cup (1-1/2 boxes) powdered fruit pectin
4 cups sugar
1/2 cup Chambord liqueur

🍓 Wash berries if they are fresh (frozen "dry pack" berries may be used). Place berries in a large saucepan. Stir in pectin.

🍓 Bring berries to a boil and boil for 1 minute, stirring constantly.

🍓 Stir in sugar and Chambord. Bring back to a rolling boil for 3 minutes, stirring constantly.

🍓 Ladle into hot, sterilized jelly jars, leaving 1/2-inch space at the top. Immediately cover with sterilized, tight-fitting lids and bands (for more detailed directions, read the pectin package).

🍓 "For best results, do not change the recipe or make in larger quantities."

Makes 6 6-ounce jars

from **The Inn at Cedar Crossing**
336 Louisiana Street
Sturgeon Bay, WI 54235
414-743-4200

Door County has more to offer than cherries, and these preserves showcase many of the fruits available locally. The preserves bring back the taste of summer whenever they are eaten.

Summer isn't the only time this inn is busy. Door County is popular all year long for guests who want to take in a variety of activities or just the scenery. Visitors can stay at this downtown inn, fill up with a hearty breakfast, spend the day out exploring and return for dinner and drinks.

Terry Wulf opened the inn in a mercantile building listed on the National Register of Historic Places. Upstairs, her nine guestrooms are decorated with antiques, down comforters, fireplaces and whirlpools. A common room with a fireplace has a well-stocked cookie jar. Downstairs, her restaurant serves three meals a day, many featuring locally-grown produce.

🏠 *Other Inn at Cedar Crossing recipes:*
Apple Walnut Coffeecake, page 35
Blueberry Grand Marnier Preserves, page 105
Chilled Cherry Soup, page 123
Dried Fruit Relish, page 190

Quick Fruit Syrup

Ingredients:

    1 cup margarine or butter (or 1/2 cup each)
    1 cup honey
    1 cup raspberry, orange or apricot preserves

- In a heavy saucepan, melt margarine.
- Stir in honey and preserves.
- Bring mixture to a boil, stirring constantly.
- After mixture boils, pour into a pitcher and serve. Store in the refrigerator. To serve again, reheat and stir.

Makes 3 cups

from **The Inn**
104 Wisconsin Avenue
Montreal, WI 54550
715-561-5180 phone or FAX

When it's ski season in Michigan's western Upper Peninsula, Innkeeper Doree Schumacher needs all the short-cuts she can get. Skiers from Indianhead, Blackjack, Big Powderhorn, Whitecap and the Porcupine Mountains pack into this four-guestroom inn, eager to enjoy the UP's legendary snowfalls. They're eager to enjoy Doree's legendary breakfasts, too, then hit the slopes.

It was skiing that brought Doree, Dick and their two sons to the area in the first place. Every weekend they drove up, they'd pass this three-story building, standing vacant. And every weekend they drove by, Doree would say, "Someone should do something with that lovely old building."

So they did. They operated a private ski school in it, where potential world-class teens studied and skied. Planning to retire from teaching to Montreal, near Ironwoood, Mich., they redid the building as a B&B in 1982.

Built in 1913, this building was the office headquarters for Oglebay-Norton Montreal Mine, said to be the largest underground iron mine in the U.S. The mine employed 700 men and yielded nearly 46 million tons of ore before it closed in 1962. The former company town is now on the National Register of Historic Places, and it's interesting to explore by foot or bike. The miners or their wives lined up at this building to collect the weekly paycheck (ask to see the vault). It also housed the super-intendent's office and the engineering and chemistry departments.

Another Inn recipe:
Banana Oat Breakfast Cookies, page 205

Rose Hip Syrup

Ingredients:

2 cups rose hip juice (see below)
2 cups sugar

☞ For Juice: In a large saucepan or kettle, crush or cut up rose hips and add water to cover. Bring hips to a boil and then simmer, covered, for 15 minutes or until soft. Strain out seeds and pulp.

☞ For Syrup: Mix juice and sugar. Boil for 5 minutes.

☞ Remove from heat and pour into hot, sterilized jelly jars, leaving 1/2-inch space at the top. Immediately cover with sterilized tight-fitting lids and bands. Process for 10 minutes in a boiling water bath. Or, if syrup will be quickly used, simply refrigerate it.

Makes about 2 cups

from **Shady Ridge Farm B&B**
410 Highland View
Houlton, WI 54082
715-549-6258

"When we moved to Shady Ridge Farm, I noticed lots of rose hips that first fall and remembered a recipe for rose hip jelly," said Sheila Fugina. "Since I didn't have enough for jelly, I made syrup, and that's been my preference ever since. Rose hips are high in vitamin C." She serves it warm over her Norwegian Pancake or baked French toast.

Homemade preserves and syrups from the B&B's organically-grown berries and fruits are part of Sheila's full breakfast. When raspberries, mulberries or other fruit is in season, guests might be able to pick some themselves.

But most guests are more fascinated by the llamas. Sheila and Britt, her husband, usually have a herd of 16 or more on the 22-acre farm, and a few lucky guests each year are present for a birth. All guests can take a llama for a walk, and llama lunches (picnics) are becoming popular.

Britt and Sheila bought this farm in 1988 after quitting their jobs, helping a friend move to Trinidad, and then spending several months inn-hopping in the Caribbean. Their version of the perfect B&B included a country home and llamas. They returned to the Twin Cities and began renovating this 1890 brick farmhouse in the St. Croix Valley, 30 miles east of the metro area. The house needed 18 months of work, "10 to 14 hour days because we had no other jobs at the time." The three-guestroom B&B opened in 1990. Each guestroom has handmade quilts, hand-stenciled walls and a view of the farm.

🏠 *Other Shady Ridge Farm recipes:*
Raspberry Bread, page 95
Mulberry Jam, page 110

Strawberry Butter

Ingredients:

1 cup butter, softened
1 tablespoon honey
3 large fresh strawberries, or 1/2 cup frozen strawberries, thawed

- Wash and hull fresh strawberries.
- Combine butter, honey and strawberries in a food processor. Blend until smooth.
- Serve in a pretty dish. Store covered in the refrigerator (Allow to soften a bit before serving.)

Tester's Comments: Mmmm. Tempting to eat plain, but save it for pancakes or muffins.

Makes 1-1/4 cups

from **Port Washington Inn**
308 West Washington Street
Port Washington, WI 53074
414-284-5583

Innkeeper Connie Evans serves this easy butter with many muffins, such as Orange Pecan. It's one of the small efforts that combine to make a stay at her inn memorable and for guests to feel pampered and special.

That's how she and her husband, Craig Siwy, felt whenever they traveled and stayed in B&Bs. And they did so often. One weekend, when they stayed at the Scofield House in Sturgeon Bay, Connie was inspired by the owners, who were heading for corporate jobs but instead chose to restore a Queen Anne Victorian home there. She and Craig were rethinking their own careers.

"I'd thought about innkeeping for a few years before I mentioned it to my husband," Connie said. "We both had corporate jobs and a large mortgage, and I didn't think Craig would be willing to adopt a new lifestyle and give up one of our corporate salaries. I'm so glad I was wrong!"

Having always lived in Chicago, they decided to stay in the Midwest. Craig and Connie decided that Connie would start "scouting" for an inn, and her first trip was to Port Washington. She booked a room at the Port Washington Inn because another B&B in town was full. "When I mentioned to the owner that I was looking for a bed and breakfast, she told me their inn was for sale. I called Craig that evening. He came up to meet me the next day and we had a finalized contract within two weeks." They opened in 1993, and had guests show up an hour after the moving van pulled away. They offer four guestrooms in this 1903 home, built by the owners of a local brewery.

Another Port Washington Inn recipe: Fresh Fruit in Orange Cream, page 124

Swiss Pear Marmalade

Ingredients:

3 cups puréed pears (cored, stemmed, unpeeled)
1/2 cup ground whole lemon (seeded)
1/2 cup ground whole orange (seeded)
1/4 teaspoon allspice
1/8 teaspoon cinnamon
1 package powdered pectin
6 cups sugar

🖝 In a food processor fitted with a steel blade, purée the pears. Grind the lemon. Grind the orange.

🖝 In a large, non-aluminum kettle or saucepan, combine pears, lemon, orange, allspice and cinnamon. Thoroughly mix in pectin.

🖝 Bring mixture to a boil, stirring often. Stir in sugar.

🖝 Bring to a full, rolling boil, stirring constantly. When mixture has come to a rolling boil, stir for 85 seconds. Remove from heat and remove spoon. Let stand for 3 minutes.

🖝 Skim off foam. Pour into hot, sterilized jelly jars, leaving 1/2-inch space at the top. Immediately cover with sterilized, tight-fitting lids and bands. Process in a hot water bath according to instructions on the pectin package.

Makes 5 to 6 8-ounce jars

from **Old Rittenhouse Inn**
301 Rittenhouse Avenue
Bayfield, WI 54814
715-779-5111

This marmalade come from some of Innkeeper Mary Phillips's grandmother's favorites. It was made for "threshing days" at the family farm in Brodhead, Wisconsin, when 15-20 neighbors were fed to thank them for their hard work. Many of Mary's family recipes are now incorporated into the gourmet breakfasts, lunches and dinners served at the popular inn she and husband Jerry bought in 1973 simply because they fell in love with the old mansion.

The 26-room Queen Anne Victorian was built in 1890 as a summer home for a Civil War general from Illinois. The Phillipses started taking in a few B&B guests the next summer after getting requests, due to a shortage of rooms in town. Today, the Phillipses have a total of 20 guestrooms in three restored historic homes in town and a widespread reputation for elegant Victorian dining. Guests at all three homes gather at the main inn for breakfast, which may include this marmalade and other preserves using local fruit.

🏠*Other Old Rittenhouse Inn recipes:*
Smoked Trout Hash, page 150
Halloween Soup, page 192
Shamrock Soup, page 196

Anyone who thinks the Great Lakes region is a frozen wasteland (and, sorry to say, there are people who do) needs to read this chapter. Cherries, cranberries, apples, pears, plums, strawberries and raspberries all make their way from summer orchards and gardens onto innkeepers' breakfast tables. Even when the winter winds do blow cold and fresh fruit is limited to supermarket imports, these clever innkeepers poach pears or apples and dress up bananas in ways that have guests asking for seconds. Try the hot compote on a cool day or one of several chilled soups for summer refreshment. Fruit is as adaptable as the remarkable innkeepers who perfected these recipes!

Fruits

Baked Apple Slices

Ingredients:

7 cups baking apples, peeled, cored and sliced
1 cup raisins
2 to 3 teaspoons cinnamon
1 teaspoon nutmeg
1 to 2 teaspoon lemon juice
2 tablespoons canola oil
1/2 cup honey

Topping:
1-1/2 cups old-fashioned oatmeal
1/2 cup whole wheat flour
1 cup chopped almonds or walnuts

Also:

Milk or half-and-half

● In a large bowl, combine apples, raisins, cinnamon, nutmeg and lemon juice.

● In a separate bowl, mix oil and honey. Pour it over the apples, then toss to coat.

● Cover bowl and refrigerate overnight.

● In the morning, mix Topping ingredients. Place apple mixture in a greased 9 x 13-inch glass baking pan. Sprinkle on the topping.

● Bake uncovered in a preheated oven at 350 degrees for about 30 minutes, or until apples are soft. Serve hot with milk or half-and-half.

Makes 8 to 10 servings

from **The French Country Inn of Ephraim**
3052 Spruce Lane
P.O. Box 129
Ephraim, WI 54211
414-854-4001

"This is not too sweet, and it's been real popular with guests," said Innkeeper Walt Fisher. Walt and spouse Joan Fitzpatrick try to use local products and to cut down on sugar and cholesterol without sacrificing taste.

Walt and Joan are the proud owners of what was a Door County summer home for a Chicago family with 10 children. The inn was built in 1912 but the family sold the place in the mid '20s, believing Ephraim was becoming "too touristy." Then it served as a boarding house for many years.

When Joan and Walt bought it in 1988, it was already an inn. They've put in countless hours of work redecorating, landscaping and upgrading, while retaining the original character of the house. Guests in the seven guestrooms enjoy the beachstone fireplace downstairs in cool weather. In summer, the inn is a block from the lake, two from an ice cream parlor.

🏠 *Another French Country Inn recipe:*
Molasses Bread, page 92

Bananas Tropicale

<u>Ingredients:</u>

> 2 to 3 tablespoons flaked coconut
> 1/2 cup slivered almonds
> 6 firm, ripe bananas
> Bottled pina colada drink mix, non-alcoholic

- In a dry non-stick skillet over high heat, quickly stir coconut until lightly toasted. Set aside.
- Toast almonds in the same manner as coconut.
- Slice bananas into six fruit or dessert dishes.
- Pour a few tablespoons of the pina colada mix over the bananas.
- Sprinkle with almonds and coconut. Serve immediately. "Garnish with edible flowers, such as nasturtiums or borage."

Makes 6 servings

from **The Inn at Elk Run**
S 4125 County Trunk Highway SS
Viola, WI 54664
608-625-2062 or 800-729-7313

"People think when they see this dish that it is simply bananas and cream, and they can never figure out what it is that makes it taste so good," said Innkeeper Janet Hugg. Her breakfasts include a fruit dish such as this, homemade muffins and an entree, often using eggs fresh from their farm.

Janet and Roger, her husband, had vacationed in Door County for 17 years, and the suburban Chicago couple thought they'd like to move there someday. But then they discovered the Kickapoo River Valley in southwestern Wisconsin's "Hidden Valleys" region. The apple orchards, Amish settlements, canoe trips and world-class bike trails appealed to them. It would, they believed, appeal to guests, as well. The area is scenic and full of wildlife, and not all that far a drive from major metro areas.

Eventually they found the old Nelson farm for sale, located near LaFarge. The farmhouse needed major work, so major that their B&B could not open for two years into the project. In addition to redoing the entire house, inside and out, they added living quarters for themselves, so guests have the run of the entire original farmhouse.

Three guestrooms opened in 1992. Guests enjoy the goats and chickens as well as the Huggs. The innkeepers serve refreshments upon arrival and feature local specialties, when possible. Even the soap is made in LaFarge. The home's deck is the perfect place to watch summer sunsets.

Chilled Berry Soup

Ingredients:

2 cups vanilla yogurt
1 cup buttermilk
1 cup sour cream
2 tablespoons fresh lemon juice
1 tablespoon honey
A dash of cinnamon
A dash of nutmeg
4 cups (1 quart) orange juice
Fresh fruit -- strawberries, blueberries and/or raspberries

Also:

Fresh mint leaves or fruit for garnish

- In a large bowl, whisk together yogurt, buttermilk, sour cream, lemon juice, honey, cinnamon and nutmeg.
- Slowly whisk in the orange juice. Taste and adjust for more spices, honey, etc. Cover and chill.
- At serving time, stir washed fruit into the soup (slice strawberries first). Pour into soup bowls.
- Top soup with mint leaves and/or a fresh whole berry.

Makes 8 servings

from **White Lace Inn**
16 North Fifth Avenue
Sturgeon Bay, WI 54235
414-743-1105

Fresh Door County berries go into this summer treat, and the mint leaves are fresh out of the inn's kitchen garden. The White Lace Inn innkeepers might use peaches in the fruit mixture, even if it is called Chilled Berry Soup.

While the 15 guestrooms at this romantic inn are located in three historic homes, the guests all gather at the main house to have breakfast in the oak-paneled dining room or in front of the parlor fireplace. Dennis and Bonnie Statz began researching opening an inn in 1980, selected Door County in 1981, and opened five rooms in the Main House in 1982. "Dennis *always* knew he wanted his own business," though he was educated as an industrial engineer.

Today, the Statzes welcome guests to 15 rooms in three restored Victorian homes, connected by the gardens in back. Laura Ashley prints, lace trim, whirlpools and fireplaces have made it the site of many special occasions.

Other White Lace Inn recipes:
Bonnie's Chocolate Zucchini Muffins, page 55
Pumpkin Apple Streusel Muffins, page 67
Lemon Herb Bread, page 89

Chilled Cherry Soup

Ingredients:

4 cups sweetened tart cherries, with juice
4 cups sweetened cherry juice
2 cups frozen peaches, diced
4 oranges, peeled and diced
2 cups sugar
1/3 cup Triple Sec liqueur
1/2 teaspoon allspice
1/2 teaspoon nutmeg
1/2 teaspoon cinnamon
4 tablespoons cornstarch
1/2 cup water

Also:

Whipped cream

- In a kettle, mix cherries, cherry juice, peaches, oranges, sugar, Triple Sec, allspice, nutmeg and cinnamon.
- In a separate bowl, mix cornstarch and water.
- Bring cherry mixture to a boil, stirring constantly.
- Slowly pour cornstarch into soup, stirring constantly. Make more cornstarch and water if soup is still too thin after it boils again.
- Chill thoroughly before serving. Serve with a dollop of whipped cream.

Makes 20 servings

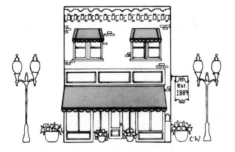

from **The Inn at Cedar Crossing**
336 Louisiana Street
Sturgeon Bay, WI 54235
414-743-4200

Door County says "cherries" to a lot of visitors, and this inn and restaurant speaks their language. This refreshing summer soup is a great way to start breakfast. Guests are treated to breakfast in the downstairs guest lobby.

Innkeeper Terry Wulf left a banking career to start her own business in this historic storefront. She removed apartments upstairs and created a nine-guestroom inn, reminiscent of a small European hotel. Guests will find antiques, hand-stenciling, poster and canopy beds and down comforters. Room service is available from her restaurant and pub downstairs.

Other Inn at Cedar Crossing recipes:
Apple Walnut Coffeecake, page 35
Blueberry Grand Marnier Preserves, page 105
Perfect Berry Chambord Preserves, page 113
Dried Fruit Relish, page 190

Fresh Fruit in Orange Cream

Ingredients:

1 cup whipping cream, chilled
3 tablespoons frozen orange juice concentrate, partly thawed
2 tablespoons honey
Sliced fresh fruit for 6 servings (berries, kiwi, peaches, nectarines, bananas, etc.)

- Place the bowl and beaters of the electric mixer in the freezer for a few minutes to chill.
- Whip cream with orange juice concentrate and honey.
- Divide whipped cream among six dessert dishes, reserving 2 tablespoons.
- Spread the cream with the back of a spoon to form a "nest" in the middle. Arrange fresh fruit on top of the whipped cream nests.
- Top with a dollop of reserved whipped cream.

Tester's Comments: Absolutely delicious, especially with blueberries. Double the amount of juice concentrate and the Orange Cream is good enough to frost a cake. I'll try some exotic juice concentrates in the future, too.

Makes 6 servings

from **Port Washington Inn**
308 West Washington Street
Port Washington, WI 53074
414-284-5583

"We serve this subtle and refreshing dish after muffins or coffeecakes and before the entree, with a sprig of fresh mint," said Innkeeper Connie Evans. It is part of the "tide you over 'til dinner" breakfast she serves daily.

Connie is an accomplished baker and cook who, with husband Craig Siwy, had traveled widely in B&Bs, preferring them to hotels. As former business travelers, these innkeepers now provide all the things they wanted when they traveled: use of the computer and fax machine, a cordless phone for privacy, and amenities like soaps, shampoos and terry robes. Guests can use both parlors downstairs, including the book or video library.

In 1993, Connie and Craig bought this 1903 home as an operating inn after researching innkeeping. They got off to a fast start: an hour after the moving van pulled away, their first guests arrived. Port Washington, 25 miles north of Milwaukee on Lake Michigan, and nine miles from historic Cedarburg, is a popular getaway, while convenient for business travelers. Their inn has four guestrooms, decorated in antiques. The original woodwork, leaded glass and gas and electric light fixtures still remain.

Another Port Washington Inn recipe:
Strawberry Butter, page 116

Fresh Peach-Raspberry Medley

Ingredients:

6 cups peeled and sliced fresh Freestone peaches
1 cup orange juice
1/4 cup sugar
1/2 teaspoon cinnamon
2 cups fresh raspberries

Also:

Whipped cream
Mint leaves

- In a large bowl, lightly mix peaches, orange juice, sugar and cinnamon. Allow to sit for at least 15 minutes to blend flavors.
- Gently fold in raspberries.
- Place in small bowls and top with whipped cream and garnish with mint leaves.

Tester's Comments: Yum. Sort of like pie without the crust. And a lot better for you!

Makes 6 servings

from **The Pebble House B&B**
15093 Lakeshore Road
Lakeside, MI 49116
616-469-1416

The Pebble House is located in southwestern Michigan's harbor country, between New Buffalo and St. Joseph. In the heart of the fruit belt, "June through September is a time for many fresh fruit medleys," said Innkeeper Jean Lawrence. "Guests often get so inspired at breakfast that they spend the day at one of the area's many 'u-pick' farms or visit one of the fruit stands."

Jean and Ed have turned more than a few guests on to the Arts and Crafts Movement, as well. This style of design and decorating, also known as Mission Style, proliferated from 1900-1916, and the Pebble House is a good example of it. Many of the seven guestrooms located in the main inn or two other cottages are decorated in Mission Style furniture. And yes, the Pebble House really is made of pebbles. The exterior of the main house, constructed as a vacation retreat in 1912, is built of decorative beach stones. It's a fitting reminder that Lake Michigan is only a stone's throw (just across the road).

Jean and Ed bought the inn in 1983. They'd renovated several buildings while living in Chicago. They wanted to continue to preserve historic buildings while having more involvement with the people using those buildings.

Another Pebble House recipe:
Everyone-Loves-It Oatmeal, page 178

Heavenly Bananas

Ingredients:

 1/2 cup sour cream (not "lite")
 2 tablespoons sugar
 1 tablespoon orange juice
 1/2 teaspoon grated orange peel
 1 banana for each serving

Also:

 Granola

- The night before serving, mix the sour cream, sugar, orange juice and orange peel.
- Cover tightly and refrigerate.
- In the morning, slice one banana for each serving into a small bowl.
- Stir the sour cream mixture. Top each banana with 1 to 2 tablespoons of the sauce.
- Sprinkle with granola and serve immediately.

Tester's Comments: If the bananas aren't quite"heavenly," they'll at least get you to Cloud 9!

Makes 4 servings

from **Whitefish Bay Farm B&B**
3831 Clark Lake Road
Sturgeon Bay, WI 54235
414-743-1560

"I serve this recipe as a first course fruit dish," said Innkeeper Gretchen Regnery. "I serve it in small glass dishes and place the dishes on a plate. When I have time, I make my own granola to put on top." During the busy season at this 80-acre Door County farm, however, there's no time to make granola. Gretchen and husband Dick are busy having guests, hosting special exhibits or openings in their gallery, making hay for their Corriedale sheep, picking cherries, and canning and freezing produce from their large garden.

Guests can come to relax, no matter what's on the Regnery's schedule. Depending on the season, some like to sit on the porch of the traditional 1908 farmhouse. Others like to bike the country roads, pet the sheep, pick cherries, or attend a nature program at neighboring Whitefish Dunes State Park.

Regnerys took five years to find the perfect farm, then eight years to restore the house, top to bottom, and open their B&B. The four guestrooms are named after pieces of original artwork that are hung in each room.

Other Whitefish Bay Farm B&B recipes:
Cherry Delicious, page 24
Oatmeal Surprise Pancakes, page 166

Hot Cranberry Compote

Ingredients:

2 cups fresh or frozen cranberries
1/2 cup sugar
1 stick of cinnamon
1 16-ounce can sliced peaches in light syrup
2 cups peeled, sliced pears
2 cups chopped apples

Also:

Sour cream
Nutmeg

- In a large, microwavable casserole, mix cranberries, sugar and cinnamon stick.
- Drain peaches, reserving 1/2 cup of the syrup. Mix it into cranberries.
- Cover and microwave on high for 4 to 5 minutes. "The mixture will boil and pop."
- Stir in peaches, pears and apples.
- Cover and cook 1-1/2 minutes on high power or until fresh fruit has softened.
- Spoon into pretty bowls and serve with a dollop of sour cream sprinkled with nutmeg.

Makes 5 servings

from **The Mustard Seed B&B**
205 California Avenue
P.O. Box 262
Hayward, WI 54843
715-634-2908

"We enjoy treating our guests to regional flavors," said former Innkeeper Betty Teske about the breakfasts she and husband Jim served. "Cranberries are plentiful in our area," and pears and apples are available in the winter.

Betty and Jim owned this inn from 1990-94. Mary and Marty Gervais bought the five-guestroom B&B in June 1994. They returned to the Midwest after 20 years in Colorado, where they taught, owned a restaurant and were Nordic ski coaches. They were especially looking forward to the famous Birkebeiner cross-country ski race, as well as being "home." Their century-old home, once owned by a lumberman, is on a residential street, close to dining, shopping and picnicking at Shue's Pond.

At any time of year, there's so much to do in the Hayward area that guests need to stoke up at the breakfast table. Outfitters offer canoeing and tubing on the Namekagon River, and there's river and lake fishing nearby (Hayward is the home of the National Fresh Water Fishing Hall of Fame, with the giant Muskie Museum). Horseback riding, golf, skiing, mountain biking, hiking and other activities are all available in or near Chequamegon National Forest.

Norwegian Fruit Soup

Ingredients:

1 cup pitted prunes
1 cup raisins
2/3 cup dried apricots
1 orange, thinly sliced
1 lemon, thinly sliced
4 tablespoons quick-cooking tapioca
1 cup (or less) sugar
1 3-inch cinnamon stick
3 apples, peeled and diced
1 16-ounce can tart pitted cherries, drained

In a large saucepan, mix prunes, raisins, apricots, orange, lemon, tapioca, sugar and cinnamon stick. Cover with water ("white grape or apple juice is very nice, too"). Refrigerate overnight.

In the morning, stir in apples and 1 more cup of water or juice.

Simmer until apples are tender, 20 to 30 minutes. Stir in cherries. Serve chilled or at room temperature.

Makes 12 servings

from **Cady Hayes House B&B**
500 Calhoun Avenue South
Lanesboro, MN 55949
507-467-2621

Innkeepers Peggy and Duke Addicks serve this in small bowls ("It is fairly rich," she notes) as a first course for breakfast, but it could be a fine dessert. Peggy has many often-requested Scandinavian recipes, and one guestroom, the Norwegian Room, has a handmade bed rosemaled by a local artist.

Peggy and Duke visited Lanesboro to bike the popular Root River state bike trail. "We fell in love with the town and one week later bought our house," a turreted Queen Anne Victorian built in 1890 by bachelor farmer Cady Hayes. The Addicks were both busy lawyers raising four kids. "We were looking for a simpler life, and most days I'd agree that we have found it," Peggy said.

For nearly three years, major restoration of the interior of the home was underway. They redid the kitchen, added a family room addition and brought back hand-stenciled designs in the living and dining rooms, among other projects. In addition to three guestrooms, guests have a game room, music room with grand piano (Duke's a fiddler) and parlor. On some weekends, Duke conducts walking tours of downtown Lanesboro, a National Historic District. And on Saturday nights August through October he's at the Sons of Norway Hall telling ghost stories.

Poached Apples in Vanilla Creme Sauce

Ingredients:

8 apples "You may substitute pears."
About 1/2 cup apple cider
1 tablespoon sugar
1/4 teaspoon cinnamon

Vanilla Creme Sauce:
1 pint (2 cups) heavy cream
1/3 cup butter
1/2 cup sugar
1/2 teaspoon cinnamon
1 tablespoon vanilla extract

- Peel and core apples. Then slice in wedges.
- Place apples in a microwave-safe container. Pour cider to a depth of about 1/4 inch.
- Sprinkle with sugar and cinnamon.
- Microwave uncovered on "high" for 2 minutes per apple. "The apple should be tender but not mushy."
- For Vanilla Creme Sauce: Combine cream, butter, sugar, cinnamon and vanilla ("I use Mexican vanilla. If you have imitation vanilla, double the amount.") in a microwave-safe container.
- Microwave 4 minutes or until very hot and bubbly. Stir until well blended.
- Place apples in individual serving dishes. Pour the sauce over the apples. Serve hot.

Makes 8 servings

from **Asa Parker House B&B**
17500 St. Croix Trail North
Marine on St. Croix, MN 54047
612-433-5248

OK, Innkeeper Marge Bush considers this "fruit," but anyone with a half a sweet tooth will know that this will make a dynamite dessert to any meal.

Marge took over as owner/innkeeper in this lumberman's mansion in 1989. She's owned other B&Bs, but this one is perfect for her. It's in the "village of Marine," located about 40 miles from the Twin Cities on the St. Croix River.

Guests come to Marine to explore the town, complete with one very old-fashioned general store, an ice cream parlor, and a marina on the river. Biking the well-maintained bike trail that runs through town, playing a game of tennis on the inn's back court, wandering down the hill for an ice cream cone or taking a canoe ride are the most taxing activities. Marge caters to getaway couples who need time and quiet to unwind and recharge. The 1856 home has four guestrooms and guests enjoy the parlors and gardens.

Other Asa Parker House recipes:
Marjorie's English Country Scones, page 62
Blueberry Grunt, page 208
Cheese Lace Crackers, page 227

Poached Pears and Craisins

Ingredients:

4 pears, peeled, cored and sliced
1 cup water
1/2 cup sugar
2 tablespoons lemon juice
2 medium cinnamon sticks
1/4 cup Creme de Noya liqueur (for almond flavor and red color)
1/2 cup craisins (dried cranberries)

- Prepare pears, set aside.
- In a medium saucepan, mix water, sugar, lemon juice, cinnamon sticks and liqueur.
- Bring mixture to a boil, then reduce to simmer. Add pears and simmer gently until pears are tender, about 15 minutes.
- Stir in craisins just before removing the pan from heat. "They need time to soften just a bit but not too long or they will lose color and get mushy."
- Serve warm in individual fruit or dessert cups (or over vanilla ice cream with toasted almonds).

Makes 4 servings

from **The Stout Trout B&B**
Rt. 1, Box 1630
Springbrook, WI 54875
715-466-2790

"After countless trips through the winter produce aisle, getting tired of oranges, apples and bananas, I decided to try my luck with the rock-like green things labeled as pears," said Innkeeper Kathleen Fredericks. Poaching was a way to make them edible, and experimenting resulted in this tasty recipe.

Winter guests at this Gull Lake B&B might be heading out for a day of cross-country skiing, and Kathy's 40 acres of property is one place they can do that. The Hayward or Spooner areas have many trails, too (Hayward is the home of the annual Birkebeiner ski marathon, afterall). The B&B's ski waxing station is downstairs. Summer guests can fish for bass out front, trout fish, canoe or tube the Namekagon River, ride horses, swim or berry pick nearby. The B&B's rowboat, paddleboat, canoes and bikes are available for guests' use.

Kathy found this former fishing lodge when she returned to her home state to enter innkeeping after living in California. The building needed a year's worth of major work, but she created four large guestrooms. "I wanted to give people the kind of retreat I always wanted and never found," she said.

Another Stout Trout recipe:
Three Muffins to the Wind, page 72

Poached Sugarplums

Ingredients:

1 vanilla bean
1/3 cup sugar
6 ripe black plums, such as Friar or Queen Anne
1 teaspoon lemon juice
1 tablespoon Fruit Fresh (to prevent fruit from darkening)

☞ With the tip of a small, sharp knife, split the vanilla bean lengthwise. Using the tip of the knife, carefully scrape out the black gummy interior (the seeds). Combine the seeds with the sugar in a 1-1/2 quart baking dish.

☞ Cut the plums in half, remove the pit and cut each half into 3 or 4 slices. Toss with lemon juice and Fruit Fresh.

☞ Mix plums with sugar. Bake, covered, in a preheated oven at 400 degrees for 8 to 10 minutes, stirring once half-way through.

☞ Remove from oven and cool, covered. Serve at room temperature.

Makes 4 servings

from **The Urban Retreat B&B**
2759 Canterbury Road
Ann Arbor, MI 48104
313-971-8110

"I think the typical fruit compote is boring so I am always looking for delicious ways to serve fresh fruit to my guests," said Gloria Krys. "There are so few recipes that feature fresh plums, so this was the happy result of experimentation with an old-fashioned recipe for Vanilla Sugar."

Breakfasts here are served on the year 'round porch Gloria and André Rosalik added to their ranch home after opening a B&B. The porch overlooks the perennial garden and the county park next door, with 127 acres of meadow.

André and Gloria opened two guestrooms to be "one of those rare establishments nowadays -- a *homestay* bed and breakfast." They are both social workers with high-stress jobs. "Home is an oasis for us, and we try to maintain the same quiet, relaxed environment for our guests," Gloria said.

Both innkeepers grew up in families where "having folks over" was a way of life. When they married, they honeymooned in Michigan B&Bs. That got them thinking about opening a B&B when they retired, but they decided not to put it off. Their home has antiques, lace, and old-fashioned wallpapers. Guests can enjoy the living room, TV and "lap cats."

🏠*Another Urban Retreat recipe:*
Baked Blueberry French Toast, page 155

Spirited Baked Apple

Ingredients:

4 Granny Smith apples
1/2 cup brown sugar, packed and divided
1/4 cup butter, plus 2 tablespoons
1 teaspoon finely chopped nuts, optional
1/2 to 1 teaspoon currants, optional
2 teaspoons cinnamon
1 teaspoon allspice
1/4 cup water
1/4 cup rum or brandy

Also:

Heavy or whipped cream

- Wash and core apples. Cut a horizontal strip around each apple to prevent bursting.

- Place apples in a glass baking dish that gives just enough room around them to be able to baste.

- Fill each apple core with 1 tablespoon brown sugar and 1 tablespoon butter. Add optional nuts and currants. Top with 1/2 teaspoon cinnamon and 1/4 teaspoon allspice.

- In the baking dish, pour in water and rum or brandy. Sprinkle in the other 1/4 cup brown sugar and dot with 2 tablespoons butter.

- Bake in a preheated oven at 375 degrees. Baste every 20 minutes for 1 hour or until tender. (If necessary, add equal amounts of water and rum to the pan.)

- Remove and cool apples to room temperature. Serve in a bowl with some of the syrup from the pan, with heavy cream or whipped cream to pass.

Makes 4 servings

from **The Log House on Spirit Lake**
P.O. Box 130
Vergas, MN 56587
800-342-2318

Innkeeper Yvonne Tweten might serve this dish on the screened porch overlooking the lake. A homemade yeast bread, fruit and a decadent main dish means "we intend that breakfast be an experience," she said.

Yvonne and Lyle Tweten and their guests have the best of two worlds in this unique B&B arrangement. Two guestrooms are available in the restored log house. Yvonne and Lyle live in another house on the property. Yvonne comes to the log house to cook breakfast for guests, who can "wake up and smell the coffee" here. The circa 1889 log house was built on Lyle's great-grandparent's homestead, then moved 80 miles intact to this site.

Another Log House on Spirit Lake recipe:
Sour Cream Soufflé, page 151

Strawberry Soup

Ingredients:

1 quart fresh or frozen "dry pack" strawberries
1 32-ounce container vanilla yogurt
Up to 1 cup powdered sugar
1 cup heavy (whipping) cream
1 tablespoon strawberry preserves

- Wash and hull fresh strawberries (leave a few fresh berries for garnish), or defrost frozen ones, saving the juice with the berries.
- In a standard blender container, purée strawberries.
- Add yogurt and powdered sugar to taste. Continue to purée until creamy.
- Add cream and preserves, puréeing again until creamy.
- Cover blender and refrigerate until thoroughly chilled.
- Pour into bowls and garnish with a sprinkling of powdered sugar and fresh berries.

Makes 8 cups

from **Cherub Hill B&B**
105 Northwest First Avenue
Faribault, MN 55021
507-332-2024

Strawberry Soup often is served as a first course with muffins and breads at Kristi and Keith LeMieux's B&B. "This is especially wonderful when strawberries are in season -- we pick our own at local berry farms," Kristi said. "I am frequently asked for this recipe."

On warm summer mornings, guests enjoy this soup while eating a leisurely breakfast on the wrap-around porch. Kristi and Keith serve a large breakfast weekdays that includes homemade pastries and fresh fruit. On weekends, wild rice crepes, apple tarts and other entrees are on the menu.

LeMieux's opened this 1896 Queen Anne home as a B&B after two years of restoration, most of which they tackled themselves. Cheerful cherubs are found throughout the decor, even on the fireplace tile. Downstairs, the decor features velour chairs and Victorian settees in the parlors. Plenty of the original oak woodwork and leaded glass windows remain. The four upstairs guestrooms are decorated with antiques and Victorian wallpapers.

Another Cherub Hill B&B recipe:
Spiced Cranberry Punch, page 30

Wild Berry Delight

Ingredients:

4 cups low-fat plain yogurt
4 cups fresh-squeezed orange juice
6 tablespoons honey
2 tablespoons Kirsch
8 to 12 cups assorted fresh berries (blueberries, strawberries, raspberries, blackberries)

- In a large bowl, whisk together yogurt, orange juice, honey and liqueur.
- Cover and refrigerate until well-chilled.
- Place berries in goblets. Cover with yogurt mixture and serve.

Makes 12 servings

from **Phipps Inn**
1005 Third Street
Hudson, WI 54016
715-386-0800 phone or FAX

This is one of the dishes that might be served during a four-course breakfast in the dining room of this home. Guests might feel like they were personally invited by the home's builders, William and Francis Phipps, as guests dine amid oak wainscotting, faceted stained glass windows and a built-in buffet.

To say the Phipps mansion is "grand" is something of an understatement. Built in 1884, the home is a full three stories, plus turret, and large enough to accommodate six guestrooms, most with fireplaces and balconies. Guests have the use of a formal music room with baby grand piano, two parlors and three porches. The handcarved staircase, geometric parquet floors, imported tile fireplaces and other architectural touches are the best money could buy.

From all accounts, few begrudged William Phipps a cent. In Hudson, he worked as a lumberman, railroad official, bank president, park commissioner, county commissioner, mayor and state senator. His philanthropy was legendary, and he was widely respected. Only one of his five children survived to adulthood, and he, too, was a respected citizen.

Cyndi and John Berglund, a former teacher/coach and an attorney and lobbyist, respectively, opened the B&B in 1990. Three previous owners had spent 12 years restoring the home from use as a nursing home and rooming house. The inn is close to Hudson's restaurants and the St. Croix River.

Another Phipps Inn recipe:
Banana Sorbet with Kiwi Sauce, page 206

Smoked Trout Hash. Breakfast Pizza. Finnish Pancake. Morel and Asparagus Quiche. Not your usual breakfast fare. But even if your tastes run to the less exotic, Lake States innkeepers still have come up with some mighty good variations on favorite themes. Gingerbread Waffles, Ham 'n Apple Pancakes and Crispy Cinnamon French Toast are but a few examples. As might be expected at these B&B inns, amazing things are done daily with the ordinary, inexpensive, always-on-hand egg. And many of their ideas are time-savers, to boot -- dishes that are made ahead the night before, refrigerated overnight and baked in the morning. No need for plain-old-bacon-and-eggs again!

Entrees

Bedeviled Ham and Eggs

Ingredients:

6 hard-boiled eggs
1/4 cup butter, melted
1/2 teaspoon white wine vinegar
1 teaspoon sugar
1/4 teaspoon dry mustard
1 2-1/2-ounce can deviled or "potted" ham
3 tablespoons finely chopped chives
6 English muffins or toast points, toasted

Sauce:

6 tablespoons butter or margarine
6 tablespoons flour
3 cups milk
1 teaspoon chicken bouillon granules
1/4 teaspoon dried dill

Also:

Roma tomato slices and/or parsley or basil

- Peel and cut the hard-boiled eggs in half. Remove yolks and mix with melted butter, vinegar, sugar, mustard, ham and chives. Blend until smooth.
- Stuff the yolk mixture into the whites as for deviled eggs. Arrange on a greased pie plate. (Note: Eggs can be covered tightly and refrigerated overnight at this point.)
- For Sauce: Melt the butter in a saucepan. Whisk in the flour to form a paste, and cook for a 1 to 2 minutes. Slowly whisk in the milk and bouillon granules.
- Cook over low heat until bubbly and thick. Stir in the dill.
- Heat stuffed eggs in a preheated oven at 350 degrees for 10 minutes.
- Toast muffin halves. Place a tablespoon or so of sauce on the muffin. Place an egg half on sauce, then top it with more sauce. Garnish with tomato slices and or parsley or basil.

Makes 6 servings

from **Morningside Bed & Breakfast**
219 Leelanau Avenue
P.O. Box 411
Frankfort, MI 49635
616-352-4008

"My mother used to make special deviled eggs with ham. I decided to try to make a hot dish with them," said Shirley Choss. "I especially like the sauce."
Guests to this hilltop B&B can feel like they were back in the 1890s, visiting this grand summer home built in a neighborhood of similar homes (actually, it's better now -- the home was built with no bathrooms, now it has six).

The home is filled with ornate woodwork and bay windows and is located just one block from a sandy Lake Michigan beach. When husband Gus retired from Ford Motor Company, Shirley had just graduated from college, so they opted for a second career as innkeepers.

Other Morningside B&B recipes:
Root Beer Muffins, page 69
Benzie Medley Conserve, page 104

Black Olive Quiche

Ingredients:

1 9-inch single pie crust, unbaked
1 tablespoon prepared mustard
4 eggs
2 cups heavy (whipping) cream
1/2 cup grated Monterey Jack cheese
1/2 teaspoon salt
1/4 teaspoon pepper
1/2 cup black olives, sliced

- Place prepared pie crust into a 9-inch quiche or pie pan.
- Brush mustard over the bottom of the crust.
- In a large bowl, beat eggs and cream until the mixture is smooth.
- Add cheese, salt and pepper and black olives. Mix thoroughly.
- Pour egg mixture into the crust.
- Bake in a preheated oven at 350 degrees for 45 minutes.
- Remove and let stand on a wire rack for a few minutes before cutting.

Tester's Comments: I don't know what got into me, but I couldn't bring myself to use 2 cups cream -- I used 1 cup 2% milk, 1 cup cream. The quiche was still plenty creamy. The mustard makes this outstanding.

Makes 8 servings

from **The Geiger House**
401 Denniston Street
Cassville, WI 53806
608-725-5419

"This quiche is a wonderful alternative for vegetarians," said Innkeeper Penny Neal. "With a full house, we serve it along with a ham-broccoli quiche." Breakfast here "would satisfy a lumberjack," Penny said, since it includes homemade muffins or breads and fresh fruit, as well as an entree.

Guests who have lots of energy can enjoy nearby bike trails or hike the bluffs above the Mississippi River. Nelson Dewey State Park and Historic Stonefield Village are only a few miles away. Canoeing on the Mississippi is another favorite pasttime, or guests can tool around town on a Geiger House bike. Those who want to curl up on the back porch or in front of the fireplace are welcome to do so. The Neals have restored the 1855 home, removing modern updating and stripping woodwork, wallpapering and refinishing floors.

Other Geiger House recipes:
Rhubarb Juice, page 28
Hearty Sausage with Apples, page 230

Breakfast Pizza

Ingredients:

1 pound bulk pork sausage
1 cup frozen hashbrown potatoes, thawed
Mushrooms, peppers, onions, olives, etc., optional
1 cup shredded Cheddar cheese
5 eggs
1/4 cup milk
1/2 teaspoon salt
Dash of pepper

Dough:
1 packet active dry yeast
1 cup very warm water
1 teaspoon sugar
1 teaspoon salt
2 tablespoons vegetable oil
2-1/2 cups flour

- Brown sausage, breaking it up as it cooks. Drain off fat.
- For Dough: Dissolve yeast in warm water. in a large bowl, mix in sugar, salt, vegetable oil and flour. Beat vigorously 20 strokes. Let rest about 5 minutes.
- Press dough on a greased pizza pan.
- Spoon sausage over dough. Layer on hashbrowns, any additional optional toppings and cheese.
- In a medium bowl, beat eggs, milk, salt and pepper. Pour over pizza.
- Bake in a preheated oven at 375 degrees for 25 to 30 minutes. Remove, cut into 8 pieces and serve hot.

Makes 8 servings

from **Red Forest B&B**
1421 25th Street
Two Rivers, WI 54241
414-793-1794

"Ever since we have been open as a B&B, we have our family over for Easter brunch," said Kay Rodewald. "The one requirement is we each bring a new breakfast recipe. Breakfast Pizza was this year's favorite and a favorite of our guests ever since." She substitutes refrigerated crescent rolls for the dough.

Breakfast is served in the wainscotted dining room furnished with grandmother's table and chairs. Many heirlooms are used here, and Kay and her mom made all the window treatments and dust ruffles. Kay and husband Alan updated the 1907 home in less than a year, and now their two children help operate the B&B. From start to present, this is a family business. That's what Kay and Alan wanted. Kay had been attending B&B seminars for a couple years, but the right house never popped up for sale. When this one did, they grabbed it and set to work, re-doing one room a month until the B&B opened. Four country Victorian guestrooms are available.

Another Red Forest B&B recipe:
Cherry Griddle Cakes, page 159

Broccoli Herb and Cheese Bake

Ingredients:

12 ounces grated sharp Cheddar cheese
1-1/2 cup broccoli flowerettes, crisp-cooked
1/4 cup chopped onions, sautéed
1/4 cup fresh chopped parsley
1/2 cup Cheddar-flavored croutons
1/4 teaspoon paprika
6 large eggs, beaten
1/4 cup bread crumbs
Pinch of salt and pepper
1 cup skimmed milk

Fresh Herb Mixture:
1/2 teaspoon fresh oregano, chopped
1/2 teaspoon fresh rosemary, chopped
1/2 teaspoon fresh sage, chopped
1/2 teaspoon fresh thyme, chopped

🍴 In the bottom of a greased 1-1/2 quart casserole, spread 3/4 of the cheese. Add layers of broccoli, onion, parsley and croutons. Sprinkle with paprika.

🍴 In a large bowl, mix eggs, bread crumbs, fresh herbs, salt and pepper, and milk.

🍴 Pour fresh herb mixture over layers in casserole. Top with remaining cheese. (At this point, dish can be covered and refrigerated overnight.)

🍴 Bake uncovered in a preheated oven at 300 degrees for 75 minutes. Remove from the oven and let rest for about 5 minutes before slicing.

Tester's Comments: My sad dried-herb winter version of this was good, so fresh herbs must be dynamite.

Makes 6 servings

from **Annie's Bed & Breakfast**
2117 Sheridan Drive
Madison, WI 53704
608-244-2224 or FAX 608-242-9611

The herbs for this creation of Anne Stuart's come out of her herb garden, and she may well have grown the broccoli and onion, too. Her jam is from her own grapes or apples. The gardens, filled with flowers and a gazebo, have been featured on botanical society tours.

Guests who don't share a green thumb still find much to like here. Anne and husband Larry's contemporary cedar shake and stucco home is on a quiet street, next to one of Madison's largest open spaces, Warner Park. The park has nature trails, biking and jogging paths, exercise course, tennis courts, Lake Mendota swimming beach and fishing, cross-country skiing and ice skating.

At the B&B, Anne and Larry have two suites that each have two bedrooms. Guests are welcome to use the library with the Belgian woodstove and the whirlpool room, with lush plants, mirrors and music. Annie's B&B opened in 1985. While the location is quiet, the B&B is convenient to the University of Wisconsin, the Capitol and Madison's many other features.

Cheese Omelette Oven-Style

Ingredients:

6 slices bacon
1-1/2 cups shredded sharp Cheddar cheese
1/2 cup shredded Swiss cheese
2 to 3 tablespoons flour
2 to 3 tablespoons diced pimento, drained
3 to 4 sprigs parsley, leaves only
8 eggs, beaten
1 cup milk

- Fry bacon until crisp. Drain.
- Butter a 1-1/2 quart casserole.
- Toss cheeses and flour together. Place in the casserole dish.
- Crumble bacon and sprinkle over cheese mixture.
- Dot cheese with pieces of pimento and parsley leaves.
- Beat eggs and milk together. Pour over ingredients in the casserole.
- Bake in a preheated oven at 350 degrees for 25 to 30 minutes, until puffed and starting to brown. "It will smell invitingly of cheese."

Tester's Comments: The "puff" doesn't fall, making this dish both pretty and delicious.

Makes 6 servings

from **Park Row Bed & Breakfast**
525 West Park Row
St. Peter, MN 56082
507-931-2495

A hot egg dish is always on the menu of Innkeeper Ann Burckhardt, along with a blended juice, hot bread and some type of fruit dessert.

Guests often come to her yellow, gingerbread-trimmed B&B because they are visiting nearby Gustavus Adolphus College. But they just as often come to visit Ann's place. Because she is a well-known food writer for the Star Tribune of the Twin Cities, the idea of having one of her breakfasts or digging into her always-full cookie jar is irresistible to many Twin Citians.

Her home, circa 1870, immediately captivated her during her search for a B&B, and it needed minimal renovation. The four guestrooms have been decorated in antiques, with queen-sized beds and down comforters.

Other Park Row B&B recipes:
Very Berry Orange Juice, page 32
June-Time Conserve, page 109

Egg and Bacon Casserole

Ingredients:

18 hard-boiled eggs, sliced
1/2 pound bacon, cooked crisp and crumbled

Also:

Parsley, dried or fresh
Buttered crumbs

Cream Sauce:
1/4 cup butter or margarine
1/4 cup flour
1 cup light cream or half-and-half
1 cup milk
2 cups grated sharp Cheddar cheese
1/2 clove garlic, crushed
1/4 teaspoon basil
1/4 teaspoon marjoram
1/4 teaspoon thyme

- In a greased 8 x 10-inch glass baking dish, spread egg slices. Top with crumbled bacon.
- For Cream Sauce: In a large non-stick skillet, melt butter. Whisk in flour and cook for 3 minutes, until bubbly and thick. Stir in cream and milk until the sauce is smooth and thick. Add cheese, garlic, basil, marjoram and thyme. Stir until cheese has melted.
- Top bacon and eggs with sauce. Sprinkle with parsley and buttered crumbs.
- Cover and refrigerate overnight or bake immediately. ("If this dish has been refrigerated, let it sit out for a half-hour before you bake it.")
- Bake in a preheated oven at 350 degrees for 30 minutes.

Makes 6 to 8 servings

from **The Nash House B&B**
1020 Oak Street
Wisconsin Rapids, WI 54494
715-424-2001 phone or FAX

"The mother of one of my fourth-grade students gave this recipe to me many years ago and I have used it many times," said Innkeeper/former teacher Phyllis Custer. "The sauce can be thinned a little and used over toasted English muffins or toast points."

The Custers opened three guestrooms in the former Nash family residence in 1988. The Nash siblings were interesting folks -- Jean co-owned her family's cranberry marsh and Philleo served as lieutenant governor. Edith, Philleo's widow, sold the home to the Custers to turn it into a B&B with her blessing (she wanted to open a B&B herself but knew she couldn't do that and run the marsh, too). Phyllis and Jim looked for an appropriate house for their B&B for two years. It's furnished with comfortable antiques and local artists' works.

Another Nash House recipe:
Mom's Molasses Cookies, page 212

Eggs Kathy

Ingredients:

8 egg roll skins
3 eggs
1-1/2 cups half-and-half (do not use milk)
1/2 cup sliced fresh mushrooms
1/2 cup diced ham
1 cup grated Swiss cheese

Also:

Salt and pepper

- Spray a muffin tin with non-stick cooking spray.
- Cut 1/2-inch off two sides of each egg roll skin to make a square.
- Place each skin in a sprayed muffin cup. (Wrap and freeze remaining egg roll skins.)
- Beat eggs and half-and-half until thoroughly mixed and light in color.
- Divide egg mixture among the eight cups.
- Divide the mushrooms, ham and cheese among the cups, too. Salt and pepper to taste.
- Bake in a preheated oven at 375 degrees for 30 minutes.

Makes 4 servings

from The Park Street Inn
RR 1, Box 254
Nevis, MN 56467
218-652-4500

"This is also good if you substitute Cheddar for Swiss cheese and add green chiles and salsa" instead of ham and mushrooms, said Innkeeper Kathy Carney. She's given out this recipe many times, once to a chef who's used it.

Kathy and spouse Jerry opened their three-guestroom inn in the 1912 home of Justin Halvorson. Halverson had moved to northcentral Minnesota to become the Nevis banker and proprietor of the Nevis Land Company, encouraging other Norwegian immigrants to settle here. He built his home overlooking Lac de Belle Taine, a 1,211-acre lake that's good bass and walleye fishing.

The Carney family spent six months restoring and improving the home before opening. "We went to lots of auctions and antique shop sales, which was the fun part," Kathy recalled. The inn has handmade quilts, oak woodwork and a parlor fireplace guests can enjoy.

The Heartland Bike Trail is only a block away with 28 miles for riders, walkers, runners and winter sports enthusiasts. Itasca State Park, headwaters of the Mississippi, and many lakes are nearby.

Fluffy Omelettes

Ingredients:

4 strips bacon, cooked crisp and crumbled
2 teaspoons finely chopped celery
1 teaspoon finely chopped onion
4 eggs
1/4 cup milk
Dash of salt and pepper
2 large slices American cheese, cubed

🐖 Fry bacon in a large non-stick frying pan, saving some of bacon grease. Sauté celery, then add onion just before celery is transparent.

🐖 In a separate bowl, beat eggs. Then beat in milk and salt and pepper.

🐖 Add egg mixture on top of celery and onions. Sprinkle cheese and bacon evenly over eggs.

🐖 Cook omelette over medium heat for 5 minutes or until eggs are about 3/4 cooked. Then loosen around the edges and gently flip over eggs with a wide spatula. (Eggs will flow back together if some of omelette is "broken.")

🐖 Continue to cook until eggs are thoroughly cooked. Invert the pan onto a serving plate, then slice.

Tester's Comments: Grated cheddar (1/2 cup) is fine instead of American. The celery is unusual and excellent!

Makes 2 to 4 servings

from **Prior's on Desoto**
1522 Desoto Street
St. Paul, MN 55101
612-774-2695

"This recipe will serve 20 hungry fishermen or two dainty ladies with equal success. I have made it in the broiler pan to serve 20 or served it on fancy china for one and have yet to have a disappointed guest," said Innkeeper Mary Prior. She developed the ingredients to find a combination pleasing to the most people. She is used to cooking breakfast for large numbers of diners, and looks for easy recipes. "We had six members in our family, and all of our relatives lived out-of-state, so we often had guests for breakfast."

Richard, her husband and a building contractor who designed this house, and Mary discovered B&Bs overseas. "We have been to Europe seven times and just loved the B&Bs there, and we always said that was something we wanted to do," she said. They tried one room when the Summer Olympics came to town, liked it, as they expected, and opened two guestrooms. Their contemporary home was built in 1991 in a quiet residential neighborhood about five minutes northeast of downtown St. Paul. The living room's 20-foot vaulted ceiling overlooks the fireplace. Tall windows are perfect for viewing sunsets. Guests have the use of the refrigerator and microwave.

John's Salsa Eggs

Ingredients:

5 eggs
2 5-inch slices salami, chopped
2 2-inch slices pepperoni, chopped
1 tablespoon favorite salsa
1/4 cup shredded "co-jack" (Cheddar and Monterey Jack) cheese
1 teaspoon chopped chives
1 teaspoon chopped parsley
Dash of salt and pepper

- In a large bowl, beat eggs with salami and pepperoni.
- Mix in salsa, then cheese. Beat in chives, parsley and salt and pepper.
- Cook in a non-stick frying pan over medium heat, stirring occasionally to scramble.
- Serve hot topped with a dollop of salsa.

Tester's Comments: Now that's an eyeopener! Sautéing meat first cooks off some of the fat. Putting a little lite sour cream on top when serving adds some of the fat back in. But it offers a cooling effect!

Makes 2 servings

from **Village Park B&B**
60 West Park Street
Fruitport, MI 49415
616-865-6289

Innkeeper John Hewett might serve up these eggs on mornings when he has breakfast duty. He cuts the chives and parsley from the herb garden.

Health-conscious visitors in the late 1800s came to visit a hotel with mineral baths that once stood just across the street from this B&B, where the village park is now. The Hewetts try to run a "heart smart" B&B with nutritious food and an exercise room, sauna and hot tub open to guests. Overlooking Spring Lake and in the "fruit belt," their B&B attracts many active guests who enjoy swimming, sailing, boating, golfing, cross-country skiing and biking.

John and Virginia started going to B&Bs for anniversaries and vacations. "We wanted a business we could do together," plus keep their jobs in Grand Rapids, Virginia said. (She is a college instructor in business and John is a customer service supervisor.) They found the large 1873 home of Joseph Ford, a local benefactor. It had been remodeled in the '50s, so they removed shag carpeting and did other major restoration, acting as their own general contractors. They opened in 1990 and have six guestrooms.

Another Village Park B&B recipe:
Rice Flour Pancakes, page 168

Mexican Mini Frittatas

Ingredients:

    10 eggs
    A splash of water
    Half of a tomato, seeded and chopped
    1 teaspoon finely chopped fresh cilantro
    1 tablespoon sliced black olives
    1 tablespoon very thinly sliced scallions, including some green tops
    1/2 cup shredded Monterey Jack cheese

Also:

    Salsa

- Beat eggs and water. Divide in half.
- Scramble eggs in two oven-proof omelette pans sprayed with a non-stick cooking spray.
- When eggs are almost set, but still wet on top, sprinkle with tomatoes, cilantro, olives, scallions and cheese.
- Broil for 1 or 2 minutes or until the cheese is melted and bubbly.
- Serve with a spoonful of salsa in the center and cilantro garnish on the side.

Tester's Comments: I like to scramble my eggs with a little milk. This is a different entree that can be "heated up" by adding chiles. It also can be made in individual casserole dishes (and then the amounts serve 5); transfer the eggs after they are scrambled and before adding toppings. Adjust topping amounts to suit you.

Makes 4 servings

from **The Inn at Union Pier**
9708 Berrien Street
P.O. Box 222
Union Pier, MI 49129
616-469-4700 or FAX 616-469-4720

Creative breakfasts are a specialty of the house here. Guests from the main house and two adjoining buildings dine in the dining room at the main house. Tables overlook the grounds and gardens.

Joyce Erickson Pitts and Mark Pitts bought this inn in 1993. On a trip to Michigan two years before, they fell in love with the idea of innkeeping. Joyce left a career in broadcast advertising sales; Mark left commercial real estate development. They sleep better working for themselves. The 15-guestroom inn was built as a 39-room hotel in the 1920s. The Lake Michigan beach, just 200 steps away, still attracts visitors as it did in the '20s.

Other Inn at Union Pier recipes:
Amaretto Sour Cream Sauce, page 102
Oven-Roasted New Potatoes, page 234

Morel and Asparagus Quiche

Ingredients:

1 9-inch pie shell, "prebaked" for 5 minutes
2 teaspoons butter or margarine
1 tablespoon minced onion
6 fresh morel mushrooms, halved (or dried morels soaked for 2 hours)
4 eggs
1-1/2 cups milk
1/2 cup plain yogurt
1 teaspoon dijon mustard
1/2 teaspoon thyme
1/4 teaspoon salt
1 cup grated Cheddar cheese
2 blanched fresh asparagus spears, cut into slices about 3 inches long
1/4 cup chopped, seeded tomato
1/3 cup Parmesan cheese

☛ Melt butter in a skillet. Sauté onion for about 2 minutes. Add mushrooms and sauté until tender. Set aside.

☛ In a bowl, food processor or blender, blend eggs, milk, yogurt, dijon mustard, thyme and salt.

☛ Stir in Cheddar cheese. Pour egg mixture into pie shell. Bake in a preheated oven at 375 degrees for 30 minutes or until the filling begins to firm up.

☛ Top with mushrooms, asparagus and tomato. Sprinkle with Parmesan. Continue to bake until a toothpick inserted in the center comes out clean, and the quiche is golden brown, about 15 minutes.

☛ Remove from oven and let stand for 10 minutes before cutting into wedges.

Makes 6 to 8 servings

from **Duley's State Street Inn**
303 State Street
Boyne City, MI 49712
616-582-7855

Morels are so popular in this neck of the woods that Boyne City has an annual festival in honor of the fungi. Sandy and John Duley host a good share of annual spring morel hunters. Sandy's hunting is improving from her first, when she found only one morel, and then by accident when she tied her shoe.

There's nothing to improve on the breakfast table here, however. This former chef and waitress from Detroit's Whitney restaurant and Rattlesnake Club, among others, have settled nicely into the pace of running a four-guestroom B&B. They spent four months restoring the 1898 home before opening in 1989. Their B&B is two blocks from downtown and Lake Charlevoix.

🏠*Another Duley's State Street Inn recipe:*
Gingerbread Waffles, page 173

Quick Crab Quiche

Ingredients:

    2 eggs
    1/2 cup mayonnaise
    1/2 cup milk
    2 tablespoons flour
    1 8-ounce can flaked crab meat, rinsed
    1 cup grated Swiss cheese
    1/2 cup chopped green onions
    1 9-inch pie shell

- Whisk together eggs, mayonnaise, milk and flour.
- Stir in crab, cheese and onions.
- Pour into the pie shell. Bake in a preheated oven at 375 degrees for 45 minutes. Let stand for a few minutes after removing from the oven before slicing.

Tester's Comments: Simple and wonderful. Don't even think of using surimi (fake crab).

Makes 6 servings

from **Victoriana 1898**
622 Washington Street
Traverse City, MI 49684
616-929-1009

"Guests often request this on return visits," said Innkeeper Flo Schermerhorn. They dine on fine china and leaded crystal at a lace-covered dining room table. After breakfast, guests might wander out to the gazebo, which was the bell tower of the city's first high school, or to see the bent tree in the backyard, which marked an Indian trail.

The artesian well, drilled when the house was built and used extensively during typhoid epidemics, still flows at the rear of the house. And the carriage house has a century-old cupola. Flo and husband Bob can tell guests more about the history of their home, built by a horse and carriage broker.

They can also fill guests in on the restoration details for those who have a yen to rehabilitate an historic home. Walls have been replaced, wallpapered and painted, floors refinished, fireplaces rebuilt, among other projects. They opened three guestrooms in 1987 after traveling in B&Bs in Europe and the U.S. When they took early retirement options, "we believed innkeeping would be an interesting.and fulfilling second career," Flo said. They furnished their B&B with heirlooms and named guestrooms after ancestors.

Another Victoriana 1898 recipe:
Puffed Swedish Pancake, page 167

147

Scotch Eggs

Ingredients:

1-1/2 pounds top quality bulk sausage
12 hard-boiled eggs, peeled
1 egg, beaten
1/2 cup seasoned bread crumbs

- Divide sausage in 12 equal parts.
- Wrap each egg in sausage, completely covering the egg. (This part can be done a day ahead. Cover eggs tightly and refrigerate overnight.)
- Dip into the beaten egg, then roll in bread crumbs.
- Place eggs on a jelly roll pan. Bake in a preheated oven at 450 degrees for 30 minutes. Serve hot.

Tester's Comments: I lowered the heat and cooked eggs a bit longer -- they're surprisingly ungreasy. A spicy Creole sausage, make by a sausagemaker at the Cross River, Minn., store, was excellent on these eggs. The bread crumbs were a nice touch, but not really necessary. To dress them up, serve with a white sauce.

Makes 6 servings

from **Stevens' White House on the Lake**
5670 West Houghton Lake Drive
P.O. Box 605
Houghton Lake, MI 48629
517-366-4567

Innkeeper Pauline Stevens still uses this recipe from the Trenton, Mich., Garden Club, to which she belonged years ago. It was always served the last meeting of the year. She serves it now with muffins and pancakes or waffles.

Pauline and Charles, her husband, bought this turn-of-the-century home, which once served as a "tourist house." "We needed to do major construction with a contractor," Pauline said. The restoration took more than three years.

"We had seen this old house for years" while vacationing in the area, she said. "I always thought it would make a great B&B. There are none in this village." Houghton Lake, in the northcentral Lower Peninsula, is about a three-hour drive from Detroit. The village is just a few miles from I-27 or I-75.

Pauline, a former teacher, sewed all the window treatments and took charge of the decorating. The four guestrooms are individually decorated in country or Victorian wallpapers and antiques. The B&B is open from May until mid-October, after "color season." Guests might be served tea during a pontoon boat ride, weather and water conditions permitting. The grassy lawn slopes down to the water, where guests can swim or just park themselves under a tree to enjoy a good book. The porch also overlooks Houghton Lake.

Smoked Salmon Quiche

Ingredients:

6 ounces smoked salmon, skinned and flaked
1 cup cooked wild rice
6 ounces grated Monterey Jack cheese
6 ounces grated Swiss cheese
3 eggs
1 cup cream
1 teaspoon dry mustard
1/4 teaspoon pepper
1/4 teaspoon dill

Crust:
1-1/4 cups flour
1/2 cup shortening
1/2 teaspoon salt
3 to 4 tablespoons cold water

- For Crust: Mix flour, shortening and salt with a pastry cutter or fork until mixture is crumbly. Add water and roll into a ball. Roll pie crust out on a floured board. Place in a 9-inch pie pan, prick bottom, and bake in a preheated oven at 425 degrees for 12 minutes.
- Onto the pre-baked crust, layer smoked salmon.
- Top with wild rice, then cheeses.
- In a separate bowl, beat eggs, cream, mustard, pepper and dill. Pour into crust.
- Bake in a preheated oven at 375 degrees for about 1 hour or until the center is no longer jiggly.
- Remove from oven and let set a few minutes before cutting.

Tester's Comments: FYI, the best smoked salmon anywhere is from Silver Lining Seafoods, Ketchikan, Alaska, and they'll air-freight it to the Midwest (you don't need king salmon - even their cheaper chum is great).

Makes 6 to 8 servings

from **Caribou Lake B&B**
County Road 38
P.O. Box 156
Lutsen, MN 55612
218-663-7489

"We also substitute lake trout sausage for smoked salmon to make an entirely different flavored quiche," said Innkeeper Leanne Wells. The Wells family is lucky to have their B&B located close to the sausagemaker at the Cross River General Store, who makes several dozen types of non-gristly sausage.

They are also lucky to live in a year-round log cabin on Caribou Lake, just a few miles inland from Lake Superior's North Shore. Leanne and Carter and their two children moved from Michigan to open the log home and an adjacent guest house as a B&B in 1990. The home is on Caribou Lake, with a boat available for fishing and a raft for swimming. The Wells let guests use the mountain bikes or direct them to the North Shore Hiking Trail access. Lutsen Resort skiing and golf is only eight miles away. The loons yodel on the lake right out in front, and the fall color change surrounds the B&B.

Smoked Trout Hash

Ingredients:

1 pound smoked trout, flaked
1/2 cup sweet onion, chopped
1/2 cup cooked wild rice
1 cup chopped fresh spinach
1 teaspoon chili powder
1/2 teaspoon white pepper
1 cup uncooked fresh hashbrown potatoes
Salt to taste
2 eggs, lightly beaten
2 tablespoons vegetable oil

Also:

8 eggs
2 cups Hollandaise sauce
8 lemon slices
Dried parsley

☛ In a large bowl, mix trout, onion, wild rice, spinach, chili powder, pepper, hashbrowns, salt and beaten eggs. Then form into 8 patties.

☛ Sauté patties using vegetable oil until hashbrowns are golden brown.

☛ As patties are cooking, poach 8 eggs and make Hollandaise.

☛ When done, place a poached egg on top of each patty. Ladle 1/4 cup Hollandaise over each. Garnish with a lemon wedge and sprinkle a little dried parsley over the top.

Makes 8 servings

from **Old Rittenhouse Inn**
301 Rittenhouse Avenue
Bayfield, WI 54814
715-779-5111

The patties can be formed ahead of time and refrigerated until cooked. Another tip is to poach the eggs in vegetable or chicken stock for more flavor. But any way these are fixed, they make a unique breakfast or brunch dish.

Using local ingredients, like Lake Superior smoked trout, and giving it some unique gourmet twist is, perhaps, the hallmark of Rittenhouse dining. Local berries, fruit, vegetables and fish make their way into soups, salads, preserves, sauces, entrées and desserts here. Rittenhouse lodging is "gourmet," too, with 20 guestrooms, all with fireplaces, in three restored Bayfield mansions. .

Other Old Rittenhouse Inn recipes:
Swiss Pear Marmalade, page 117
Halloween Soup, page 192
Shamrock Soup, page 196

Sour Cream Soufflé

Ingredients:

6 eggs, divided
1 cup sour cream, divided
1/4 teaspoon salt
3 tablespoons butter or margarine
2 cups fresh blueberries, sweetened to taste
2 tablespoons wild berry liqueur

- Beat egg whites until stiff. Set aside.

- Beat egg yolks until thick and lemon colored, about 5 minutes.

- Fold in 1/2 cup of the sour cream and the salt. Then fold in egg whites.

- Melt butter or margarine in a 10-inch oven-proof skillet. Pour in the egg mixture, gently smoothing the top. Cook over very low heat 8 to 10 minutes.

- Carefully move skillet to an oven preheated to 325 degrees. Bake for 12 to 15 minutes or until the soufflé is puffy and golden brown.

- Cut into 4 wedges and place wedges on a plate. Dollop with remaining sour cream. Top with blueberries and a little of the liqueur, letting some of the berries fall to the plate.

Makes 4 servings

from **The Log House on Spirit Lake**
P.O. Box 130
Vergas, MN 56587
800-342-2318

"This is a dish my family has enjoyed over the years and I felt it would go over equally well for the B&B," said Innkeeper Yvonne Tweten. She serves it with locally-made sausage, bacon or ham, homemade bread and fruit.

Visitors to this two-guestroom inn are treated to breakfast cooked by Yvonne in the kitchen there. Yvonne and Lyle, her husband, live in their own house on the 115 acres, so guests have privacy in the log house.

They also have some family history. Lyle lived in this log house until he was 12. At the time, it was part of his great-grandparents' homestead 80 miles away. After the farm was sold and the house deteriorated, the owners offered it to Lyle and Yvonne, who moved it to their land on Spirit Lake. It took two years of work by Lyle and local craftsmen, one of whom was an 83-year-old carpenter. The house was furnished with antiques, primitives and wicker and opened in 1990. Guests can hike, swim and fish right out front, or enjoy other water-based activities in the many lakes of Otter Tail County.

Another Log House on Spirit Lake recipe:
Spirited Baked Apple, page 132

151

Three Cheese Casserole

Ingredients:

3 cups shredded mild Cheddar cheese
3 cups shredded Mozzarella cheese
6 heaping tablespoons flour
2 cups small curd cottage cheese
1 medium onion, chopped
6 tablespoons margarine or butter
6 eggs, beaten
1 10-ounce package frozen chopped spinach, thawed and drained

Also:

Sour cream
Dill

- In a large bowl, mix Cheddar and Mozzarella. Sprinkle with flour and toss to coat all the cheese.

- Stir in cottage cheese. Set aside.

- Sauté onion in margarine until soft and transparent.

- Stir onion and margarine into beaten eggs.

- Mix eggs into cheese mixture. Stir thoroughly. Then spread in a 9 x 13-inch pan.

- Squeeze all moisture from thawed spinach. Separate spinach and spread over cheese mixture.

- Bake in a preheated oven at 350 degrees for 55 minutes. Remove from oven. Let stand 15 minutes or more before cutting. Serve with a dollop of sour cream, topped with dill.

Tester's Comments: This is a hearty, filling main dish. While a quiche-like consistency might have been expected, this was firm and substantial. I might try a fourth cheese sometime -- Feta -- for a Greek taste.

Makes 12 servings

from **Walden Woods B&B**
16070 Highway 18 Southeast
Deerwood, MN 56444
612-692-4379 or 800-892-5336

Guests here have worked up an appetite -- or are ready to. Located on a small lake, guests can hike or ski the wooded trails, canoe the lake, or head off to all the activities at Lake Mille Lacs and the smaller lakes near Brainerd. When they do return to this log home-turned-B&B, they sleep like logs in the quiet surroundings, says Innkeeper Richard Manly, who built the home. Outside the four guestrooms, the most frequent guests are beaver, otter, herons, loons, wood ducks and owls. Anne and Richard welcome human guests year 'round, and the sitting room, library and screened porch are for guests' use.

Other Walden Woods recipes:
Maple Muffins with Maple Butter Glaze, page 61
Mother's Blueberry Bread, page 93

Very Good

Apple Cinnamon French Toast

Ingredients:

1 loaf French bread
8 extra large eggs
3-1/2 cups milk
1/2 cup sugar
1 tablespoon vanilla extract
4 to 6 medium to large cooking apples (Red Rome, Cortland, et al.)

Topping:
1/2 cup sugar
1 tablespoon cinnamon
1 teaspooon nutmeg

Also:

Butter
Warmed maple syrup

- Slice bread into slices 1-1/2 inches wide. Place them together tightly in a 9 x 13-inch baking dish that has been sprayed with non-stick cooking spray.

- In a large bowl, beat eggs, milk, 1/2 cup sugar and vanilla for 30 seconds. Pour half of the mixture over the bread.

- Peel, core and slice apples. Place slices on top of the bread to cover all of it.

- Pour other half of egg mixture over the apples.

- In a small bowl, make Topping: Mix sugar, cinnamon and nutmeg. Sprinkle evenly over the top of the apples. Dot with butter. Cover dish tightly with plastic wrap and refrigerate overnight.

- In the morning, uncover dish and bake in a preheated oven at 350 degrees for 1 hour. Remove from oven and let stand for 5 minutes before cutting. Serve with warmed maple syrup.

Tester's Comments: The finished dish is light and custardy, though it nearly spilled out of the pan!

Makes 10 to 12 servings

from **The Scofield House B&B**
908 Michigan Street
Sturgeon Bay, WI 54235
414-743-7727

This is one of the hearty breakfasts about which Scofield House guests have been known to write, "we were too full for lunch!" Bill, a former health care administrator, and Fran Cecil, a registered nurse, are sold on Door County.

In 1987, the Cecils took a wrong turn in Sturgeon Bay and found this 1902 Queen Anne Victorian home for sale. They were leaning towards taking new jobs in Boston, but decided to give innkeeping a try. After major round-the-clock renovation, they now offer six guestrooms in this home. Recently they acquired three rental houses on Lake Michigan near Baileys Harbor.

🏠*Other Scofield House recipes:*
Baked Bananas, page 204
Butter Pecan Turtle Cookies, page 225

Apricot Baked French Toast

Ingredients:

16 slices French bread, sliced diagonally about 1/2-inch thick
9 eggs, beaten
1 cup orange juice
1 cup milk
1/3 cup Grand Marnier or orange-flavored liqueur
3 tablespoons sugar
1 teaspoon vanilla extract
1/4 teaspoon salt
2 tablespoons butter, cubed

Filling:
12 ounces cream cheese
1/4 cup apricot preserves
1 teaspoon finely grated orange peel
1/4 cup chopped pecans
1 tablespoon sugar

Peach Topping:
1 16-ounce package frozen peaches
1 11-ounce jar mandarin oranges
1/2 cup apricot preserves
1 tablespoon Grand Marnier
1 tablespoon cornstarch

For Filling: Combine cream cheese, preserves, orange peel, pecans and sugar. Spread it on 8 slices of bread, then top with other eight slices. Place slices close together in a greased 9 x 13-inch pan.

Beat eggs, orange juice, milk, liqueur, sugar, vanilla and salt. Pour over bread. Cover with plastic wrap and refrigerate overnight.

In the morning, dot with butter. Bake in a preheated oven at 350 degrees for 45 minutes.

For Peach Topping: Heat peaches, oranges and their liquid, and preserves. In a separate bowl, mix liqueur and cornstarch. Pour into peach mixture. Bring to a boil, stirring often. Serve warm.

Tester's Comments: I cut eggs to 7 and it was just fine. The liqueur really adds a punch to this dish. Use all the cream cheese filling because it sort of soaks in overnight.

Makes about 6 servings

from **Bluff Creek Inn**
1161 Bluff Creek Drive
Chaska, MN 55318
612-445-2735

When Anne Delaney bought this picture-perfect brick farmhouse B&B in 1988, she intended to make mouths water. Her breakfasts might include fresh-baked caramel rolls, spiced apples or poached pears, this French toast, and a dessert. (Her husband, Gary, says he's gained 20 pounds since he met her.) Anne and Gary have four guestrooms in the main house, built by a pioneer on land granted by President Abraham Lincoln before Minnesota was a state. Many of the original brick walls remain exposed, combined with designer linens and wallpapers. A separate cottage also is available.

Other Bluff Creek Inn recipes:
Bubbly Holiday Punch, page 186
Herbed Cheese Puffs, page 231

Baked Blueberry French Toast

Ingredients:

4 thin slices French or Italian bread
4 tablespoons cream cheese, softened
1/2 cup fresh or frozen "dry pack" blueberries
3 eggs
3/4 cup milk
2 tablespoons maple syrup

Also:

Blueberry syrup

- Spread 2 slices of bread with cream cheese. Top with the other 2 slices.
- Slice the cream cheese "sandwiches" into 1-inch cubes. Divide the cubes and place in two individual casserole dishes that have been sprayed with non-stick cooking spray.
- Sprinkle on the blueberries.
- Mix eggs, milk and maple syrup. Pour over the bread cubes and berries.
- Cover dishes with aluminum foil and refrigerate overnight.
- In the morning, place the covered dishes in a preheated oven at 350 degrees for 25 minutes. Then remove foil and bake for another 15 minutes.
- Remove from oven and cool for 5 minutes. Drizzle with blueberry syrup and serve.

Makes 2 servings

from **The Urban Retreat B&B**
2759 Canterbury Road
Ann Arbor, MI 48104
313-971-8110

"Guests love it," said Gloria Krys about this recipe. "This dish is filling and needs little more than juice and fresh fruit to round out the meal. It's another way to showcase the state's abundance of fresh fruit," which she loves to do.

She also loves to garden, as guests can tell by the "active" perennial garden, created to attract butterflies, bees and birds. Guests have a garden view from the breakfast room, added on to the back of the house.

Gloria and André Rosalik, her spouse, opened their contemporary home with two guestrooms in 1986. They had honeymooned at B&Bs throughout Michigan, and thought about opening a B&B after retiring from social work. But they decided not to put it off, so they offer a low-key homestay.

Another Urban Retreat recipe:
Poached Sugarplums, page 131

Crispy Cinnamon French Toast

Ingredients:

4 eggs
1/2 cup half-and-half
1 teaspoon vanilla extract
2 tablespoons sugar
1/2 teaspoon cinnamon
A pinch of nutmeg
2 cups crushed crispy rice cereal (4 cups before crushed)
16 slices swirled or marbled cinnamon bread
6 tablespoons margarine, melted

Also:

Cinnamon, optional
Maple syrup, warmed

- Beat eggs, half-and-half and vanilla. Mix in sugar, cinnamon and nutmeg, stirring until well blended.
- Place the crushed cereal in a pie plate.
- Dip one side of a slice of bread into egg mixture, then the other side.
- Place bread on cereal, then turn to coat the other side.
- Grease a cookie sheet. Place coated bread on cookie sheet, then repeat with remaining bread.
- Drizzle melted margarine over top of the bread. Sprinkle lightly with additional cinnamon.
- Bake in a preheated oven for 10 to 12 minutes. Serve hot with warmed maple syrup.

Tester's Comments: It's fun to hear a little snap and crackle and pop after the bread is dipped in cereal. Don't put all the cinnamon in egg mixture at once -- it floats and the first piece of bread dipped gets nearly all of it.

Makes 4 to 8 servings

from **Dr. Joseph Moses House B&B**
1100 South Division Street
Northfield, MN 55057
507-663-1563

Innkeepers Kathleen Murphy and Ron Halverson combined a number of recipes "until we came up with something good to eat and easy to make," two important criteria to innkeepers. "Typically, we would serve this casually on Ron's collection of Fire King, accompanied by warm maple syrup, possibly ham, fresh fruit, muffins and beverages," Kathleen said. Kathleen and Ron opened this 1929 home as a B&B in 1990. They have four guestrooms for travelers coming to Carleton or St. Olaf Colleges, or to explore historic Northfield, about 35 minutes south of the Twin Cities.

Another Moses House recipe:
Rhubarb Cake, page 42

Apple Nut Pancakes

Ingredients:

1 cup flour
1 cup whole wheat flour
1/4 teaspoon salt
3 teaspoons baking powder
2 cups buttermilk
2 eggs
2 tablespoons vegetable oil
1 cup peeled and chopped apple
1/3 cup chopped nuts

Also:

Warmed maple syrup

- In a large bowl, combine flours, salt and baking powder.
- In a separate bowl, whisk together the buttermilk, eggs, oil, apple and nuts.
- Stir the buttermilk mixture into the flour mixture, stirring just until all ingredients are blended.
- Pour batter onto a hot (350 to 400-degree) greased griddle. Flip when bubbles show through and batter appears dry. Cook thoroughly on the other side. Serve hot with butter and pure maple syrup.

Tester's Comments: What the heck -- add raisins, cinnamon and a little cloves, too!

Makes 8 large pancakes

from **The Oak Street Inn**
506 Oak Street
Prescott, WI 54021
715-262-4110

These pancakes might follow servings of strawberries and raspberries from the Inn's garden. The apples come from nearby apple orchards, plentiful in this part of Wisconsin, where the St. Croix and Mississippi rivers meet.

Ann-Marie and Stan Johnson serve breakfast on grandmother's china in the dining room of this 1854 Italianate home. Set at the top of the old rivertown of Prescott, this family home also has housed a church, parsonage, a piano factory and a hospital annex. The Johnson family bought it as an operating B&B in 1990. They furnished the house and landscaped. Roses or other flowers from their gardens are found in the two guestrooms.

Located less than an hour from the Twin Cities, Prescott has access to the St. Croix for swimming or boating, just before it merges with the Mississippi. It's one of the historic towns on the Great River Road. A nature center, state parks and winery are nearby. The B&B is within walking distance of downtown, with antique shops and restaurants.

Banana Cinnamon Pancakes

Ingredients:

1 cup flour
1 cup whole wheat flour
2 tablespoons sugar
1-1/2 teaspoons cinnamon
1 teaspoon salt
3 teaspoons baking powder
1/2 teaspoon baking soda
2 cups buttermilk
1/4 cup oil
2 eggs
2 medium ripe bananas, mashed

Raspberry Butter:
1/2 cup butter, softened
1/4 cup powdered sugar
1/2 cup raspberries, fresh or frozen,
    thawed and drained

Also:

Warmed maple syrup

- In a large bowl, combine flours, sugar, cinnamon, salt, baking powder and baking soda.

- In a separate bowl, mix buttermilk, oil and eggs.

- Combine the wet and dry ingredients. When thoroughly beaten, mix in bananas.

- Spoon batter onto a hot, greased griddle. When the top bubbles, flip and cook for 1 minute.

- For Raspberry Butter: Beat butter, powdered sugar and raspberries until light and fluffy, or place ingredients in a blender or food processor and process on "whip."

- Serve pancakes hot with Raspberry Butter and warmed maple syrup.

Tester's Comments: These are very hearty pancakes, serving 4 lumberjack appetites. They take a little longer to cook than thinner griddle cakes.

Makes 4 to 6 servings

from **Big Bay Point Lighthouse B&B**
#3 Lighthouse Road
Big Bay, MI 49808
906-345-9957

Appetites are a little larger in this neck of the woods, 30 miles up the road from Marquette in Michigan's beautiful Upper Peninsula. Hiking to waterfalls or through the woods, fishing, mountain biking, cross country skiing, rock climbing and canoeing are all offered near Big Bay, pop. 250, and one of the sites of the Otto Preminger classic, "Anatomy of a Murder." The lighthouse went into operation in 1896, housing two families on this cliff 60 feet above Lake Superior. In 1986, it was converted into a B&B, and it has seven guestrooms. Step up to the lantern, 125 feet above the lake surface, to get a view of the lake and the Huron Mountains. There's a sauna, and two miles of groomed ski trails are in the 50 acres of woods around the inn. The three innkeepers are former guests, ex-Chicagoans and avid preservationists.

Cherry Griddle Cakes

Ingredients:

2 cups flour
1/3 cup plus 3 tablespoons sugar
2 tablespoons baking powder
1/2 teaspoon salt
2 eggs, separated
2-1/2 cups milk
1/2 cup butter, melted and divided
2 tablespoons lemon juice

Cherry Sauce:
4 cups pitted tart red cherries
1 cup sugar
1/4 cup cornstarch
1 cup water

- In a large mixing bowl, mix flour, 3 tablespoons sugar, baking power and salt.

- In a separate bowl, beat egg yolks. Whisk in milk.

- Pour all at once into flour mixture. Mix just until batter is smooth. Stir in 1/4 cup butter.

- Beat egg whites until stiff peaks form. Fold into the batter. Allow batter to stand a few minutes.

- For Cherry Sauce: Pour cherries and water into a large kettle. Cook over medium heat. In a small bowl, mix sugar and cornstarch. Stir into cherries. Cook, stirring often, until thick and bubbly.

- For each griddle cake, pour about 1/2 cup batter onto hot, lightly-buttered 10-inch non-stick skillet. Tilt pan to spread batter evenly. Cook for about 1 minute or until golden; turn when griddle cake has a bubbly surface and slightly dry edges. Cook 30 seconds more and remove from pan.

- Brush the surface of the finished cakes with the remaining 1/4 cup butter and the lemon juice. Sprinkle lightly with some of the 1/3 cup sugar.

- Spread about 3 tablespoons cherry sauce over one end of each cake, then roll up like a jelly roll or crepe. Place rolled cakes in a glass baking dish. Keep warm in oven until ready to serve. Spoon remaining sauce over all before serving.

Makes 8 servings

from **Red Forest B&B**
1421 25th Street
Two Rivers, WI 54241
414-793-1794

This is a good dish for when all of Kay and Alan Rodewald's four guestrooms are booked, Kay said. Since Two Rivers, located on Lake Michigan, is not far from Door County, there's no shortage of cherries in their freezer. Kay and Alan opened their B&B in 1990 after redecorating a 1907 three-story shingle-style home. They stripped, refinished, rewallpapered and repainted one room a month until opening. The period furnishings are comfortable and homey, and many are heirlooms. Kay and her mom made all the window treatments and the Rodewald's two children help operate the family business.

Another Red Forest B&B recipe:
Breakfast Pizza, page 138

Chris' Crepecakes

Ingredients:

1 cup buttermilk
1 egg
1 tablespoon vegetable oil
1 cup flour
1 teaspoon baking powder
1/2 teaspoon baking soda
1/4 teaspoon salt

Also:

Vanilla yogurt
Fresh sliced fruit
Dark brown sugar

- In a large bowl, preferably one from which pouring is easy, beat together buttermilk, egg and oil.

- Beat in flour, baking powder, baking soda and salt with an egg beater.

- Heat griddle or skillet to medium high and oil pan with margarine or non-stick cooking spray (re-grease every three or four crepes). Pour batter in and swirl to spread batter about 1/8-inch thick.

- Flip crepe when top has nearly lost its gloss. Cook about 45 seconds on the other side.

- Remove to a covered dish and stack while other crepes cook.

- To serve, microwave crepes one or two at a time so they are very hot. Spread top side with yogurt, then put fresh fruit down the middle. Fold sides in. Spread top with more yogurt, sprinkle with dark brown sugar and serve.

Tester's Comments: The batter easily can be made in the blender. Filling options are nearly endless.

Makes 6 to 8 crepecakes

from 1900 Dupont
1900 Dupont Avenue South
Minneapolis, MN 55403
612-374-1973

Innkeeper Christine Viken serves these half-crepes, half-pancakes as part of her continental breakfast. It's a creative way to serve fresh fruit. "My guests say they enjoy it as a guilt-free indulgence," she said.

There are plenty of other indulgences not far from this Lowry Hill home. Restaurants and bakeries abound on south Hennepin Avenue. The Guthrie Theatre, Walker Art Center and Sculpture Garden are only five blocks away. Many guests enjoy the walk past 19th century mansions on the way to Lake of the Isles pathways, which connect with paths around Lakes Calhoun and Harriet. This three-guestroom B&B is in a renovated 1896 home. The second floor library has a fireplace, tufted leather sofas and stained glass windows. The home has dark woodwork and is furnished with Victorian antiques.

Finnish Pancake

Ingredients:

8 eggs
1/2 cup sugar
1-1/4 cups flour
1/2 teaspoon salt
4 cups milk
3/4 cup butter, divided

🛥 In a large bowl or blender, mix the eggs, sugar, flour, salt, milk and 1/2 cup of butter, melted.

🛥 Melt the other 1/4 cup butter in the bottom of a 9 x 13-inch pan while oven preheats to 400 degrees.

🛥 Pour the batter into the pan. Bake in the preheated oven for 30 minutes.

🛥 Remove from oven and cool for several minutes before cutting into squares (entire dish can be refrigerated and individual portions reheated in the microwave before serving).

Tester's Comments: A rich, sweet custard. The flour forms a thin bottom crust. No topping is needed.

Makes 12 servings

from **Michigamme Lake Lodge**
U.S. Highway 41
P.O. Box 97
Champion, MI 49814
906-339-4400 or 800-358-0058

This custard-like "pancake" puzzles guests at first, but it's love at first bite when they try it, said Manager Barbara Sacks. The recipe is from Gail Landtroop, the Lodge's Finnish housekeeper.

But that's just one minor jaw-dropper here. Sam Cohodas, a businessman, financier and philanthropist of near legendary proportions in the Upper Peninsula, built his own getaway in 1934. Reminiscent of the Adirondack style, the two-story log lodge has a 33-foot high stone fireplace in the grand room, log railings, some twig furniture and an impressive staircase. The nine guestrooms all have down comforters and many original furnishings, custom-made by furniture craftsmen downstate in Grand Rapids.

Linda and Frank Stabile, who own a motel in Marquette, 30 miles east, were lucky enough to purchase this gem in 1988. Listed on the National Register of Historic Places, it was one of the last intact "great camps" in the U.P. Cohodas' property includes 1700 feet of Lake Michigamme and Peshekee River shoreline, which guests can explore by canoe. Other details include an oak floor secured by wooden pegs and a cedar stump chandelier. The B&B is open each year from May 1 through October.

French Baked Pancake

Ingredients:

1/2 cup butter
4 teaspoons sugar
3 eggs
1-1/4 cups milk
2 cups flour
1-1/2 teaspoons baking powder

Filling:
1-1/2 pounds (24 ounces) cottage cheese
2 eggs
3 tablespoons butter, melted
1 teaspoon salt

Blueberry Sauce:
1 12-ounce package frozen "dry pack" blueberries
1/4 cup sugar
1/4 teaspoon cinnamon extract, optional
1 tablespoon cornstarch
1/4 cup water

- In a large bowl, cream butter and sugar. Then beat in eggs.

- Mix in milk alternately with flour and baking powder.

- Place half the batter in a well-greased 9 x 13-inch baking pan.

- For Filling: Mix cottage cheese, eggs, butter and salt. Spread over batter in pan.

- Top filling with the remaining batter.

- Bake in a preheated oven at 350 degrees for 45 minutes or until golden brown.

- For Blueberry Sauce: Place blueberries, sugar and optional extract in a microwavable covered casserole. Cook on medium or medium low for 5 to 10 minutes until berries soften. Mix cornstarch and water. Stir it into blueberry mixture, cook for 1 minute, stir, then cook for 1 more minute.

- Serve pancake hot, cut into squares, with Blueberry Sauce ladled over the top.

Makes 6 to 10 servings

from **The Victorian Rose Inn**
609 West Fountain Street
Albert Lea, MN 56007
507-373-7602 or 800-252-6558

Innkeeper Linda Roemmich serves this dish in six or eight large portions. The original recipe, she said, called for sour cream, preserves, honey or maple syrup, "but none of them measure up to the blueberry sauce!"

Linda and Darrel, her husband, stayed in B&Bs on a European trip in 1986. When they came home, they wanted to restore a building and share it with others. They drove by this three-story Queen Anne Victorian sitting empty, bought it and opened for business a year later, in 1990. They worked weekends and evenings to restore and redecorate and open four guestrooms. The home is listed on the National Register of Historic Places. Guests are welcome to enjoy the living room, parlor or library as well as the porches. The B&B is close to downtown, Fountain Lake and the Community Theater.

Fruit-Filled Breakfast Crepes

Ingredients:

6 eggs
1 cup milk
1/4 cup butter, melted
1 cup flour
1 tablespoon sugar
1/2 teaspoon salt

Also:

Powdered sugar

Fruit Filling:
2 cups diced rhubarb
1/2 to 3/4 cup sugar
2 cups sliced strawberries, peaches
    or apples

🥄 In a large bowl, whisk eggs well. Whisk in milk and butter.

🥄 In a separate bowl, sift together flour, sugar and salt.

🥄 Add flour mixture to egg mixture. Whisk slowly until batter is smooth (it will be thin).

🥄 Ladle 1/4 cup batter into a non-stick 10-inch crepe pan over medium high heat. Swirl the pan so the batter covers the bottom. When the edges are slightly dry, turn and cook for 30 seconds more, then remove crepe to a plate. Keep crepes covered with a clean towel in a warm oven.

🥄 For Fruit Filling: In a saucepan, mix rhubarb and sugar. Cook over medium heat until bubbly and smooth. Mix in fruit and cook for about another 10 minutes or until fruit is soft, but not mushy.

🥄 To serve, place two crepes on a plate. Spoon filling down the centers of each, then roll up the crepes. Sprinkle with powdered sugar and serve hot.

Tester's Comments: I used a blender for smoothness and used an 8-inch pan, and it made 14 crepes.

Makes 10 to 14 pancakes

from **Oak Hill Manor B&B**
401 East Main Street
Albany, WI 53502
608-862-1400

"I learned this recipe from watching my mother," said Innkeeper Mary DeWolf. "She used to make these pancakes for Saturday supper, with smoked sausages." Mary and Lee, her spouse, serve them with baked ham.

Now retired, the DeWolfs think they have it easier cooking for B&B guests. They sold their restaurant in Northern Wisconsin, so "cooking for eight or 10 is such a pleasure, allowing us to really pamper our guests," Mary said. This 1908 brick home had been sitting vacant for two years when they bought it in 1990. It had been built as a retirement home for a wealthy farmer. The DeWolfs spent seven months getting the home up to snuff for guests. Each of the four guestrooms is a corner room in the 3500-square-foot home.

🏠*Another Oak Hill Manor recipe:*
Nutty Apple Cinnamon Waffles, page 174

Ham 'n Apple Pancakes

Ingredients:

2 cups buttermilk baking mix
1 cup milk
2 eggs
3/4 cup diced fully-cooked, smoked ham
1/2 cup shredded Cheddar cheese
2 tablespoons sliced green onions (with tops)

Apple Topping:
1 cup plus 2 tablespoons sugar
1/4 cup cornstarch
1/2 teaspoon cinnamon
Pinch of nutmeg
2-1/2 cups water
3 tablespoons lemon juice
3 apples, peeled, cored and sliced

🖙 For Apple Topping: In a large saucepan, mix sugar, cornstarch, cinnamon, nutmeg and water. Bring it to a boil, stirring often. Stir in lemon juice. Reduce heat. Mix in apples. Cook until apples are soft. Keep sauce warm, stirring occasionally, until serving.

🖙 In a large bowl, beat baking mix, milk and eggs with a whisk until smooth.

🖙 Fold in ham, cheese and onions.

🖙 Pour about 1/4 cup batter onto a hot, greased griddle. Cook until pancakes are dry around the edges, flip and cook another minute or so until golden brown.

🖙 Serve hot with warm Apple Topping.

Tester's Comments: The house smells like apple pie baking when the topping cooks. The pancakes are delicious, sort of like potato pancakes, and are good served with lite sour cream (in place of the topping).

Makes about 15 pancakes

from **Duncan's Country B&B**
4738 Clark Road
Prescott, MI 48756
517-873-4237 phone or FAX

Innkeeper Nancy Duncan serves these filling pancakes at the solid wood trestle table in the dining room. Her large country breakfast might include fruit, homemade biscuits, country-fried potatoes and homemade jams.

Her turn-of-the-century farmhouse is one of the original homes in the Prescott area, near West Branch in the central Lower Peninsula. Restoration began in 1981, and "the house was stripped to the outside walls." New interior walls and woodwork copied from the original were installed, and the family room wall was paneled with barnwood from an ice house on the grounds.

"I enjoy meeting people and making new friends and I had this large home with extra rooms, so it just seemed natural to want to share it," Nancy said. The B&B is near canoeing on the Rifle River, golf, boating, fishing and swimming. Nancy counts 26 lakes within 26 minutes, including the sandy beaches of Lake Huron at Tawas.

Honey Puff Pancake

Ingredients:

6 eggs
1 cup milk
3 tablespoons honey
3 ounces cream cheese, softened
1 cup flour
1/2 teaspoon salt
1/2 teaspoon baking powder
3 tablespoons butter

Honey Butter Spread:
1/2 cup honey
1/2 cup powdered sugar
1/2 cup butter, softened
Cinnamon to taste

- Place eggs, milk, honey, cream cheese, flour, salt and baking powder in the blender.
- Grease a 10-inch oven-proof skillet with 1 tablespoon butter. Place remaining 2 tablespoons butter in the skillet. Put skillet in the oven as oven preheats; watch carefully and remove when butter sizzles.
- Blend ingredients in the blender at high speed for 1 minute or until smooth.
- Pour batter into the hot skillet.
- Bake at 400 degrees for 20 to 25 minutes or until puffed and golden brown. Serve with a sprinkle of powdered sugar on top and pass the Honey Butter Spread.
- For Honey Butter Spread: Beat the honey, powdered sugar, butter and cinnamon until smooth.

Tester's Comments: If you go for the Butter Spread, more power to you -- it was rich enough "plain" for me!

Makes 6 servings

from **Pleasant Lake Inn**
2238 60th Avenue
Osceola, WI 54020
715-294-2545 or 800-294-2545

"This is a favorite with many guests," said Innkeeper Charlene Berg. "When it comes from the oven, it's two inches above the pan and it shrinks quickly." The honey in this recipe comes from the hives kept by Richard and Charlene (Charlene might grind her own wheat, too, for the flour). The Berg family has farmed their land for generations, and the 48-cow dairy farm has been in the family since 1857. Six acres are taken up with a 500-tree apple orchard, where guests can see the blossoms in the spring and pick a few apples in the fall.

The inn itself is on 34 wooded acres on a small lake, a quarter-mile from the farm. The Bergs built this custom-designed contemporary pine home with a B&B in mind. Two guestrooms were originally built, and two more have been added. "We wanted an open, warm feeling and with privacy," Charlene said. Guests can join them in the vaulted-ceiling living room or retreat to their quiet quarters. There are ski trails by the inn and a ski hill nearby, or skating out on the lake. In the summer, guests can tube the Apple River or canoe the St. Croix. The inn is located an hour northeast of the Twin Cities.

Oatmeal Surprise Pancakes

Ingredients:

2 cups old-fashioned oatmeal
2 cups skim milk
2 tablespoons lemon juice
1/2 cup margarine, melted
1/2 cup flour, sifted
2 tablespoons sugar
1 teaspoon baking powder
1 teaspoon baking soda
1/2 teaspoon cinnamon
1/2 cup dried cherries, cut into smaller pieces (raisins can be substituted)
1/4 cup diced, dried apricots
1/2 cup diced walnuts
2 eggs

Also:

Maple syrup and butter

- The night before serving, mix the oatmeal, milk and lemon juice in a large bowl. Cover and refrigerate overnight.
- In the morning, melt the margarine. Let it cool while sifting together the flour, sugar, baking powder, baking soda and cinnamon.
- Stir the fruits and nuts into the oatmeal mixture.
- Beat the eggs into the cooled margarine. Then stir the margarine-egg mixture into the oatmeal.
- Mix in the flour mixture. The batter will be very thick.
- Scoop out about 1/4 cup batter per pancake and cook on a greased, preheated griddle (350 degrees). Spread batter to form a 4-inch circle.
- Cook until the top of the pancakes are bubbly (at least 2-3 minutes), then flip and cook another 1 to 2 minutes.
- Serve with maple syrup and butter.

Tester's Comments: These are VERY hearty pancakes that are good before a day of skiing or hiking.

Makes 18 or more 4-inch pancakes

from **Whitefish Bay Farm B&B**
3831 Clark Lake Road
Sturgeon Bay, WI 54235
414-743-1560

"Guests with hearty appetites may be able to eat three -- these are very filling!" Innkeepers Gretchen and Dick Regnery fill their guests up before travelers head out for a day exploring the sheep farm or Door County.

Other Whitefish Bay Farm B&B recipes:
Cherry Delicious, page 24
Heavenly Bananas, page 126

Puffed Swedish Pancake

Ingredients:

    1 cup flour
    2 tablespoons sugar
    3/4 teaspoon salt
    2 cups milk
    3 eggs
    4 to 6 slices bacon, diced

Also:

    Whipped cream
    Cinnamon
    Honey

- Sift flour, sugar and salt into a bowl.
- In a separate bowl, mix milk and eggs.
- Pour egg mixture into flour mixture. Beat until the batter is smooth.
- In a 9-inch oven-proof skillet, sauté bacon until it is crisp.
- Pour out all but 1/4 cup of drippings. Pour egg mixture over the 1/4 cup drippings and bacon.
- Place the skillet in a preheated oven at 375 degrees. Bake for 30 minutes or until puffed and golden.
- Remove from oven and cut into 6 wedges. Top each wedge with a teaspoon of whipped cream, sprinkle with cinnamon and drizzle with honey.

Tester's Comments: Mixing egg mixture in the blender is easy. We preferred no toppings at all on this.

Makes 6 servings

from Victoriana 1898
622 Washington Street
Traverse City, MI 49684
616-929-1009

"I grew up in northern Minnesota among Swedes, Norwegians and Germans," said Innkeeper Flo Schermerhorn. "This is one of the glorious recipes passed from neighbor to neighbor." As a special treat, she'd get to "stay over" at a friend's house. "I couldn't seem to get enough of these pancakes, so I liked to stay at that farm often."

Flo and Bob's guests who "stay over" seem to get their fill every morning at the dining room table. Whether outdoors in the gazebo or in by the fire, there's plenty to enjoy in this architectural gem with three guestrooms. Close to West Grand Traverse Bay, there's also plenty to do in this resort area.

Another Victoriana 1898 recipe:
Quick Crab Quiche, page 147

Rice Flour Pancakes

Ingredients:

    2-1/4 cups brown rice flour
    4 teaspoons baking powder
    1 teaspoon baking soda
    1 teaspoon salt
    1-3/4 cups water
    4 eggs
    1/2 cup canola oil

Also:

    Natural fruit syrups

- In a large bowl, sift together flour, baking powder, baking soda and salt.
- In a separate bowl, beat water and eggs. Then beat in oil.
- Pour egg mixture into flour mixture, stirring just until all ingredients are blended.
- Let mixture set for 20 minutes.
- Heat a lightly-greased griddle to 400 degrees. Spoon batter on to make medium-sized pancakes. Turn when bubbles form.
- Serve in a stack, hot, with blueberry and raspberry syrups.

Makes 16 4-inch pancakes

from **Village Park B&B**
60 West Park Street
Fruitport, MI 49415
616-865-6289

"A guest with an allergy to wheat products and milk was very grateful that we served these pancakes," said Innkeeper Virginia Hewett. "Others accustomed to the usual breakfast fare were surprised by the light but wholesome taste of these pancakes." Brown rice flour can be purchased in health food stores and should be kept in a cool place or refrigerated, she said.

B&B guests won't be weighed down with a calorie-rich breakfast here. Fresh fruit from Michigan's "fruit belt" and whole-grain, low-salt, low-cholesterol and fruit-sweetened breakfasts are Virginia's specialty. Then guests might be off to climb up a sand dune at Gillette Nature Center, hike in Hoffmaster State Park, or bike or cross-country ski in the Grand Haven-Muskegon area. A tennis court and a Spring Lake boat launch are across the street, and the B&B has an exercise room, hot tub and sauna. Virginia and John, her husband, offer six guestrooms in their 1873 home, which overlooks Spring Lake.

Another Village Park B&B recipe:
John's Salsa Eggs, page 144

Scandinavian Plattar Cakes

Ingredients:

- 3 eggs
- 1-1/4 cups milk
- 3/4 cup flour
- 1 tablespoon sugar
- 1/4 teaspoon salt

Also:

- Lingonberries
- Powdered sugar
- Whipped butter

- In a large bowl, beat eggs until they are thick and lemon-colored. Stir in milk.
- In a separate bowl, sift together flour, sugar and salt. Add to egg and milk mixture and mix until smooth.
- Allow batter to set for 20 minutes.
- In a buttered, 10-inch non-stick skillet, pour in 1/4 cup batter, tilting pan to coat bottom evenly. Cook over medium high heat until golden brown. Flip and cook on the other side.
- Keep cooked pancakes warm in a covered pan in the oven until all are cooked. Spread lingonberries down the middle and roll pancakes up like a crepe. Dust with powdered sugar and serve with whipped butter.

Tester's Comments: A first-class crepe recipe. If lingonberries aren't in your grocery store, diced fresh strawberries are a wonderful substitute. (Folding lingonberries into stiffly-beaten whipped cream, then topping a rolled crepe with the mixture, is absolutely scrumptious!)

Makes 12 pancakes

from **Triple L Farm**
Route 1, Box 141
Hendricks, MN 56136
507-275-3740

"When I was in Norway, one of my Norwegian relatives made these Plattar Cakes," said Innkeeper Joan Larson. "All her measurements were metric and some were dump-style." Joan re-created the recipe at home.

It was Joan's travels in Europe before she married Lanny that acquainted her with B&Bs. "I thought it was a great way to experience the culture of the area, meet the people and find out what to do and see in the area," she said. Joan also worked in the Trapp Family Lodge in Stowe, Vermont. Travelers now come to Joan and Lanny and their kids on their 283-acre farm. They remodeled their 1890 farmhouse and opened a B&B in 1986. One of the two guestrooms can accommodate an entire family, and kids are welcome. They can even walk country roads to the South Dakota border.

Spicy Pancakes with Sautéed Apples

Ingredients:

1 cup flour
1 cup milk
1 egg, beaten
1 teaspoon baking powder
1/2 teaspoon cinnamon
1/2 teaspoon cloves
1/8 teaspoon baking soda
1 teaspoon vanilla extract
1 to 2 tablespoons margarine

Also:

Warmed maple syrup

German Sautéed Apples:
1 large apple per two guests
1/2 tablespoon corn syrup per apple
1 tablespoon butter per apple
1 tablespoon brown sugar, lightly
     packed, per apple
Dash of cinnamon

🌿 In a large bowl, mix flour, milk, egg, baking powder, cinnamon, cloves, baking soda and vanilla with a wire whisk.

🌿 Heat margarine in a skillet or griddle (use less in a non-stick pan). Drop batter from a large spoon to make 1-1/2 to 2-inch small pancakes.

🌿 Flip pancakes when bubbles appear. Cook about 1 minute on the other side.

🌿 For German Sautéed Apples: Peel and slice apple(s). In a non-stick frying pan, mix corn syrup, butter, brown sugar and cinnamon. Stir in apples and cook, stirring often, until apples are soft (but not mushy), about 10 minutes.

🌿 To serve, overlap the pancakes in a semi-circle around half of a dinner plate, 5 to 6 pancakes per person. Place apples next to the pancakes. Serve with warmed maple syrup.

Tester's Comments: The pancakes are the perfect flavor to go with apples and maple syrup. Raisins and nuts added at the last minute to the apples also are good; serve them on top of the pancakes and syrup isn't needed.

Makes 10 to 12 pancakes (2 servings)

from **The Linen & Lace B&B**
26060 Washington Avenue
Kansasville, WI 53139
414-534-4966

Innkeeper Nancy Reckhouse combined these two recipes in order to provide guests with a good start while still serving something memorable. Guests at this historic Racine County farmhouse are often off to start a busy vacation. The 1874 farmhouse, which took Nancy 18 months to restore, top to bottom, has three guestrooms with linens, lace and antiques. Set on 4-1/2 acres adjacent to a large game farm, the gardens are respected by local gardeners and appreciated by guests. The wrap-around porch is perfect for relaxing.

🏠*Another Linen & Lace recipe:*
Blueberry Cherry Pie, page 224

Wild Rice Buttermilk Pancakes

Ingredients:

2 to 4 eggs (use 2 eggs for thick pancakes, 4 for thin)
1-1/4 cups buttermilk
1/2 teaspoon baking soda
1-1/4 cups flour
1 teaspoon baking powder
1 teaspoon sugar
1/2 teaspoon salt
2 tablespoons butter or margarine, melted
1/2 cup cooked wild rice
1/4 cup sunflower seeds, optional

Also:

Butter
Warmed fruit or warmed maple syrup

- In a large bowl, whisk together eggs, buttermilk and baking soda.
- In a separate bowl, combine the flour, baking powder, sugar and salt. Add to egg mixture.
- Whisk in the butter, rice and sunflower seeds.
- Pour batter onto a hot, greased griddle. Cook until pancakes are dry around the edges.
- Flip and cook on the other side for about 1 minute, depending on thickness of pancakes.
- Serve hot with butter and warmed fruit or maple syrup.

Makes 16 thin pancakes

from **Elm Street Inn**
422 Elm Street
Crookston, MN 56716
800-568-4476 or FAX 218-281-1756

These pancakes are often part of a candlelight breakfast, served on fine china in the formal dining room of this 1910 home. Designed by the architect who also designed the Cathedral and Carnegie Library in town, it was built for a lawyer, then owned by a doctor and a banker. John and Sheryl Winters bought it in 1976 from the school board, which was considering demolition.

Since the Winters were being asked for tours of the house and had rented rooms to students, these attorneys opened a B&B in 1992. The four guestrooms are decorated with antiques and handmade quilts. The rest of the place is, as they say in their advertising, "No nightmare on this Elm Street!"

The indoor municipal pool is next door (free passes provided), and guests are within walking distance of Crookston's historic business district. Pankratz Nature Trail is two miles away, and Grand Forks, N.D., is 25 miles west.

Belgian Waffles

Ingredients:

1-3/4 cups flour
1 tablespoon baking powder
2 tablespoons malted milk powder, optional
2 eggs, separated
1-3/4 cups milk
1/2 cup vegetable oil
1/2 cup chopped nuts, optional

Also:

Blueberries or strawberries
Whipped cream

- In a large bowl, mix flour, baking powder and (optional) malted milk powder.
- In a separate bowl, beat egg whites until stiff peaks form. Set aside.
- In a medium bowl, beat egg yolks. Mix in milk and oil.
- Stir milk mixture into flour mixture, combining only until all ingredients are mixed, but still lumpy.
- Gently fold in egg whites, being careful not to overmix.
- Pour about 1/4 of the batter onto a hot Belgian waffle iron. Top with 1 tablespoon chopped nuts. Bake until steaming stops.
- Serve hot, topped with berries and whipped cream.

Makes 4 8-inch waffles

from **East Highland B&B**
W4342 Highway D
Phillips, WI 54555
715-339-3492

A large country breakfast, with two kind of muffins, fruit and coffeecake or rolls as well as these waffles, is served in the dining room, next to Jeanne Kirchmeyer's collection of blue willow china.

Their B&B is in the East Highland State Graded School, complete with the old cupola from which the school bell still rings. "Guests love to ring it," Jeanne said. One end was built in 1905, the other in 1920.

Jeanne and her husband, Russell, bid on it just to have an old home to restore -- and restore they did. It had to be taken to the bare walls to insulate, and they did all the work themselves. Once finished, local folks wanted tours and remarked they'd like to stay here. With Jeanne's cooking skills, the Kirchmeyers opened three guestrooms in 1990. Located in northcentral Wisconsin, there is year 'round recreation.

Gingerbread Waffles

Ingredients:

1-1/2 cups flour
1/4 cup sugar
1 teaspoon baking soda
1 teaspoon baking powder
1 teaspoon ginger
1/2 teaspoon salt
1/2 teaspoon cinnamon
1/3 teaspoon nutmeg
3 eggs, beaten
1 cup buttermilk
1/2 cup molasses
1/3 cup shortening, melted

Also:

Fresh peaches, peeled and sliced
Honey butter (honey whipped into butter or margarine)
Powdered sugar and maple syrup

- In a large bowl, mix flour, sugar, baking soda, baking powder, ginger, salt, cinnamon and nutmeg.

- In a separate bowl, mix eggs, buttermilk, molasses and shortening.

- Add egg mixture to flour mixture, stirring just until blended.

- Pour batter into a preheated, oiled waffle iron. Bake for 2-1/2 minutes.

- Sauté peaches in honey butter. Sprinkle waffles with powdered sugar and garnish with peaches. Serve with warmed maple syrup.

Tester's Comments: These are dark (don't wait for the waffle iron to judge doneness by color) and yummy, and no egg whites to beat. Try topping them with Aunt Josie's Lemon Butter, p. 103, or Peach Topping, p. 154.

Makes 6 to 7 waffles

from **Duley's State Street Inn**
303 State Street
Boyne City, MI 49712
616-582-7855

This might be on the breakfast table, set with fine china and fresh flowers and accompanied by seasonal fruit and homebaked muffins or pastries. Sandy and John Duley have an extensive background in restaurants and catering, and their culinary skills are put to good use in their four-guestroom inn. They opened Boyne City's first B&B in 1989 after relocating from Detroit and restoring this 1898 home. They uncovered oak and maple hardwoods and brass hardware in what was the first house in the city to have electricity.

Another Duley's State Street Inn recipe:
Morel and Asparagus Quiche, page 146

Nutty Apple Cinnamon Waffles

Ingredients:

3 eggs
1/4 cup butter-flavored shortening
1 cup buttermilk
1/2 cup flour
1/2 cup whole wheat flour
1 tablespoon baking powder
1 tablespoon sugar
1/2 teaspoon baking soda
1/2 teaspoon salt
1/2 teaspoon cinnamon
2 cooking apples, grated
1/2 cup chopped walnuts

Also:

Warmed maple syrup

- In a large bowl, whisk eggs and shortening together. Mix in buttermilk.
- In a separate bowl, sift together flours, baking powder, sugar, soda, salt and cinnamon.
- Beat flour mixture into egg mixture. Fold grated apples into the batter.
- Spoon batter onto a hot, non-stick waffle iron. Sprinkle with 2 tablespoons of walnuts.
- Bake waffles just until steaming stops. Keep warm in a 200-degree oven. Serve with warm syrup.

Tester's Comments: These are good, and no egg whites to beat! We preferred pecans over walnuts.

Makes 5 or 6 waffles

from **Oak Hill Manor B&B**
401 East Main Street
Albany, WI 53502
608-862-1400

"This is the result of experimenting in the kitchen. We find the apple makes the waffles moist inside and crisp outside," said Innkeeper Mary DeWolf. She and her husband, Lee, former restaurateurs, know their waffles.

They also know the value of an historic 3,500-square-foot home sitting empty. That's the way they found this three-story, 1908 brick home. They repaired, rebuilt and redecorated for seven months before opening four guestrooms in 1991. Each room is a corner room, all decorated in period furniture. The home, built for a wealthy farmer, is on an acre of gardens. Albany, 30 minutes from Madison in the beautiful Hidden Valley region, is great for canoeing the Sugar River or biking the Sugar River Bike Trail (it runs next to the B&B).

🏠*Another Oak Hill Manor recipe:*
Fruit-Filled Breakfast Crepes, page 163

Whole Wheat Waffle Mix

Ingredients:

2-1/2 cups flour
2-1/2 cups whole wheat flour
1 cup non-fat dry powdered milk
1/4 cup sugar
3 tablespoons baking powder
1-1/2 teaspoons cinnamon
1-1/2 teaspoons nutmeg

- In a large bowl, mix flours, powdered milk, sugar, baking powder, cinnamon and nutmeg.
- Store mix in a jar with a tight-fitting lid. The mixture keeps for 4 weeks.
- To make waffles, mix 1/2 cup Whole Wheat Waffle Mix, 1/2 cup water, and 1 tablespoon vegetable oil for each waffle. Bake in a greased waffle iron until steaming stops.

Makes 12 to 14 waffles

from **Afton Country B&B**
210 South Indian Trail
Afton, MN 55001
612-436-6964

Innkeeper Dee Cullen makes these waffles in a heart-shaped waffle iron. She covers two waffles with a scoop of non-fat frozen vanilla yogurt, then drizzles strawberry syrup over all. The syrup is also homemade, made from strawberries grown in her organic garden.

Guests might sip a glass of iced tea or cup of hot tea made with herbs from her garden, as well. Dee teaches workshops in the summer and fall on cooking with herbs and how to make herb vinegar.

Dee and Mark Cullen built this new country home in a Victorian manner and opened two barrier-free guestrooms in 1990. Dee decided to get into innkeeping after doing lots of entertaining for 25 years as a minister's wife. The home, set on six acres, overlooks a scenic ravine. From the breakfast table, guests have a good view of the gardens and bird houses.

The B&B is located 12 miles east of St. Paul and just a few miles from the St. Croix River. Upriver is historic Stillwater, with restaurants and shops along the main street. Downriver is historic Afton, still a small village. Across the river is Hudson, Wis., with greyhound racing and other attractions. All up and down the St. Croix River Valley are hiking, biking, golf and ski trails. Afton Alps ski area is close, as is Afton State Park, with miles of cross-country skiing and hiking trails and a St. Croix River swimming beach.

Cherry Sausage Roulade

Ingredients:

1/4 cup butter
1/4 cup flour
1/4 teaspoon salt
1/4 teaspoon pepper
3/4 cup milk
6 eggs, separated
1/2 teaspoon cream of tartar
1/4 cup Parmesan cheese
1/2 cup grated Swiss cheese

Sausage Filling:
1 pound bulk pork sausage
1 cup sliced green onions
1 cup sour cream
1/4 cup Parmesan cheese
1/2 teaspoon sage
1/2 teaspoon oregano
1 cup dried cherries

- Grease a jelly roll pan. Line it with waxed paper, then grease the waxed paper.
- In a non-stick saucepan, melt butter over low heat. Stir in flour, salt and pepper until smooth.
- Cook for 1 minute, then slowly whisk in milk. Cook until thick. Remove from heat.
- In a separate bowl, beat egg yolks until thick. Gradually beat in white sauce. Set aside.
- In a separate bowl, beat egg whites until foamy. Add cream of tartar. Beat until stiff peaks form.
- Fold egg white and egg yolk mixtures together.
- Spread egg mixture in the jelly roll pan. Bake roulade in a preheated oven at 350 degrees for 15 to 18 minutes, until puffy and firm in the middle.
- Meanwhile, make Sausage Filling: Brown and drain sausage. Add onion and cook 1 minute. Then add sour cream, Parmesan, sage, oregano and dried cherries. Keep warm until used.
- Turn roulade out onto a clean towel sprinkled with a little of the Parmesan. Peel off waxed paper immediately. Spread the warm sausage mixture on the roulade. Roll up jelly-roll style from the short side. Place on a cookie sheet seam side down. Top with the remaining Parmesan.
- Broil until cheese melts, then cut into slices 1-inch thick. Serve immediately.

Makes 6 servings

from **The Cottage B&B**
503 St. Joseph Avenue (M-22)
P.O. Box 653
Suttons Bay, MI 49682
616-271-6348

"This recipe is not as complicated as it seems," said Innkeepers Linda Jacobs.
"To cut time in the morning, I prepare the sausage filling the evening before.
In the morning, I heat it through in the microwave." Linda and Dave, her
spouse, like to use local products, and cherries are prolific in the Traverse City
area. They bought this operating B&B in 1986 after a long process of looking
at large, historic homes. Theirs is a 1920s home with a stone foundation and
three guestrooms. The large screened front porch is filled with wicker.
Guests enjoy the rose garden and can walk to the beach on Suttons Bay. The
town of Suttons Bay is located on the scenic Leelanau Peninsula.

Easterly Inn Breakfast Pudding

Ingredients:

4 cups milk, divided
1/2 cup uncooked rice
1 cup raisins
1/4 cup margarine
4 eggs
1/2 cup brown sugar, packed
2 tablespoons vanilla extract
Pinch of salt
1 cup granola or quick-cooking oatmeal
1/4 cup ground pecans
1/2 teaspoon cinnamon and/or nutmeg

- In a large saucepan, bring 2 cups of the milk, the rice and raisins to a boil.
- Reduce heat. Add margarine and stir until boiling stops, about 5 minutes. Remove from heat.
- In a mixing bowl, blend eggs, remaining milk, brown sugar, vanilla and salt.
- Add rice mixture to the egg mixture and stir.
- Pour into a 9 x 9-inch pan. Sprinkle granola on top.
- Bake in a preheated oven at 325 degrees for 20 minutes.
- Sprinkle pecans, cinnamon and nutmeg on top and bake for an additional 20 minutes.
- Remove from oven and serve immediately.

Makes 6 servings

from **Easterly Inn B&B**
209 Esterly Street
P.O. Box 366
East Jordan, MI 49727
616-536-3434

"We serve vegetarian breakfasts, including a hot entrée," said Innkeeper Cindi Dalian. She created this recipe as a heartier version of her husband's favorite dessert, rice pudding, and made it suitable for a main dish.

Cindi and Dennis Myers opened this 1906 Queen Anne Victorian on Esterly and Third in 1988. They started with one guestroom and now have four. They wanted to be able to live in a resort area, and their inn is just two blocks from popular Lake Charlevoix.

Guests can wind down on the wrap-around porch or head off for golf, canoeing, boating, swimming and hiking. Boyne Mountain skiing is less than 10 minutes away, and cross-country skiing trails are also nearby.

Excellent

Everyone-Loves-It Oatmeal

Ingredients:

4 cups milk
1/2 cup brown sugar, packed
2 tablespoons butter
1 teaspoon cinnamon
1/2 teaspoon salt
2 cups old-fashioned oatmeal
3 cups chopped apples
1 cup chopped walnuts or pecans

Also:

Cinnamon-sugar mixture

- In a large saucepan, bring milk, brown sugar, butter, cinnamon and salt to a boil.
- Stir in oatmeal, apples and nuts. Bring mixture to a boil again.
- Pour into a greased cast iron frying pan.
- Bake in a preheated oven at 350 degrees for 30 to 35 minutes.
- Remove from the oven, top with cinnamon-sugar mixture, and serve.

Makes 6 servings

from **The Pebble House B&B**
15093 Lakeshore Road
Lakeside, MI 49116
616-469-1416

"Even oatmeal-haters love this one! We sometimes tell guests it's called 'Baked Apples with Oatmeal,' which makes it even more appealing," said Innkeeper Jean Lawrence. Jean sets this entree on the breakfast buffet in the frying pan, hot from the oven. The Scandinavian-style buffet breakfasts here might also include fresh hot nut breads or muffins, local seasonal fruits, cheese, sausage, herring, yogurt and a choice of cereals.

Guests from the seven guestrooms in three buildings gather at the main inn for breakfast in the glass-walled dining room. Summer guests breakfast on the porch, then often head across the road to a Lake Michigan beach or to the inn's tennis court. There is plenty to do in this area between New Buffalo and St. Joseph, including swimming, hiking, wind-surfing, antiquing and wine-tasting. Art galleries, shops and Warren Dunes State Park also are nearby.

Jean and Ed are former Chicagoans who love the Arts and Crafts (Mission) style architecture of their home and restoring old buildings. Jean, an artist, and Ed, a real estate investment analyst, opened this B&B in 1984.

Another Pebble House recipe:
Fresh Peach-Raspberry Medley, page 125

Oatmeal Soufflé

Ingredients:

1 cup milk
2 tablespoons butter
3/4 cup quick-cooking oatmeal
1/3 cup low-fat cream cheese
1/4 teaspoon salt
1/4 cup brown sugar, packed
1/2 teaspoon nutmeg
1/2 teaspoon cinnamon
3 eggs, separated
1/2 cup raisins
1/2 cup nuts, chopped ("I use hickory nuts")

- Butter and sugar a 1-1/2 quart soufflé dish or casserole, then set aside.

- Put the milk and butter into a large saucepan. Heat until barely boiling.

- Slowly add the oatmeal, stirring constantly. Cook until the oatmeal is thick, about 5 minutes.

- Remove from heat. Add the cream cheese, salt, sugar, nutmeg and cinnamon. Stir briskly to blend and smooth the mixture.

- Beat the egg yolks slightly and add to oatmeal. Stir in raisins and nuts.

- Beat the egg whites until they are stiff but still moist. Using a rubber spatula, gently stir and fold the whites into the oatmeal mixture.

- Spoon the mixture into the soufflé dish. Bake in a preheated oven at 325 for 35 to 40 minutes or until the center still trembles a bit but most of the soufflé is set.

Makes 4 servings

from **Hill Street B&B**
353 Hill Street
Spring Green, WI 53599
608-588-7751

"Bike groups love it," said Marie Neider about her recipe. "The Oak Park (Illinois) bike group put it in their newsletter!"

Marie and Jim Neider owned this Queen Anne Victorian for 20 years, restoring it themselves into a seven-guestroom B&B. Kelly and Jay Phelps bought the inn from the Neiders and welcomed their first guests in May 1994. They promise there'll be no blues on this Hill Street. They were eager to try innkeeping and to continue to work with the Neiders, who own a B&B, The Bettinger House, in nearby Plain.

This part of Wisconsin, with rolling hills, parks and back roads, is a favorite of bikers. The B&B is also convenient to the American Players Theater, which is renown for its Shakespearan summer stock.

Potato Hot Dish

Ingredients:

8 cups cooked potatoes, diced
6 slices uncooked bacon, diced
1 large onion, diced
4 ounces process American cheese, diced or grated
1/4 cup green olives, chopped
1 cup mayonnaise

- In a large bowl, mix potatoes, bacon, onion, cheese, olives and mayonnaise.
- Cover and refrigerate overnight.
- In the morning, spread mixture into a greased 9 x 13-inch baking pan.
- Bake in a preheated oven at 350 degrees for 1 hour.

Tester's Comments: I made this with almost-fully cooked bacon and wished I'd greased the pan more heavily and used another 1/2 cup or so of mayonnaise. It's so good I'll make it again like that.

Makes 10 servings

from **Chicago Street Inn**
219 Chicago Street
Brooklyn, MI 49230
517-592-3888 or FAX 517-592-9025

"This recipe belonged to a delightful pair of 75-year-old twins" who visited the inn of Karen and Bill Kerr. As with all hot dishes, it's perfect for potlucks.

Most of the guests at the Kerr's B&B are city folks looking for some small town peace and quiet. Located near Jackson, Brooklyn is within 15 minutes of 54 hills and offers places to visit in the Irish Hills, as well as antiquing, shopping, and just strolling around town. The B&B has three common rooms, one with a fireplace, for guests' use, and seven antique-filled guestrooms.

Karen and Bill opened this home as an inn in 1986, just four months after buying it. Built by the family that ran a local mercantile store, the 1886 Queen Anne Victorian had been kept in good condition over the years. Kerrs needed only to redecorate, add bathrooms and "hang out the shingle."

Many of the home's original features remain. The cherry and oak woodwork found throughout the house is from the family's farm. Glass light fixtures, stained glass windows and fireplace tiles are all original. The home's first owners were said to have had their own generating system for electricity.

Other Chicago Street Inn recipes:
Strawberry Rhubarb Muffins, page 71
Sour Cream Ripple Coffee Cake, page 217

Sausage Ring

Ingredients:

1 pound turkey breakfast sausage
1 cup soft bread crumbs
3 egg whites
1/2 teaspoon sage
1/4 cup chopped parsley
1/4 cup chopped onion
A dash of oregano, basil, garlic, thyme or other favorite spices

- In a large bowl, mix sausage, bread crumbs, egg whites, sage, parsley, onion and optional spices. It may be easiest to mix with your hands.
- Spray a ring mold with cooking oil spray.
- Lightly press the sausage mixture into the mold. Cover and refrigerate no longer than 24 hours.
- Unmold the ring and place on a baking rack in a shallow pan, or on a broiler pan.
- Bake in a preheated oven at 350 degrees for 1 hour.

Makes 12 servings

from **Dutch Colonial Inn**
560 Central Avenue
Holland, MI 49423
616-396-3664

Innkeeper Diana Klungel serves this Sausage Ring with many of her French toast entrees. She developed the recipe using turkey sausage, rather than pork, and served it to the folks at Bil-Mar Foods who were testing their "Mr. Turkey" brand products. "They enjoyed it so much they requested permission to use it in their official 'Mr. Turkey' cookbook," she said.

Many of the foods served at the formal dining room table in Pat and Bob Elenbaases' home are low-fat and low-cholesterol. As many as 10 guests from the five guestrooms might gather at the table and compare notes about the best Lake Michigan beaches, cross-country ski trails or local dining.

The Elenbaases opened their large 1928 home as a B&B in 1988. The family already had pitched in and completed a major restoration project after they bought the home in 1983. Even more work was done -- adding baths, a porch and back room -- after it was a B&B. Guests are welcome to rock on the porch on summer nights or sit by the fireplace in cooler weather. Guests come to visit Holland for its famous annual tulip festival, and to visit Hope College or to enjoy the area's fine dining, shopping and bike paths.

Another Dutch Colonial Inn recipe:
Pineapple Tradewind Muffins, page 66

Anyone who has had to travel over a major holiday can understand how being on the road and away from home could make for a depressing event. But many B&Bs actually attract travelers over the holidays. These wonderful homes are decorated to the rafters with boughs and bows for Christmas. Another holiday that's popular at romantic inns is Valentine's Day, where lovers treat themselves to rooms with whirlpools or a four-poster bed. Whatever the holiday, innkeepers rise to the occasion with fantastic fare. They've generously shared their treasured recipes, many of them long-time family favorites, so now those recipes can be a family tradition at your home, as well.

Holiday Fare

An Affair to Savor

Ingredients:

12 ounces thawed orange juice concentrate
12 ounces thawed cranberry juice concentrate
1-1/4 cups strawberry Schnapps
6 12-ounce cans (from frozen juice) water

Also:

Mint sprigs

▰ In a punch bowl, combine juice concentrates, liquor and water. Float small sprigs of washed mint on top. Add an ice ring and serve.

▰ To make individual drinks, combine 1 jigger of strawberry Schnapps with equal amounts of the juice concentrates. Add crushed ice and blend in a blender. Serve daiquiri-style.

Makes about 12 servings

from **The Grapevine Inn**
702 Vine Street
Hudson, WI 54016
715-386-1989

"I serve this every year around Christmas time," said Innkeeper Barbara Dahl. "It has great color and flavor and is a light drink and punch." She and co-workers invented it years ago when she worked as a waitress "and we were playing around after work." She's made it every year since.

Barbara and her spouse, Avery, opened their B&B in 1993 in the Hans J. Andersen home. Andersen founded what is now the largest window manufacturer in the world, the Andersen Corporation in nearby Bayport, Minn. Plans and activities surrounding the founding took place around the dining room table here, with Hans revealing his plans to the "family board."

Andersen, a Danish immigrant, came to Hudson and managed a lumber company operated by his father-in-law. In 1891, just five years later, he was doing well enough to build this 10-room Arts and Crafts-style home. Local legend says he personally inspected each piece of wood used. He began investigating how to mass produce standardized window frames for home construction. His initial investment was $10,000.

"We stayed one night on our honeymoon in a B&B, and by morning I was saying, 'Can we do this?' I don't think Avery believed I was serious. Two years later we moved into this home," Barb said. The Dahls have three guestrooms in the home where Andersen lived until his death. Guests are treated to a three-course breakfast plus hors d'oeuvres in the afternoon. In the summer, guests can swim in the in-ground pool.

Bread Pudding Cake

Ingredients:

8 slices day-old whole wheat bread
1-3/4 cups milk
1/4 cup butter
1/4 cup dark brown sugar, firmly packed
1/2 cup raisins
1/2 cup currants
1 teaspoon cinnamon
1 teaspoon ginger
1/2 teaspoon nutmeg
2 eggs, beaten

Also:

Ice cream or whipped cream

- In a medium bowl, crumble bread. Set aside.

- In a saucepan, heat milk, butter and brown sugar until butter is melted and mixture boils.

- Stir hot milk into bread. Let stand 15 minutes, stirring occasionally. Meanwhile, grease an 11 x 7-inch baking dish.

- Stir raisins, currants, cinnamon, ginger, nutmeg and beaten eggs into bread. Pour into baking dish.

- Bake in a preheated oven at 350 degrees for 40 to 45 minutes.

- Remove from oven and sprinkle with additional brown sugar. Cut into squares. Serve plain or with ice cream or whipped cream.

Makes 6 to 8 servings

from **Greystone Farms B&B**
N9391 Adams Road
East Troy, WI 53120
414-495-8485

"This is great for Christmas breakfast," said Innkeeper Ruth Leibner. "Use golden raisins or snipped prunes if you don't have currants." While some people like whipped cream or ice cream on top, she prefers it "just plain." Whether or not it's Christmas, Ruth and daughter Alane, who operate the B&B together, assure that guests can hardly walk away from the dining room table. The meal might include eggs, sausage, pancakes, homemade bread and jams, muffins and fruit. Even French toast is made from homemade bread.

The house and four upstairs guestrooms are decorated in antiques, and the 1880s farmhouse is on 17 acres guests can wander. The farm is near Southern Kettle Moraine State Forest and Old World Wisconsin outdoor museum.

Another Greystone Farms recipe:
Low-Fat Banana Prune Bread, page 90

Bubbly Holiday Punch

Ingredients:

1 12-ounce package frozen "dry pack" raspberries
2 limes, thinly sliced
2 6-ounce cans frozen lime juice
2 cups light rum
3 bottles Cold Duck

☛ Pour water into a ring mold about 1-inch deep. Freeze to make an ice ring.

☛ Remove from freezer. Arrange berries and sliced limes on top of the ice. Add enough water to anchor fruit and freeze again. Add more water later to fill the ring mold, and freeze again.

☛ In a punch bowl, combine lime juice and rum.

☛ Unmold ice ring carefully by dipping it in hot water until it loosens. Place design-side up in the punch bowl.

☛ Pour in Cold Duck and serve.

Makes 20 5-ounce servings

from **Bluff Creek Inn**
1161 Bluff Creek Drive
Chaska, MN 55318
612-445-2735

Innkeeper Anne Delaney might serve this to guests at holiday time or for many special holiday parties that are booked at the inn. Her culinary skills are near legendary (13 days after she took possession of the B&B, she hosted a wedding and dinner for 20), and she's taught cooking classes for years.

Small weddings are often held here -- she's had several since she bought the farmhouse inn in 1988. One of her favorites was a summer wedding on the wide front porch, surrounded by the blooming perennial garden. "The harpist played on the porch," outside the kitchen where Anne was working. "I don't know if the wedding people enjoyed it, but I thought it was wonderful!" Winter weddings often are held fireside in the parlor.

Anne and husband Gary have four guestrooms in the main inn, an 1860 brick farmhouse. The bricks were made on site by the builder, and many of the original brick walls are exposed on the inside. The guestrooms have designer linens and family antiques, in keeping with the "country" feel. Guests enjoy breakfast on the side porch overlooking the farm in the summer, or in the dining room in cooler weather. A separate guest cottage also is available.

🏠 *Other Bluff Creek Inn recipes:*
Apricot Baked French Toast, page 154
Herbed Cheese Puffs, page 231

Chocolate Joy

Ingredients:

1 cup butter, melted
4 cups powdered sugar
5-1/2 cups crisp rice cereal
1 18-ounce jar of chunky peanut butter
1 12-ounce bag semi-sweet chocolate chips
8 ounces milk chocolate chips or an 8-ounce milk chocolate bar
6 ounces butterscotch chips

- In a large bowl of an electric mixer, combine melted butter and powdered sugar.
- Mix in cereal and peanut butter by hand.
- Roll mixture in small balls, squeezing tightly in the palm of the hand 5 or 6 times. Refrigerate.
- In a microwave-safe bowl, melt three kinds of chips together. Stir.
- Using two forks or spoons, coat the cereal balls with chocolate mixture. Place coated treats on waxed paper. After coating thoroughly hardens, store covered in the refrigerator.

Tester's Comments: I might eliminate butterscotch chips (and replace them with semi-sweet) next time to intensify chocolate flavor. Folks gobbled these up. They froze beautifully.

Makes 6 dozen 1" to 1-1/2" balls

from **Historic Bennett House**
825 Oak Street
Wisconsin Dells, WI 53965
608-254-2500

"I first tasted this candy while visiting a pumpkin festival in Illinois. I bought a small plate of cookies and this was on it," said Gail Obermeyer. "I absolutely loved it and spent hours figuring out what was in it!" Innkeepers Gail and husband Rich serve these as part of a holiday cookie tray.

If you see historic photos of the beauty of the dells of the early Wisconsin River, chances are the photos were taken by H.H. Bennett, who bought this house in 1891. Bennett came to the area during the lumber boom, when the undammed Wisconsin River attracted lumbermen. Bennett developed and printed his now-famous nature photos in his studio down the street, which is still family-operated. The house is on the National Register of Historic Places.

The Obermeyers bought this three-guestroom inn in 1988 to enter a second career as innkeepers. They gave it "a face lift," Gail said, and offer a relaxing and quiet B&B just one block from downtown.

Another Historic Bennett House recipe:
Mini Cheese Balls, page 195

Cinnamon Strawberry Soup

Ingredients:

2 pints (4 cups) fresh strawberries, washed and hulled
3 cups water
1/3 cup sugar
1 2-inch cinnamon stick
A pinch of salt
1 lemon slice
1 tablespoon cornstarch dissolved in 2 tablespoons water
1 cup heavy (whipping) cream
1/2 cup fruity semi-dry white wine (Riesling or Chenin Blanc) or Catawba Juice

Also:

Whipped cream or sour cream

- In a 3-quart saucepan, combine berries, water, sugar, cinnamon stick, salt and lemon slice.
- Boil slowly until berries are soft and have rendered their color.
- Stir in dissolved cornstarch. Cook, stirring constantly, until thick. Discard cinnamon stick and lemon slice.
- Transfer soup to blender or food processor. Purée mixture.
- Return soup to the saucepan. Stir in heavy cream and wine. Cover and chill thoroughly.
- Serve chilled in soup bowls or mugs, garnished with a dollop of whipped or sour cream.

Makes 4 to 6 servings

from **Thorwood and Rosewood Inns**
4th and Pine
Hastings, MN 55033
612-437-3297

"We serve this as the first course of our Sweetheart Dinner served in February," said Innkeeper Pam Thorsen. Pam, Dick and their staff host extended celebrations of Valentine's Day at these two inns, known for romantic getaways. Valentine's is, understandably, one of their most-requested holidays, and it's impossible to fit everyone in on one weekend.

The Thorsens bought Thorwood in 1979 and began turning the former home of a steamboat captain and private hospital into a B&B. They opened two guestrooms in 1983 after extensive renovation from a six-plex apartment house. Since then, work has continued almost without end until they have seven guestrooms. Rosewood, another historic home that once served as a hospital, was purchased from the city in 1986. It's located just across the small town from Thorwood. They "gutted" it, Dick acting as general contractor, and made eight suites, each with a different look and theme. Hastings is an historic Mississippi River town close to the Twin Cities. A winery, nature center, antiquing, state parks and "u-pick" farms are all nearby.

Cranberry Holiday Punch

Ingredients:

1 6-ounce can frozen cranberry juice concentrate
1-1/3 cups water
3 tablespoons honey
8 inches of stick cinnamon
6 whole cloves
4 cardamom pods, opened
2 cups dry red wine
1 cup cranberry liqueur

Also:

10 to 12 small sticks of cinnamon

- In a large saucepan, heat juice concentrate, water, honey, cinnamon stick(s), cloves and cardamom pods until mixture boils.
- Reduce heat, cover and simmer for 10 minutes.
- Stir in wine and liqueur. Heat thoroughly but do not boil.
- Serve hot in mugs or punch cups with a small stick of cinnamon.

Makes 10 to 12 servings

from **Quill & Quilt**
615 West Hoffman Street
Cannon Falls, MN 55009
507-263-5507 or 800-488-3849

"This punch is so good that it gets me to sing along on Christmas carols," said Innkeeper Denise Anderson, who rarely sings in public. She and David Karpinski served this punch by the parlor fire during the holidays.

The "quill" was for David, a writer and public relations professional, and the "quilt" was for Denise, also a professional who enjoys quilting and has made the quilted bedspread in each of the four guestrooms. This couple visited more than 40 B&Bs before they bought this 1897 home in Cannon Falls, about 40 minutes southeast of the Twin Cities.

In June 1994, Marcia and Dennis Flom bought the B&B. The three-story Colonial Revival home was built by Dr. Alonzo T. Conley, a prominent physician from a family of area doctors and dentists. The house was in good shape when it was restored as a B&B, but bathrooms were added and the home was redecorated. The B&B is just a short walk to the Cannon River, and the popular Cannon Valley Bike Trail is at the end of the block.

Another Quill & Quilt recipe:
Scottish Shortbread, page 237

Dried Fruit Relish

Ingredients:

2 cups dried cranberries
2 cups dried cherries
1-1/2 cups dried apricots, diced
4 cups fresh-squeezed orange juice
1 cup sugar
1/2 teaspoon cloves
1/2 teaspoon cinnamon
1/8 cup cornstarch
1/4 cup cold water

- In a kettle or large saucepan, mix cranberries, cherries, apricots, orange juice, sugar, cloves and cinnamon.
- Place over low heat. Cook until fruit has softened, stirring often.
- In a separate bowl, combine cornstarch and water. Slowly pour mixture into relish, stirring constantly. Stir and cook until bubbly and sauce is clear.
- Chill before serving.

Makes 12 servings

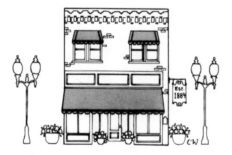

from **The Inn at Cedar Crossing**
336 Louisiana Street
Sturgeon Bay, WI 54235
414-743-4200

This fruit relish is on the Thanksgiving table at the inn's restaurant, where guests have three seatings from which they can choose to feast. Dried fruit is available in many Door County stores and orchards, in gourmet shops or in bulk food or natural food sections of grocery stores.

Innkeeper Terry Wulf and her staff decorate the inn, pub and restaurant for the holidays. While the restaurant might be the focus on Thanksgiving, the business actually began with the inn. Terry took an historic downtown mercantile building and replaced upstairs apartments with nine antique-filled guestrooms. Guests who don't have a fireplace in their room can enjoy the one in the common area, close to the cookie jar. Three years later, Terry opened the restaurant, which was followed by the pub in 1991. Inn guests can enjoy the specialties of the house delivered to their guestroom.

Other Inn at Cedar Crossing recipes:
Apple Walnut Coffeecake, page 35
Blueberry Grand Marnier Preserves, page 105
Perfect Berry Chambord Preserves, page 113
Chilled Cherry Soup, page 123

Frances Spicer's Candied Citrus Peels

Ingredients:

6 to 8 citrus fruit (pink grapefruit, oranges, lemons and/or limes)
6 cups sugar, plus some extra for rolling finished peels

- Cut fruit into quarters and peel fruit away from the rinds. Chill fruit for other uses.
- Boil the peels in a kettle of water for 20 minutes.
- Drain, then boil again in fresh water for another 20 minutes.
- Drain peels and let cool.
- Carefully scrape away any membrane from peels. Cut peels into 1/4-inch strips.
- In the kettle, combine 6 cups sugar and 6 cups water. Bring to a boil.
- Add peels and boil gently for 20 minutes.
- Drain peels. Then roll each peel in sugar. Place on waxed paper to dry.
- Store in an air-tight container.

Makes about 60 pieces

from **Spicer Castle**
11600 Indian Beach Road
Spicer, MN 56288
800-821-6675 or FAX 612-796-4076

"I remember my grandfather wandering in and out of the kitchen with a large smile on his face as he recalled his youth and his grandmother making candied citrus peels," said Innkeeper Mary Latham Swanson. This recipe, which Mary still makes for her sons, is at least 100 years old and named for Mary's great-grandmother.

It was Mary's great-grandfather, John Spicer, who founded the town and built this large home as a summer cottage on his experimental farm. Today, the home is on five acres and 500 feet of Green Lake shoreline, which guests can use to fish or swim. Allen and Marti Latham, Mary's parents, had the family home winterized, replumbed and redecorated to open to guests. But little has changed from Allen's boyhood when he spent his summers here. The home is listed on the National Register of Historic Places.

Eight guestrooms are offered in the main house, plus two cottages, all named after a member of the Spicer family. Many of the rooms have a view of Green Lake, and all are filled with antiques. The innkeepers serve breakfast on the dining porch in the summer, with a lake view, or in the dining room by the fireplace in cooler weather. They also host special meals for groups. Spicer is two hours west of the Twin Cities.

Another Spicer Castle recipe:
Peaches and Cream Muffins, page 65

Halloween Soup

Ingredients:

2 cups cooked pumpkin, fresh or canned
1/4 cup chopped onion
2 tablespoons butter, melted
1/2 cup dry sherry
4 cups chicken stock
1/4 cup maple syrup
1/2 teaspoon curry powder
1/2 teaspoon mace
1/2 teaspoon minced fresh sage
1/4 teaspoon cumin

Hazelnut Cream:
2 ounces finely chopped roasted
    hazelnuts (filberts)
1 teaspoon hazelnut liqueur or
    several drops of hazelnut oil
1/2 cup whipped cream or sour
    cream

Also:

Dill sprigs and nasturtium or violet petals

- In a food processor fitted with a steel blade, blend the pumpkin until smooth.

- In a small pan, sauté onion in butter until the onion is translucent.

- Add onion and butter, sherry, chicken stock, maple syrup, curry, mace, sage and cumin to the pumpkin in the food processor. Process until smooth.

- For Hazelnut Cream: In a small bowl, fold nuts and liqueur or oil into whipped or sour cream.

- To serve, ladle soup into bowls. Top with hazelnut cream. Garnish each bowl with a sprig of dill and edible flowers.

Makes 6 servings

from **Old Rittenhouse Inn**
301 Rittenhouse Avenue
Bayfield, WI 54814
715-779-5111

For this autumn favorite, walnuts and walnut oil may be substituted for the hazelnuts and liqueur. Either way, holidays are special at this inn. Seasonal foods are always served in the dining parlors of the 1890 Queen Anne Victorian. But holidays mean special decorations and special menus. At Christmas, Valentine's Day and fall harvest, the Rittenhouse Chamber Singers put on dinner concerts under Innkeeper Jerry Phillips' direction (he was a choir director). Mary Phillips (a former music teacher) is in the kitchen, overseeing the timing of the five-course meals in between concert numbers. Mary and Jerry bought this three-story hilltop mansion in 1973. They opened a B&B long before the "industry" was born in the Midwest, and long before percale sheets (Mary ironed them). They now have three guesthouses.

Other Old Rittenhouse Inn recipes:
Swiss Pear Marmalade, page 117
Smoked Trout Hash, page 150
Shamrock Soup, page 196

Holiday Fruit Cup

Ingredients:

1 20-ounce can pineapple chunks
1 cup apple juice
1 cinnamon stick
1 tablespoon grated orange rind
2 tablespoons cornstarch
2 tablespoons "red hot" cinnamon candies
2 large apples, cut into chunks
1 11-ounce can mandarin oranges, drained
2 bananas

Also:

Kiwi slices, whipped cream and nutmeg, or red cherries

- Drain pineapple chunks, saving juice.
- In a 2-quart saucepan, mix pineapple juice, apple juice, cinnamon stick, orange rind, cornstarch and cinnamon candies. Over medium heat, bring mixture to a boil, stirring often. Boil for 1 minutes, stirring constantly.
- Place pineapple, apples and oranges in a container with a cover. Pour sauce over the fruit. Refrigerate until thoroughly chilled (or overnight).
- Before serving, slice bananas and fold them into the mixture. Serve in fruit bowls garnished with a slice of kiwi or a dollop of whipped cream topped with nutmeg or a cherry.

Makes 6 to 8 servings

from **The Wooden Heart Inn**
11086 Highway 42
Sister Bay, WI 54234
414-854-9097

Marilyn and Mike Hagerman created this recipe to bring some much-needed holiday color to winter fruit. Breakfast at their B&B always features some type of Door County fruit, fresh, baked or in a fruit soup.

Their Wooden Heart Inn is a new log home they built and opened in 1992. "After 26 years with a major corporation, Mike decided it was time for a change of pace," Marilyn said. "We had fallen in love with Door County many years before and dreamed of living here someday."

After selling their home in Waukesha, they moved north. They designed their B&B to include three guestrooms on the second floor with a separate loft for guests. The country decor has apple, heart and Door County cherry themes. Marilyn also operates The Back Porch, a gift shop that's "for the birds," specializing in bird-related items, such as bird houses, feeders and books.

June's Sugar Cookies

Ingredients:

1 cup sugar
1 cup powdered sugar
1 cup butter, softened
1 cup vegetable oil
2 eggs, beaten
1 teaspoon vanilla extract
4-1/4 cups flour
1 teaspoon baking soda
1 teaspoon salt
1 teaspoon cream of tartar

Also:

Sugar
Red and green sugar

- In the large bowl of an electric mixer, cream sugars and butter.
- Beat in oil. Then mix in eggs and vanilla.
- In a separate bowl, sift flour with soda, salt and cream of tartar. Add half of the flour mixture to the sugar mixture. When it has combined well, mix in the other half.
- Roll dough into small balls about 1-inch in diameter. Place on a greased cookie sheet.
- Flatten each cookie with a glass dipped in sugar. Sprinkle on a little red and/or green sugar.
- Bake in a preheated oven at 375 degrees for 10 minutes.

Tester's Comments: These are rich and shortbread-like. Store in a tightly-covered container.

Makes 7 to 8 dozen cookies

from **Country Quiet Inn**
37295 112th Avenue Way
Cannon Falls, MN 55009
612-258-4406 or 800-258-1843

Innkeeper June Twaites' mother-in-law used to make these cookies and June made them each Christmas while raising five children. Now she bakes them up for B&B guests whom she and her husband, Dave, welcome.

June and Dave moved their family to this 80-acre farm in 1971 where they raised dairy cattle and farmed the land. They began remodeling the farm house, built in 1894, a few years ago with a B&B in the back of their minds, Dave said. Major remodeling was underway in early 1994 before opening. Both the Twaites enjoy gardening and invites guests to wander the lawn. Cannon Falls boasts the popular Cannon Valley Bike Trail.

Mini Cheese Balls

Ingredients:

   8 ounces cream cheese
   2 cups shredded Cheddar cheese
   2 tablespoons minced onion
   3 tablespoons minced green pepper
   6 chopped green olives
   1/4 cup pickle relish
   2 tablespoons chopped pimento
   3 chopped hard-boiled eggs
   1 cup crushed saltine crackers
   1/2 cup mayonnaise (not "lite")
   1 teaspoon salt
   1/2 teaspoon pepper

Also:

   Chopped parsley, chopped pecans or walnuts, and/or Ritz cracker crumbs

- In a large bowl of an electric mixer, combine all ingredients ("I use the bread hooks.")
- Cover and refrigerate the mixture for at least 2 hours.
- Place parsley, pecans, walnuts and/or cracker crumbs in a pie plate. You may use just one ingredient, a combination of ingredients or a mixture of all four.
- Form the cheese mixture into 1-inch balls. Roll each in the parsley/nut/crumb pan.
- Cover and refrigerate Mini Cheese Balls until use. Serve as holiday hors d'oeuvres.

Makes 6 dozen 1-inch balls

from **Historic Bennett House**
825 Oak Street
Wisconsin Dells, WI 53965
608-254-2500

Years ago, Innkeeper Gail Obermeyer was presented a tray of these as a gift. She asked for the recipe. "With a few changes, I have been serving them ever since and almost always have a request for the recipe." She and her husband, Rich, serve it on a festive table on New Year's Eve. "It's easy to double or triple the recipe." Plus, it freezes well -- "thaw these in the refrigerator."

The Obermeyers host guests all year 'round at this 1863 home, located a block from downtown. They originally are from the area and came back in 1988 to begin a retirement career as innkeepers. This three-guestroom inn was home and studio to H.H. Bennett, a famous nature photographer who recorded the Wisconsin River Dells in their wild and scenic condition in the late 1800s.

Another Historic Bennett House recipe:
Chocolate Joy, page 187

Shamrock Soup

Ingredients:

1-1/2 pounds broccoli (3 average stalks)
2 cups chicken stock or broth
3 to 4 "good sized" garlic cloves, minced
1/4 cup minced green onions (tops included)
1 cup heavy cream
3/4 teaspoon curry
1/2 teaspoon nutmeg

☛ Cut off the heads (flowerettes) of broccoli. Wash and set aside for garnish.

☛ Peel the stalks. Mince stalks or run through the food processor in several bursts.

☛ Place broccoli purée, chicken stock, garlic and onion in a large saucepan. Bring to a boil. Lower heat and simmer uncovered for 15 minutes.

☛ Place hot soup in the food processor and blend until smooth. Then return to saucepan and simmer on low heat.

☛ Stir in cream, curry and nutmeg. Serve when cream is heated through. Garnish with reserved flowerettes.

Makes 6 to 8 servings

from **Old Rittenhouse Inn**
301 Rittenhouse Avenue
Bayfield, WI 54814
715-779-5111

This flavorful soup recipe is one found in the cookbook published by this inn in 1992, the 100th birthday of the Queen Anne Victorian mansion that dominates a hilly corner of downtown Bayfield.

In recent years, the elegant meals and overnight lodging at the Rittenhouse have enticed many visitors to this small harbor town, where ferries to Madeline Island in the Apostle chain dock. Mary and Jerry Phillips' inn has been featured in "Gourmet" and other publications nationwide, highly praised for its creative regional cuisine.

Those who pull back from their table too full to drive far need only go upstairs in the main inn or up the street to two other restored guesthouses. Twenty guestrooms decorated in period antiques are available. After breakfast in the morning, guests can take home "Bayfield in a jar" in the form of the Rittenhouse kitchen's favorite preserves and sauces.

🏠*Other Old Rittenhouse Inn recipes:*
Swiss Pear Marmalade, page 117
Smoked Trout Hash, page 150
Halloween Soup, page 192

Soft Sugar Cookies

Ingredients:

    1/2 cup butter
    1-1/2 cups sugar
    2 eggs
    1 teaspoon vanilla extract
    1 cup sour cream
    2-2/3 cups flour
    1/2 teaspoon salt
    1/2 teasoon baking powder
    1/2 teaspoon baking soda

- With an electric mixer, cream butter and sugar.
- Mix in eggs and vanilla.
- Beat in sour cream.
- Sift flour before measuring. Then sift again with salt, baking powder and baking soda.
- Mix flour mixture into sour cream mixture.
- Drop dough by the teaspoonful onto a lightly greased cookie sheet.
- Bake in a preheated oven at 350 degrees for 10-12 minutes, or until cookies appear "set" and firm. Or take out of the oven at 5 minutes and sprinkle with sugar, then bake 5 minutes more.

Tester's Comments: These wonderful cookies are a cardiologist's nightmare, so don't even bother substituting margarine and "sour lean." A half-teaspoon of lemon extract is a nice addition, however.

Makes 48 cookies

from **The Kraemer House**
1190 Spruce Street
Plain, WI 53577
608-546-3161

At Christmas time, Innkneeper Gwen Kraemer serves up a plate of these cookies with coffee at 7 a.m. in the upstairs hallway. She notes the cookies can be frosted with a powdered sugar frosting and decorated with colored sugars.

"This recipe is from my 100-year-old mother-in-law, who, by the way, is the real chef of the family," Gwen notes. Gwen and Duane, her husband, have been sharing family recipes with guests for several years. They have four guestrooms in their 1965 home, which appeal to visitors to the nearby American Players Theater, Frank Lloyd Wright's Taliesin and the House on the Rock. Guests return to the Kraemer House because of the sun-dried sheets and other special touches.

Another Kraemer House recipe:
Orange Froth, page 27

Wine Slush

Ingredients:

1 12-ounce can frozen lemonade concentrate
1 12-ounce can frozen grape juice concentrate
2 quarts 7-Up or lemon-lime soda
2 quarts favorite red wine

- In a large container that can be covered and frozen, mix lemonade and grape juice concentrates, 1 quart of soda pop, and 2 quarts of the wine.
- Freeze mixture overnight or until almost solid.
- To serve, scoop mixture into a wine glass until it is half full. Fill remainder of the glass with soda pop from the remaining quart. Offer a demitasse spoon for stirring.

Makes about 40 servings

from **The Rectory B&B**
1575 Second Avenue
Cumberland, WI 54829
715-822-3151

"This Wine Slush is offered to guests in the parlor during the Christmas season, when they gather to enjoy the holiday decorations, music and crackling fire," said Innkeeper Ethel Anderson. The grape juice and red wine make it a pretty color. "The mixture keeps indefinitely in the freezer. This is also a refreshing summer drink, much like a wine cooler."

If having a little wine seems odd in a former rectory, think of it as historic hospitality. This brick-turreted home was built in 1905, the year Father Stephen Leinfelder came to serve St. Mary's Parish (the church is next door). Local lore says the good Father used his own funds to build the three-story house where he graciously welcomed traveling clergy and other friends.

The Rectory had been sold by the church in 1985, and Ethel and Jerry, her spouse, became the third owners in 1991. They had stayed in a guesthouse in Wyoming and loved the experience. "It was something I thought I'd enjoy doing if I had the right house," Ethel said. "The Rectory was for sale in my home town, so we came home" to Cumberland. "Jerry is humoring me but enjoying it just the same," she jokes about her innkeeping profession.

They found much work to be done before they could open their four guestrooms. "Structurally, the house was sound but it had been neglected for many years," Ethel said. They have rewired, refinished floors, added bathrooms and a deck and completed other projects. Guests can explore some of the 50 lakes within 10 miles of Cumberland, which is called "the Island City" and is, indeed, built on an island.

Years ago, when the first *Wake Up & Smell the Coffee* was published, only a few innkeepers actually served a dessert course. Boy, has that changed! Now this leisurely meal is capped off in many inns with a dessert. Dessert for Breakfast rarely means a banana split, but it might mean banana sorbet. Or it could be a rich coffeecake or cookies. Often it's a sweet fruit dish, like a cobbler, crunch or grunt. Sometimes it's a dessert that could be served after lunch or dinner, too, like carrot cake or a pie or pudding. Whatever, dessert for breakfast is a concept that's long overdue and heartily welcomed. Note that many of the fruit dishes or recipes in the Other Favorites chapter could be served for dessert, as well.

Dessert for Breakfast

Apple and Raisin Cobbler

Ingredients:

 1 cup raisins
 2 tablespoons orange-flavored liqueur, such as Grand Marnier, optional
 2 tablespoons blackberry brandy, optional
 12 cups peeled and sliced apples, such as Granny Smith
 1/2 cup brown sugar, packed
 1-1/4 cups flour
 1/2 cup sugar
 1 teaspoon baking powder
 1/2 teaspoon baking soda
 1 cup buttermilk

Also:

 Fresh mint
 Vanilla yogurt

☛ In a small microwavable bowl, combine raisins, liqueur and brandy (or water). Microwave on high for 1 to 2 minutes and let stand until plump.

☛ In a large bowl, mix raisins and liquid with apple slices. Stir in brown sugar. (Mixture can be covered and refrigerated overnight at this point.)

☛ In a medium-sized bowl, mix flour, sugar, baking powder, baking soda and buttermilk until smooth.

☛ Divide apple/raisin mixture into 8 to 10 one-cup ramekins. Spoon batter over fruit to cover.

☛ Bake ramekins in a preheated oven at 350 degrees for about 30 minutes, until top is brown and bubbly.

☛ Serve hot, garnished with mint. Pass the yogurt to spoon over cobbler.

Makes 8 to 10 servings

from **Evelo's Bed & Breakfast**
2301 Bryant Avenue South
Minneapolis, MN 55405
612-374-9656

"This recipe is great for all seasons," said Innkeeper Sheryl Evelo, and it works with any combination of seasonal fruits. "You can combine bananas with strawberries, sliced peaches with raspberries, blueberries and nectarines." Sheryl and her husband, David, might serve this dish with a basket of muffins, rolls and bagels.

The Evelos opened their 1897 Victorian home as a three-guestroom B&B in 1979. Both teachers, they wanted to offer European-style B&Bs to American travelers in their eight-bedroom South Minneapolis home. Their home is within walking distance of Uptown-area attractions.

Apple Crunch

Ingredients:

5 to 6 tart apples, peeled, cored and thinly sliced
2 tablespoons lemon juice
1 cup sugar
1 teaspoon cinnamon
1/2 teaspoon cloves
1/4 teaspoon nutmeg
2 teaspoons grated orange peel
2/3 cup honey oatmeal granola
2/3 cup oatmeal
2/3 cup flour
2/3 cup brown sugar, packed firmly
2/3 cup margarine, softened

Also:

Plain or vanilla yogurt or frozen yogurt

- In a large bowl, combine apples and lemon juice.
- Add sugar, cinnamon, cloves, nutmeg and orange peel. Mix well.
- In a separate bowl, mix granola, oatmeal, flour and sugar. Cut in margarine with a fork or a pastry cutter.
- Place apples into an 8 x 10-inch baking dish. Sprinkle top with granola mixture.
- Bake in a preheated oven at 350 degrees for 30 to 35 minutes, until top is golden brown.
- Scoop into individual serving dishes. Serve warm with yogurt or frozen yogurt.

Makes 8 servings

from **Candlewick Country Inn**
300 West Mill Street
Cannon Falls, MN 55009
507-263-0879

This is one of the heart-healthy recipes Dona Morgan serves at her B&B. She's enjoyed baking for years and the B&B allows her to bake all she wants.

Dona and her spouse, Tom, a former police officer, bought this 1880 Queen Anne Victorian home in 1992. They had plenty of long days before their two-guestroom B&B opened more than a year later. It had been turned into a triplex apartment and needed to be turned back into near-original condition.

Dona, a Sauk Centre native, and Tom had been living in the Twin Cities and looked forward to returning to small town life. They selected Cannon Falls because it offers visitors hiking, biking and skiing along the Cannon Valley Bike Trail, tubing or canoeing the Cannon River, an antique mall, shops and restaurants. It's also only about 40 minutes from the Twin Cities.

Apple Pecan Quick Cake

Ingredients:

2 eggs
1/2 teaspoon vanilla extract
1 cup sugar
1 cup flour
2 teaspoons baking powder
Dash of salt
2 cups baking apples, peeled and diced
1/2 cup raisins
1/4 cup chopped pecans

Also:

Whipped cream or topping
Pecan halves or apple slices

- In the bowl of an electric mixer, beat eggs and vanilla until frothy.

- Beat in sugar.

- Beat in flour, baking powder and salt.

- By hand, stir in apples, raisins and pecans.

- Spread batter in a 9-inch square pan that has been sprayed with non-stick cooking spray.

- Bake in a preheated oven at 325 degrees for about 50 minutes, or until a knife inserted in the middle comes out clean.

- Serve warm, cut in squares. Top with whipped cream or topping and a pecan half or apple slice.

Makes 6 to 9 servings

from **A Country Rose**
13452 90th Street South
Hastings, MN 55033
612-436-2237

Innkeeper Helen Schneider says this cake is a popular dessert for breakfast, which might be served outdoors in the gazebo, in the sun room or in the formal dining room. The recipe was handed down from her mother.

Helen, an interior designer, and her husband, Buster, who farms their 200 acres, opened their home as a two-guestroom homestay in 1992. They built and designed their home 28 years ago. It is located between Afton, a town on the St. Croix River, and Hastings, on the banks of the Mississippi.

The house is surrounded by a spacious lawn and rose, perennial and herb gardens. Helen enjoys gardening and has added several arbors and a fish pond to her gardens. Guests are welcome to explore the acreage, and they may see deer on the trails in the nearby woods.

Apple Walnut Torte

Ingredients:

1 egg
3/4 cup sugar
1/2 teaspoon vanilla extract
1/2 cup flour
1 teaspoon baking powder
Dash of salt
1 cup Granny Smith apples, peeled and chopped
1/2 cup walnuts

Also:

Whipped cream or ice cream
Fresh berries

- Beat together the egg, sugar and vanilla.
- In a separate bowl, mix flour, baking powder and salt. Then stir them into egg mixture.
- Stir in apples and walnuts.
- Spray a 9-inch pan or pie plate with non-stick cooking spray. Pour in batter.
- Bake in a preheated oven at 350 degrees for 30 minutes.
- Serve warm, cut into squares or wedges, topped with whipped or ice cream and fresh berries.

Tester's Comments: Yes, the recipe is correct without butter or oil; the cake is rather delicate but still holds together without it. It was great with pecans instead of walnuts, topped with a generous layer of whipped cream and fresh raspberries.

Makes 4 to 6 servings

from **The Pepin House**
120 South Prairie Street
Lake City, MN 55041
612-345-4454

"Jim's grandparents had an apple orchard and fruit farm in LaCrosse, Wisconsin," said Innkeeper Darlyne Lyons about her husband, Jim. So their family passed on many recipes featuring the fruits they grew. "This recipe was always a favorite. I always had the ingredients, and it's so simple but so good that everybody always wanted the recipe."

Darlyne had thought about opening a B&B for years, and she always enjoyed the Lake City area. After the children were gone, she and Jim found this restored 1905 home, built by a local brewer, John C. Schmidt. They literally were driving through town looking at homes when they turned down this street and saw the "for sale" sign. They have three guestrooms and are located four blocks from Lake Pepin on the Mississippi River and the marina.

Baked Bananas

Ingredients:

4 firm bananas
1/4 cup brown sugar, packed
1/2 cup orange juice ("Freshly-squeezed works best")
1/4 teaspoon cinnamon
1/2 cup rum
1 tablespoon butter, melted

Also:

Vanilla ice cream

☛ Peel bananas and cut in half lengthwise. Place in a glass baking dish.

☛ In a saucepan, mix brown sugar, orange juice, cinnamon, rum and butter. Stir and bring to a boil, then simmer for a minute on low heat.

☛ Pour some of the sauce over bananas, turning gently to coat both sides.

☛ Bake in a preheated oven at 400 degrees for 3 to 5 minutes, until tender (or microwave for 90 seconds on high, checking to see when bananas are tender).

☛ Remove from oven and place on serving plates. Dollop with vanilla ice cream and spoon more rum sauce on top. Serve immediately.

Tester's Comments: For non-alcoholic version, I used heavy cream instead of rum. Either way was delicious, even more so with a few chocolate chips sprinkled on top during the last couple of minutes of baking.

Makes 4 servings

from **The Scofield House B&B**
908 Michigan Street
Sturgeon Bay, WI 54235
414-743-7727

Innkeeper/Head Chef Bill Cecil triples this recipe to serve a full house of 12 guests. Guests say this recipe is the best way they know to get their potassium, he said, and Bill believes "it's fun to have dessert with breakfast." Guests in the six guestrooms gather in the dining room of this 1902 home, built by Herbert Scofield, the owner of Wisconsin's largest hardware store. His building materials and woodwork were, understandably, top notch.

Bill and spouse Fran worked around the clock in 1987 to restore the Queen Anne Victorian home. They were on their way to Boston to pursue new jobs when friends at an Ellison Bay inn persuaded them to look at properties for a B&B. They took a wrong turn on their way to lunch and saw a "for sale" sign on this house. The rest is history, and a lot of work.

🏠*Other Scofield House recipes:*
Apple Cinnamon French Toast, page 153
Butter Pecan Turtle Cookies, page 225

Banana Oat Breakfast Cookies

Ingredients:

- 1-1/2 cups flour
- 1/2 teaspoon baking soda
- 3/4 teaspoon cinnamon
- 1/2 teaspoon salt
- 3/4 cup butter or margarine
- 1 cup sugar
- 1 egg
- 1-3/4 cups old-fashioned oatmeal
- 1 cup mashed banana (2 to 3 bananas)
- 1/2 cup chopped nuts

- Sift the flour, baking soda, cinnamon and salt together into a large bowl. Set aside.
- In a large bowl of an electric mixer, cream butter and sugar. Beat in the egg and mix thoroughly.
- Stir in oats, bananas and nuts.
- Add the flour mixture and stir.
- Drop dough by the spoonful onto an ungreased cookie sheet, about 1-1/2 inches apart.
- Bake in a preheated oven at 400 degrees for 15 minutes.

Tester's Comments: Just great for folks on the run. If you have leftover mini-chocolate chips from Bonnie's Chocolate Zucchini Muffins, page 55, consider adding them or substituting them for the nuts - yum!

Makes 24 to 32 cookies

from **The Inn**
104 Wisconsin Avenue
Montreal, WI 54550
715-561-5180 phone or FAX

"This is a hearty, moist, tasty cookie -- and they keep very well," said Innkeeper Doree Schumacher. She serves them as a change from muffins. Her guests often are looking for a breakfast that will stick with them. In the winter, skiers are heading from her Inn to the Big Snow Country ski areas or cross-country ski trails near the Porcupine Mountains. In spring, summer or fall, they might be mountain biking, hiking, canoeing or fishing in the area.

Doree and Dick, formerly teachers in Oshkosh, converted this 1913 building to an inn in 1982. They'd first bought the former iron mining company's office building as a private ski school. It had housed the Oglebay-Norton headquarters until the rich mine shut down in 1962. The former company town, which employed 700, is now on the National Register of Historic Places.

Another Inn recipe:
Quick Fruit Syrup, page 114

Banana Sorbet with Kiwi Sauce

Ingredients:

2/3 cup sugar
2/3 cup water
2 large, ripe bananas
1 cup orange juice
1 tablespoon lemon juice

Kiwi Sauce:
2 kiwi fruit
2 teaspoons sugar

🦂 In a small saucepan, mix sugar and water. Bring mixture to a boil, stirring until sugar is dissolved. Cool, then refrigerate until thoroughly chilled.

🦂 In the blender, purée bananas.

🦂 Add orange juice, lemon juice and sugar-water mixture. Blend until smooth.

🦂 Pour mixture into a 9-inch square pan. Cover. Freeze until firm, about 4 to 6 hours, or overnight, stirring several times during the process.

🦂 For Kiwi Sauce: Peel kiwis. In the blender, purée 1 kiwi and the sugar. Slice other kiwi, set aside.

🦂 Scoop sorbet into 6 dessert bowls. Top with Kiwi Sauce. Garnish with a slice of the remaining kiwi.

Tester's Comments: Move over Ben & Jerry, here come Cyndi & John. I only remembered to stir once, and it worked just fine.

Makes 6 1-/2 cup servings

from **Phipps Inn**
1005 Third Street
Hudson, WI 54016
715-386-0800 phone or FAX

Innkeeper Cyndi Berglund created this dish to end a four-course breakfast at her inn. The half-cup serving sizes are more than sufficient for guests who have dined on homemade pastries, fruit and, perhaps, a quiche.

Cyndi, a former high school teacher and coach, and John, a Minneapolis attorney and lobbyist, opened the "grand dame" of Hudson homes as a B&B in 1990. Impressive from the outside, the three-story mansion is no less so inside. One example: the parquet floors' geometric designs make use of five types of wood. Six upstairs guestrooms are available, some with views of the St. Croix River, all with special amenities.

Over the years, the home had been used as a nursing home and rooming house, and restoration efforts outlasted three owners before the Berglunds. Today, Frances and Williams Phipps would be pleased by the condition of their home, built in 1884 and listed on the National Register of Historic Places.

🏠*Another Phipps Inn recipe:*
Wild Berry Delight, page 134

Bananas Royale

Ingredients:

6 ounces flaked coconut
1/2 cup nuts, ground
1/4 cup sour cream
1/2 cup mayonnaise
2 tablespoons brown sugar
4 ripe but firm bananas

Also:

Fresh cherries or strawberries and kiwi slices

- On a jelly roll pan, spread coconut and nuts. Toast in a preheated oven at about 300 degrees, watching carefully, until coconut is a light golden brown and nuts turn a darker golden. Stir as needed while toasting.
- In a small bowl, blend sour cream and mayonnaise. Stir in brown sugar.
- Slice bananas in half lengthwise, or slice in chunks about 1/2-inch wide. Dip in the mayonnaise mix, then roll them in the coconut/nut mix.
- Place bananas on waxed paper and chill until serving. Serve with other fruits for color.

Tester's Comments: Almonds or macadamia nuts are both good bets in this recipe.

Makes 4 servings

from **Summit Place B&B**
1682 West Kimmel Road
Jackson, MI 49201
517-787-0468

Innkeeper Marlene Laing serves this dessert for a tropical feel in the dead of winter or any other time for a change of pace. Breakfast at the B&B she and husband Douglas operate is on heirloom china, served in the formal dining room or, on summer mornings, outside on the deck overlooking the garden.

Located 10 minutes from downtown Jackson, the Laings' home is in the countryside, surrounded by trees and gardens. Their tri-level contemporary home is decorated in Victorian wallpapers and with fine art, antiques and reproductions and designer linens.

"We have stayed at inns in Europe and in our country and it is something I have wanted to do for a long time," said Marlene about opening her home as a B&B. They opened two guestrooms in 1992. "I do everything I can for our guests to feel comfortable and at home." That once included providing a tuxedo shirt for a soloist who forgot his shirt for a symphony program. The B&B is located a half-mile from the Dahlem Environmental Center. The Jackson area offers exceptionally good antiquing and dining.

Blueberry Grunt

Ingredients:

7-1/2 cups fresh or frozen "dry pack" blueberries
1 tablespoon lemon juice
3/4 cup sugar
1 tablespoon cornstarch
1 teaspoon cinnamon
1 cup water

Also:

Heavy cream or ice cream

Dumplings:
1 cup flour
2 tablespoons sugar
1 teaspoon baking powder
1/2 teaspoon baking soda
A pinch of salt
2 tablespoons butter, melted
1/2 cup buttermilk

- In a large bowl, toss blueberries with lemon juice. Stir in sugar, cornstarch, cinnamon and water.
- Put berries into a deep frying pan or kettle with a cover. Bring to a gentle boil.
- For Dumplings: In a large bowl, combine flour, sugar, baking powder, baking soda and salt.
- Stir in the butter, then buttermilk (use a little more if needed to make a soft dough).
- Drop spoonfuls of dough onto the blueberries. Cover pan tightly.
- Simmer for 15 minutes — do not lift the lid or dumplings won't rise.
- Serve hot in individual serving dishes, topped with heavy cream or ice cream.

Makes 8 servings

from **Asa Parker House B&B**
17500 St. Croix Trail North
Marine on St. Croix, MN 54047
612-433-5248

"Even if you lift the lid and the dumplings don't rise, they are still wonderful," said Innkeeper Marjorie Bush. She's been serving this recipe as a dessert since her second B&B, where she made "dessert for breakfast" a staple on the menu. She's now at her fourth (and last) B&B, and many of her guests choose her place repeatedly because of the reputation of her breakfasts.

Marge bought this huge home in 1989, adding an extra guestroom and all private baths to make four guestrooms. The home was built in 1856 by Asa Parker, a Vermont lumberman working along the St. Croix River, who modeled this home after one in his home state.

The house is one of the most grand in the village of Marine, nearly all of which is an historic district and is perfect for strolling and exploring. Guests enjoy cross-country skiing in winter, or biking, canoeing, hiking and picnicking in other seasons.

🏠*Other Asa Parker House recipes:*
Marjorie's English Country Scones, page 62
Poached Apples in Vanilla Creme Sauce, page 129
Cheese Lace Crackers, page 227

French Doughnuts

Ingredients:

3 cups flour
1 packet active dry yeast
1/2 teaspoon nutmeg
1 cup milk
1/4 cup sugar
1/4 cup vegetable oil
3/4 teaspoon salt
1 egg

Also:

3/4 to 1 cup powdered sugar
Vegetable oil for frying

- In a large bowl, combine 1-3/4 cups flour, yeast and nutmeg.
- In a saucepan, heat milk, sugar, vegetable oil and salt just until warm, stirring occasionally.
- Pour milk mixture over the flour mixture and stir.
- Add egg. Beat with an electric mixer or wooden spoon for 3 to 4 minutes.
- Stir in enough flour (the other 1-1/4 cups) to make a soft dough. Turn into a greased bowl. Cover with a lid or plastic wrap and chill (can refrigerate overnight).
- When dough is well-chilled, turn out onto a well-floured surface. Cover and let rest 10 minutes.
- Roll into an 12 x 18-inch rectangle. Cut into pieces that are 2 x 3 inches. Cover and let dough rest 30 minutes (the dough will *not* double).
- Fry the rectangles in oil that is preheated to 375 degrees. When they are golden brown, turn and fry on the other side. Remove from oil, drain on paper towels and roll in powdered sugar.

Makes about 36 doughnuts

from **Ty-Bach**
3104 Simpson Lane
Lac du Flambeau, WI 54538
715-588-7851

These homemade doughnuts resemble those Janet and Kermit Bekkum enjoyed in the French Quarter in New Orleans. They finish off a full country breakfast at the Bekkum's lakeside B&B.

The Bekkums opened their contemporary lake home in 1987 with two guestrooms. "We enjoyed staying in B&Bs," said Janet. "Kermit was able to retire after working 30 years at General Motors and we moved to the northwoods." Guests may swim or use the bikes, canoe or paddleboat. They can hike or ski on the cleared logging roads through Bekkums' 80 acres. Some simply come to listen for the call of the loons. The Native American Cultural Center and a casino are nearby.

Mama Esther's Baked Custard

Ingredients:

3 eggs ("Egg substitute may be used.")
1/2 cup sugar
3 cups milk

Also:

Nutmeg or fresh, sliced strawberries

- With an electric mixer, beat eggs and sugar.

- Beat in milk, thoroughly combining all ingredients.

- Pour mixture into 6 individual ramekins. Sprinkle with nutmeg. Set ramekins into a 9 x 13-inch baking pan filled with water that comes 1/2-inch up on the sides of the ramekins.

- Bake in a preheated oven at 300 degrees for 75 minutes or until a sharp knife inserted in the middle comes out clean. "Do not overbake or the custard will curdle."

- Remove the ramekins from the pan of water and cool. Then refrigerate, covered with plastic wrap.

- To serve, top with fresh sliced strawberries.

Makes 6 servings

from **The Parsonage 1908**
6 East 24th Street
Holland, MI 49423
616-396-1316

"This recipe is from my Swedish grandmother, who was an excellent cook," said Innkeeper Bonnie McVoy-Verwys, who credits her cooking skills to "Mama Esther." "I didn't realize how many things I 'borrowed' or 'inherited' from her when I was growing up."

From 1908 until the early 1970s, this American Four Square house was home to seven ministers and their families who served one of Holland's early Dutch churches. "The church took excellent care of the Parsonage over the years," said Bonnie, and the oak woodwork, pocket doors and stairway are still in their original condition. Bonnie has decorated all of it -- including the closets.

"When I bought this house in 1974, I worked as a supervisor in a sheltered workshop with the adult handicapped, and I had no idea that I would open Holland's first B&B in 1984," she said. She was raising three children alone, and then lost her job. She wanted to work for herself, so she started the B&B. Since then she's also modeled for local companies, designed B&B flags and won a bronze medal in the Michigan Senior Olympics in tennis doubles.

The Parsonage 1908 is located three minutes away from Hope College. Holland also has Tulip Time in May, Lake Michigan beaches, swimming, golf, antiquing, summer theater, fall colors, cross-country skiing and fine dining.

Mom's Carrot Cake

Ingredients:

3 cups flour
2 cups sugar
2 teaspoons cinnamon
2 teaspoons baking soda
2 teaspoons baking powder
1 teaspoon salt
2 cups grated carrots
1-1/2 cups corn or canola oil
1/2 cup chopped nuts
4 eggs, beaten

- In a large bowl, sift twice flour, sugar, cinnamon, baking soda, baking powder and salt.
- Mix in carrots, oil, nuts and beaten eggs.
- Pour batter into a greased 9 x 13-inch pan.
- Bake in a preheated oven at 350 degrees for 1 hour or until a knife inserted in the center comes out clean.

Tester's Comments: For a traditional cream cheese frosting, beat 1/2 cup margarine, 1 8-ounce package cream cheese, 1 teaspoon vanilla extract and 2 cups powdered sugar until light and fluffy. Refrigerate leftover cake.

Makes 18 large servings

from **Dreams of Yesteryear**
1100 Brawley Street
Stevens Point, WI 54481
715-341-4525 or FAX 715-344-3047

"I knew whenever mom made this cake, company was coming," said Innkeeper Bonnie Maher. "She would serve it as a midnight snack to card-playing guests. This has always been my favorite cake." Bonnie serves slices of it as a dessert for breakfast, served in the formal dining room. After the meal, guests might wander off to the gardens, porches or the parlors.

There are plenty of rooms to explore in this 1901 Queen Anne Victorian, designed by J.H. Jeffers, who designed the Wisconsin Exhibition Building at the 1904 St. Louis World's Fair. Three generations of the Jensen family owned it until 1987, when the Mahers bought it. Bonnie, Bill and their daughters turned the home into a four-guestroom B&B in 1990. Another local innkeeper, Joan Ouellette at the Victorian Swan on Water, suggested a B&B, and the Mahers love it. The home is on the National Register of Historic Places.

Other Dreams of Yesteryear recipes:
Gramma's Beer Bread, page 86
Rhubarb Cobbler, page 216

Mom's Molasses Cookies

Ingredients:

3/4 cup shortening or margarine
1 egg
1/4 cup molasses
1 cup sugar plus 1/4 cup
2 cups flour
2 teaspoons baking soda
1 teaspoon salt
1 teaspoon cinnamon
1 teaspoon cloves
1 teaspoon ginger

- With an electric mixer, cream shortening, egg and molasses. Beat in 1 cup sugar.

- In a separate bowl, mix flour, soda, salt, cinnamon, cloves and ginger.

- Beat flour mixture into molasses mixture. Dough will be stiff.

- Roll dough into 1-inch balls. Place on a lightly-greased cookie sheet. Flatten by pressing lightly with a glass dipped in 1/4 cup sugar.

- Bake in a preheated oven at 350 degrees for 8 to 10 minutes.

Tester's Comments: My mom had this recipe for gingersnaps. We rolled the balls in sugar and didn't bother to press them with a glass. Use shortening for chewy cookies and double the batch! They freeze well.

Makes 2 to 3 dozen

from **The Nash House B&B**
1020 Oak Street
Wisconsin Rapids, WI 54494
715-424-2001 phone or FAX

"There were always cookies in our cookie jar when I was growing up and it is something that I have continued with my own family," said Innkeeper Phyllis Custer. She puts a pretty plate of these on the breakfast table.

Breakfast is served in the dining room or on the screened porch, which gets a lot of guest use in the summer. So does the front porch with its porch swing.
Phyllis and Jim bought this Victorian home in 1988 to open a B&B. They opened two months later and have three guestrooms. Most of the restoration necessary has been cosmetic, with one bedroom converted to two baths. The B&B is named for the remarkable family who owned a local cranberry marsh. Two Nash kids grew up here. Jean was one of the first women to manage a marsh, and the office was in this home. Philleo was an anthropologist and lieutenant governor. His widow, Edith, sold the home to the Custers.

Another Nash House recipe:
Egg and Bacon Casserole, page 141

Peach-Berry Cobbler

Ingredients:

1/4 cup sugar
1/4 cup brown sugar, packed
1 tablespoon cornstarch
1 cup water
1 tablespoon lemon juice
3 cups peeled and sliced fresh peaches
1 cup fresh blueberries

Also:

Heavy cream

Topping:
1/2 cup sugar
1 cup flour
1-1/2 teaspoons baking powder
1/4 teaspoon salt
1/2 cup milk
1/4 cup butter, melted
2 tablespoons sugar
1/4 teaspoon nutmeg

🍃 In a saucepan, combine sugar, brown sugar, cornstarch and water. Cook over medium heat, stirring constantly until thick.

🍃 Remove from heat and add the lemon juice, peach slices and blueberries.

🍃 Turn the peach mixture into a greased two-quart glass baking or casserole dish.

🍃 In a separate bowl, make the Topping: Mix sugar, flour, baking powder and salt. Beat in milk and butter until smooth. Spoon the topping batter over the fruit (it rises and spreads as it bakes). Mix sugar and nutmeg and sprinkle over the batter.

🍃 Bake in a preheated oven at 375 degrees for 40 to 45 minutes. Remove from oven and serve in small dishes. Pass a pitcher of cream or dollop on whipped cream.

Tester's Comments: Everyone had seconds. I used frozen fruit and suggest increasing peaches to 4 cups.

Makes 7 to 8 servings

from **South Cliff Inn B&B**
1900 Lakeshore Drive
St. Joseph, MI 49085
616-983-4881 or FAX 616-983-7391

Innkeeper Bill Swisher always tries to use fruit grown locally, and this cobbler takes advantage of southwestern Michigan's peaches and blueberries. Guests might enjoy it in the sunroom overlooking Lake Michigan.

Bill, a former court administrator and chef, bought this large brick home a short walk from downtown St. Joseph in 1986. "The home had not been lived in for four years," he said, meaning "everything had to be restored or redone. It had 1-1/2 bathrooms and now has seven," for example. His goal was to give the inn "a very luxurious as well as inviting feeling." Furniture is either antique or custom made with imported fabrics, and each of the seven guestrooms is different. He was able to open the inn a year later. Many guests enjoy the sandy beach in front of the inn or other beaches, including nearby Warren Dunes State Park. The St. Joseph area also offers sailing, antiquing, theater, fine dining, historic sites, wineries and unique shopping.

Puff Danish

Ingredients:

Crust:

>1 cup flour
>1/2 cup butter, softened
>1 tablespoon water

Puff:

>1 cup water
>1/2 cup butter
>3 eggs
>1 teaspoon vanilla extract

Also:

>Buttercream frosting, optional

🡒 For Crust: In a small bowl, mix flour, butter and water until the mixture holds together and forms a ball.

🡒 With your fingers, press dough onto a cookie sheet into the shape of a large "S." Keep dough about 1/2-inch thick in all places.

🡒 For Puff: In a medium saucepan, bring water to a boil. Carefully drop in butter.

🡒 When butter is completely melted, remove pan from heat. Quickly add eggs, one at a time, mixing after each addition until blended. Stir in vanilla.

🡒 Spread egg mixture on top of the crust.

🡒 Bake in a preheated oven at 425 degrees for 30 minutes. Then turn the oven off and leave puff in a closed oven for 10 minutes.

🡒 Remove from oven. Frost with buttercream frosting, if desired.

Makes 18 large slices

from **The Stagecoach Inn B&B**
W61 N520 Washington Avenue
Cedarburg, WI 53012
414-375-0208

"This recipe originated with my great aunt," said Innkeeper Marge Jorgensen, who serves this treat to guests on an antique platter. It's rich enough so that it often follows cereal and muffins as dessert for breakfast, she said.

Today, guests can sleep in this 1850s inn much more comfortably than the original stagecoach passengers did. Owners Liz and Brook Brown have insisted on historically-accurate renovation, but added modern comforts like central air, private baths and, in some suites, whirlpool tubs.

🏠*Another Stagecoach Inn recipe:*
Sour Cream Coffeecake, page 44

Raspberry Meringue Pie

Ingredients:

Crust:
- 5 egg whites
- 1/2 tablespoon baking powder
- 1/2 teaspoon salt
- 1-1/2 cups sugar
- 1 cup instant oatmeal
- 3/4 cup nuts, coarsely chopped
- 1 teaspoon vanilla extract

Also:
Whipped cream

Filling:
- 10 ounces frozen raspberries
- 1 tablespoon cornstarch
- 1 tablespoon sugar

- Whip egg whites, baking powder and salt, adding sugar gradually, until stiff peaks form.
- Fold in oatmeal, nuts and vanilla.
- Press crust into a 9-inch pie pan that has been sprayed with non-stick cooking spray.
- Bake crust in a preheated oven at 350 degrees for about 35 minutes. Then remove and let cool (the center will fall).
- Meanwhile, thaw raspberries and save juice. Add juice to cornstarch and sugar.
- In a saucepan or in the microwave, cook juice mixture, stirring often until thick.
- Fold in berries. Pour into cooled crust. Refrigerate until serving. Garnish with whipped cream.

Makes 6 to 8 slices

from **Rum River Country B&B**
5002 85th Avenue
Princeton, MN 55371
612-389-2679

Raspberry recipes are collected by Innkeeper Millie Schimming. She and Wally, her husband, grow two acres of raspberries on their farm, enough so that July is busy with a pick-your-own or ready-picked business. The freezer is full and guests are promised raspberries in some form any time of year.

The Schimmings opened their B&B in 1987 on the 320-acre farm. "We believe the farm is a necessary place for 'city people' to visit," Millie said. Their contemporary home has four guestrooms, plus two in the original farmhouse located adjacent to the main B&B.

Decor is an unusual mix of collectibles, crafts, family pieces and handmade beds and lamps the Schimmings construct in their ironworks shop; one room, "The Birds Room," includes bird wallpaper and a stuffed flamingo. Guests are welcome to explore the farm fields, woods and river. Princeton is a one-hour drive from the Twin Cities.

Rhubarb Cobbler

Ingredients:

Dough:
- 1/2 cup butter
- 1 cup sugar
- 1 egg
- 1/2 cup milk
- 1 cup flour
- 1 teaspoon baking powder

Filling:
- 3 cups fresh or frozen "dry pack" rhubarb
- 1 cup sugar
- 1 tablespoon butter, melted

Also:

Vanilla, plain or strawberry yogurt or whipped cream

- For Filling: In a large bowl, mix rhubarb and sugar. Place in a 9 x 9-inch pan or 1-1/2 quart casserole dish. Drizzle melted butter over rhubarb.
- For Dough: Cream butter and sugar. Beat in egg. Slowly add milk. Beat in flour and baking powder.
- Spread the dough over the rhubarb.
- Bake in a preheated oven at 350 degrees for 40 to 50 minutes until rhubarb is bubbly and dough is golden brown. Serve warm with yogurt or whipped cream.

Tester's Comments: A very good basic cobbler that could be used with other fresh fruit. Seems like dough is a little thick and I could have done without about a third of it -- or another cup or two of fruit could've been used.

Makes 7 to 9 servings

from **Dreams of Yesteryear**
1100 Brawley Street
Stevens Point, WI 54481
715-341-4525 or FAX 715-344-3047

"This dessert is hard to cut into squares because of its soft consistency. However, it looks great in a saucedish with yogurt spooned over the top," said Innkeeper Bonnie Maher. "Even guests who claimed not to like rhubarb like this dessert and even ask for seconds -- and thirds!"

Bonnie is a firm believer in a hearty breakfast, topped off with dessert, served in the formal dining room. She describes her breakfasts as "something special that you wouldn't make for yourself." Most guests wouldn't undertake the restoration of this 1901 Queen Anne Victorian home themselves, but they now enjoy Bonnie and Bill's work. The National Register of Historic Place's home features oak woodwork, hardwood floors, leaded glass windows, clawfoot bathtubs and antique furnishings. The Mahers opened it as a B&B in 1990.

Other Dreams of Yesteryear recipes:
Gramma's Beer Bread, page 86
Mom's Carrot Cake, page 211

Sour Cream Ripple Coffee Cake

Ingredients:

1 cup margarine
2 cups sugar
2 eggs
1 cup sour cream
1/2 teaspoon vanilla extract
2 cups flour, preferably cake flour
1 teaspoon baking powder
1/4 teaspoon salt

Topping:
1/2 cup chopped pecans
1/4 brown sugar, packed
2 teaspoons cinnamon

- With an electric mixer, cream margarine and sugar. Beat in eggs.

- At low speed, add sour cream, vanilla, flour, baking powder and salt.

- Grease and flour a a 10-inch Bundt tube pan. Spoon in half of the batter.

- For Topping: Mix pecans, sugar and cinnamon. Sprinkle half the topping over the batter in the pan.

- Spoon remaining batter into the pan, covering the topping layer. Then sprinkle the remaining topping over all.

- Bake in a preheated oven at 350 degrees for 1 hour. Invert while still slightly warm.

Tester's Comments: This got rave reviews. It's also delicious made with poppyseeds stirred into the batter and the pecans deleted. Sprinkling powdered sugar on top is all that's necessary for a pretty, rich dessert.

Makes 12 to 14 servings

from **Chicago Street Inn**
219 Chicago Street
Brooklyn, MI 49230
517-592-3888 or FAX 517-592-9025

"This recipe was shared with us by a fellow innkeeper and very dear friend who has since sold her inn," said Karen Kerr. She and spouse Bill serve it from a silver tray as a dessert to a hearty breakfast, along with lots of hot coffee. Guests at this inn usually have two options for breakfast -- a light one of fruit and cereal at 8 a.m., or a full breakfast at 9. Breakfast is served in the formal dining room, under an ornate, wood-beamed ceiling.

Karen and Bill hadn't intended to become innkeepers when they stayed at their first B&B. They ended up there because all other lodgings in the area were booked. But they returned to Brooklyn, bought this 1886 Queen Anne Victorian, and opened four months later. Their B&B has seven guestrooms.

Other Chicago Street Inn recipes:
Strawberry Rhubarb Muffins, page 71
Potato Hot Dish, page 180

Strawberry Shortcake Muffins

Ingredients:

2 cups flour
2 teaspoons baking powder
3/4 cup sugar
1/2 cup butter or margarine
1 egg
1 cup heavy (whipping) cream
1 teaspoon vanilla extract
1 cup diced fresh strawberries, well drained

Strawberry Butter:
4 tablespoons butter, softened
2 tablespoons diced, ripe strawberries

Also:

Powdered sugar

- In a medium bowl, mix flour, baking powder and sugar. Cut in butter with a pastry cutter or fork.
- In a separate bowl, mix egg, cream and vanilla.
- Add egg mixture all at once to flour mixture and mix well with a wooden spoon.
- Gently fold in strawberries.
- Spoon batter into 12 greased muffin tins.
- Bake in a preheated oven at 350 degrees for 25 minutes. Remove and cool ("muffins are very rich and warm muffins may fall apart"). Dust with powdered sugar and serve with Strawberry Butter, or split muffins and top with sliced, sugared strawberries and whipped cream.
- For Strawberry Butter: Beat butter and strawberries. Serve in a pretty bowl.

Tester's Comments: I made these without the strawberries, then served them split with sliced strawberries and whipped cream. No reason to ever make "regular" shortcake again!

Makes 12 to 15 muffins

from **The Inn at Ludington**
701 East Ludington Avenue
Ludington, MI 49431
616-845-7055

These rich muffins make a good strawberry shortcake at Innkeeper Diane Shields' place. Strawberries are just one of the fresh fruits that the Ludington area produces, and Diane tries to make good use of them all. She tries to use as many "Made in Michigan" products as she can, down to locally made maple syrup and butter. And she makes her own preserves.

Diane's inn is an 1889 Queen Anne Victorian that was turned into a B&B in 1986. She has six guestrooms open for travelers taking the Lake Michigan car ferry or just exploring the area beaches, golf courses and other attractions.

Another Inn at Ludington recipe:
Whole Wheat Oatmeal Bread, page 99

Warm Apple Pudding

Ingredients:

6 cups peeled, sliced apples ("Harolsons are great")
1 egg
1/4 cup butter, softened
1/4 cup milk
1/2 cup sugar
1 teaspoon baking powder
3/4 cup flour

Topping:
1/2 cup sugar
1 cup water
1 tablespoon cornstarch
1 tablespoon butter
1 teaspoon vanilla extract

🐂 Place the apple slices in a 9 x 9-inch baking pan.

🐂 In the bowl of an electric mixer, beat egg, butter, milk, sugar, baking powder and flour for 2 minutes on low speed, then 1 minute at high speed.

🐂 Pour batter over apples.

🐂 Bake in a preheated oven at 325 degrees for 1 hour.

🐂 For Topping: In a saucepan, mix the sugar, water and cornstarch. Cook, stirring often, over medium heat until thick and bubbly. Remove from heat and add butter and vanilla.

🐂 Serve the apple pudding in bowls with the warm topping ladled over the pudding.

Makes 6 large servings

from **Evergreen Knoll Acres**
Box 145, RR 1
Lake City, MN 55041
612-345-2257

"This is a family recipe -- my mother made it for as long as I can remember," said Innkeeper Bev Meyer. Bev serves it on cold fall and winter mornings as part of her large country breakfast.

Families often head for Evergreen Knoll Acres, a working dairy farm B&B just outside of town. Guests can watch mechanized milking, try their hand at milking the old-fashioned way, and get a tour through the area where calves are born year 'round. "Our farm is a family farm -- the house, barn and another small building were built by Paul's parents in 1919 when they were married," said Bev. "Paul and I have lived here since 1956." Paul and Bev have raised four children on their farm. Now they have at least 65 Holsteins on this 240-acre farm.

Bev and Paul have three guestrooms upstairs in their farmhouse, or a family can rent a restored four-bedroom cottage nearby. Either way, the Meyers like to "acquaint city people with the rural life on a farm and give their children some idea where milk comes from." Kids like the barn cats and farm dog, too.

Wisconsin Cranberry Pudding Cake

Ingredients:

2 cups flour
1 cup sugar
1 tablespoon baking powder
1/4 teaspoon salt
1 cup milk
3 tablespoons butter, melted
Grated peel of 1 lemon, optional
2 cups whole cranberries, fresh or frozen (or blueberries)

Sauce:

2 cups sugar
1 cup butter
1-1/2 cups half-and-half

- In a large bowl, mix the flour, sugar, baking powder, salt, milk, butter and optional lemon peel with a wooden spoon.
- Fold in the cranberries. Pour the mixture into a buttered 9 x 13-inch pan.
- Bake in a preheated oven at 350 degrees for 25 to 30 minutes or until cake is golden brown.
- For Sauce: In a large saucepan, mix sugar, butter and half-and-half. Heat over medium heat, stirring often, until butter is melted and mixture is hot, but do not boil.
- Pour the warm sauce over individual servings of the cake.

Tester's Comments: I made one 8-inch cake with blueberries, one with cranberries. Both were good, but the tart cranberries seemed best with the sweet sauce.

Makes 12 servings

from **The Inn at Wildcat Mountain**
Highway 33
P.O. Box 112
Ontario, WI 54651
608-337-4352

"This recipe is so simple, but so good," said Innkeeper Patricia Barnes. She garnishes the servings with cranberries that have been dipped in egg white and rolled in sugar, then dried. "The recipe came from an acquaintance whose family owns the cranberry bog where we purchase 50 to 100 pounds of fresh cranberries each fall. I freeze them for use during the year."

Her breakfasts always include dessert and are served in the dining room of this 1910 mansion, built by Charles Lord. Lord, an early ginseng grower, built it as a hotel on the rumor the railroad was coming through. It never did, but he worked as a photographer and kept the house in the family until the '40s.

Patricia and her husband, Wendell, bought the B&B in 1987. They uncovered wood floors, stripped woodwork, raised ceilings, re-roofed and replicated the 165-spindle rail that edges the roof. They offer four guestrooms next to the Kickapoo River, where canoeing is popular. They're also close to Wildcat Mountain State Park, the Elroy-Sparta Bike Trail and Amish shops.

Homemade cookies in a bottomless cookie jar. A piece of pie after returning from dinner. Appetizers in the parlor with other guests, sharing conversation before dinner. A wonderful side-dish that rounds out a meal. All are symbols of hospitality, and savvy innkeepers know that food can help a guest feel at home. So something wonderful to eat isn't limited to breakfast. The following recipes are innkeepers' favorites, but either weren't served for breakfast or didn't fit well into another category. Innkeepers find themselves making these recipes over and over again, often by request of repeat visitors. Perhaps they will make your list of frequent favorite recipes, as well!

Other Favorites

Apple Bars

Ingredients:

1-3/4 cups quick-cooking oatmeal
3/4 cup margarine, softened
1 cup brown sugar, packed
1-1/3 cups flour
1/4 teaspoon baking soda

Filling:
2-1/2 cups apples, peeled and sliced
1/2 cup sugar
3/4 teaspoon cinnamon
2 tablespoons margarine, melted

- In a large bowl, mix oatmeal, margarine, brown sugar, flour and baking soda.
- Spread half of the mixture into the bottom of a greased 9 x 13-inch pan.
- For Filling: Mix apple slices with sugar and cinnamon, tossing gently.
- Arrange apple slices over the crust. Then drizzle margarine over apples.
- Pat remaining oat mixture over filling.
- Bake in a preheated oven at 350 degrees for 30 minutes or until golden brown.

Tester's Comments: These are buttery and wonderful and would be good with other fillings, like date.

Makes 24 bars

from **The Kingsley House**
626 West Main Street
Fennville, MI 49408
616-561-6425

Innkeeper Shirley Witt might have a batch of these sitting on the buffet for guests after check-in. They might enjoy them on the porch with a glass of lemonade or in front of the fireplace with hot apple cider from area orchards.

Apples are important here. Harvey Kingsley, for whom the home was built, introduced apple trees to the area. The eight guestrooms are named after Michigan apples -- including Duchess, Granny Smith, Golden Delicious, McIntosh, Jonathan, Cortland and Northern Spy.

Shirley and Dave Witt are former teachers (this recipe came from the mother of one of Shirley's students 30-some years ago). Their first B&B was in nearby Holland, but they wanted an historic inn. This home, designed by a New York architect, needed major work, which Dave undertook. Eight bathrooms, 150 porch spindles and miles of wallpaper were among the additions. They opened in 1989. One guestroom's tub is in the turret.

Fennville is within minutes of Saugatuck and Holland. Guests can use the inn's bicycles to explore Fennville, and there is fishing and x-c skiing nearby.

Another Kingsley House recipe:
Chopped Apple Bread, page 80

Artichoke Toasts

Ingredients:

1 14-ounce can artichoke hearts, drained and chopped
6 green onions, finely chopped
3/4 cup grated Parmesan cheese
1/2 cup mayonnaise (not "lite")
1 loaf sliced cocktail rye bread

- In a large bowl, mix artichoke hearts, onions, Parmesan and mayonnaise. Cover and refrigerate at least 1 hour to blend flavors.
- Spread about 1 tablespoon of the mixture on each rye bread slice.
- Place slices on a cookie sheet. Broil until the artichoke spread bubbles and browns.
- Serve warm with hearty wine or cider.

Makes about 30 servings

from **Red Gables Inn**
403 North High Street
Lake City, MN 55041
612-345-2605

Innkeepers Mary and Doug DeRoos serve hors d'oeuvres in the parlor with Victorian settees and lace-covered tables, or perhaps on the screened porch.

This eye-catching Victorian B&B -- painted a deep red with black trim -- has five guestrooms. Mary and Doug bought this operating B&B in 1990. "After 22 years traveling and living around the U.S. and Europe, we decided to retire from the military here as it is close to our native state of Iowa," said Mary. "During our assignments in Germany, staying at small inns and homes while traveling allowed us to meet people and learn their ways," she said. "Our interest to have our own inn grew over several years."

The home was built in 1865 by a local wheat merchant. It was later owned by one of the partners in the Neal-Johns Wagon Works, which produced 5,000 wagons a year. Since the 1940s, it had changed hands several times. The DeRooses made additional changes and added some personal antiques collected during their own travelers.

Lake City, the birthplace of waterskiing, is located on Lake Pepin in the Mississippi River. With advance notice, the DeRooses will pick up boating guests at the marina. They can help with plans for picnics, biking, antiquing, visits to orchards or wineries, or traveling the Great River Road along the Upper Mississippi. Lake City is about 90 minutes from the Twin Cities.

Blueberry Cherry Pie

Ingredients:

1 double pie crust
2 16-ounce cans water-packed tart cherries, drained
1 12-ounce package frozen "dry pack" blueberries
1-1/2 cups sugar
1/4 cup flour
1-1/2 tablespoons tapioca
1/4 teaspoon salt
1/4 teaspoon almond extract

🞽 Prepare a double pie crust. ("Hint: Refrigerate dough for at least 1 hour to rebuild the shortening particles and create a very flaky crust.")

🞽 In a large bowl, mix cherries, frozen blueberries, sugar, flour, tapioca, salt and extract.

🞽 Pour into pie crust. Cover with top crust, piercing to vent.

🞽 Bake in a preheated oven at 375 degrees for 1 hour or more. Remove from oven and allow to cool quite a bit before slicing and serving.

Tester's Comments: Combining two favorite pies in one is one of those "why didn't I think of this before?" ideas. It's made for ala mode.

Makes 6 to 8 servings

from **The Linen & Lace B&B**
26060 Washington Avenue
Kansasville, WI 53139
414-534-4966

"This is one of those recipes that people ask for," said Innkeeper Nancy Reckhouse. It's a recipe handed down through her family.

The wrap-around porch of this restored farmhouse seems like the place to enjoy her afternoon snack. The porch was falling off when Nancy bought this house, and "all nine pillars were homes to woodpeckers." The roof leaked, the hardwood floors had carpet glued to them, and the horror stories go on and on. But 18 months of hard work later, the Reckhouses have a three-guestroom B&B in the three-story house, set on 4-1/2 acres near Racine.

Nancy, a former teacher and systems analyst, got into innkeeping because "it allows me to do all of the things that I like most." A crafter, she also has a business specializing in one-of-a-kind antique dolls and rabbits. A gardener, she has several gardens on the grounds, all open to curious guests.

🏠*Another Linen & Lace recipe:*
Spicy Pancakes with Sautéed Apples, page 170

Butter Pecan Turtle Cookies

Ingredients:

Crust:
   2 cups flour
   1 cup brown sugar, packed
   1 cup butter, softened
   1 cup pecan halves

Topping:
   1 cup semi-sweet chocolate chips

Caramel:
   2/3 cup butter
   1 cup brown sugar, packed

🍬 For Crust: In a large bowl, mix flour, brown sugar and butter with a fork or pastry cutter until crumbly. Pat down firmly into an ungreased 9 x 13-inch pan. Sprinkle with pecans.

🍬 For Caramel: In a saucepan, mix butter and sugar over medium heat. Stir constantly until the entire surface has boiled hard for 1 minute. Pour mixture over pecans and crust.

🍬 Bake in a preheated oven at 350 degrees for 18 to 22 minutes, until golden brown.

🍬 Remove from oven and immediately sprinkle with chocolate chips. When they have melted a bit, swirl them over the cookies with a knife. Allow to cool completely and cut into squares.

Tester's Comments: These bar cookies taste like chewy toffee candy. It's difficult to improve on perfection, but I "upped" the chocolate chips to 1-1/2 cups to cover every smidgeon of cookie.

Makes 24 squares

from **The Scofield House B&B**
908 Michigan Street
Sturgeon Bay, WI 54235
414-743-7727

"It's hard to keep the cookie jar filled. Fran bakes four to six dozen cookies every other day, plus other treats," said Innkeeper Bill Cecil of his spouse/co-innkeeper. They offer "sweet treats" to guests each day from 4 p.m. on. "That's probably why guests are always back to the house by tea time!" They can sit by the fire or on the porch to enjoy their refreshments.

Bill and Fran rarely get time to put their feet up, however. Their six guestrooms in this 1902 Queen Anne Victorian, plus three rental homes in Baileys Harbor, keep them busy. It has been that way from the start. When they bought the house in 1987, Bill moved in and worked with local workers. He kept working after they left for the day, slept on a cot and ate pork and beans. But just nine weeks after the previous owners moved out, the first guests arrived. Work has since continued, adding baths and an 800-square-foot suite on the third floor. Furnishings are antiques and heirlooms.

🏠*Other Scofield House recipes:*
Apple Cinnamon French Toast, page 153
Baked Bananas, page 204

Butter Tarts

Ingredients:

For Filling:
- 1/2 cup currants
- Boiling water
- 1/4 cup butter
- 1/2 cup brown sugar, lightly packed
- 1/4 teaspoon salt
- 1/2 cup corn syrup
- 1 egg, beaten
- 1/2 teaspoon vanilla extract
- A few drops lemon juice

For Pastry:
- 2 cups flour
- 1 teaspoon salt
- 3/4 cup shortening
- 4 to 5 tablespoons cold water

🍂 For Filling: Pour enough boiling water over the currants to cover. Soak them until the edges begin to turn white, about 5 minutes. Meanwhile, make the pastry.

🍂 For Pastry: Mix flour and salt. Cut in shortening with a pastry cutter or fork. Sprinkle with cold water and mix lightly with a fork until all the flour is dampened. Form into a ball. Chill, if desired. Then roll pastry to 1/8-inch thickness on a floured board. Cut with a 2-1/2-inch circular cookie cutter. Line 24 mini-muffin cups with the circles.

🍂 With an electric mixer, cream butter and brown sugar. Mix in salt, corn syrup, egg, vanilla and lemon juice. Drain currants; fold them in. Spoon filling into unbaked tart shells, filling about 3/4 full.

🍂 Bake in a preheated oven at 375 degrees for 20 to 25 minutes. "Do not allow filling to boil."

Tester's Comments: Bless Bess for sending this delicious recipe. (I almost ate one in Marathon, Ont., but we left them in the car with the dog and she ate every one, with no apology.) I had trouble keeping the tarts from boiling. Bess said a frothy-topped, slightly liquid filling is perfectly OK, and just don't fill pastry too full.

Makes 24 tarts

from **Courthouse Square B&B**
210 East Polk Street
Crandon, WI 54520
715-478-2549

Innkeeper Bess Aho, an Ontario native, serves these at afternoon teas or tucked into the breakfast basket, with two other baked treats. She grew up eating Butter Tarts at Christmas time and enjoys introducing guests to them.

After Les, her husband, took early retirement, the Ahos looked for three years before they found this home for their Northern Wisconsin B&B. It's situated on a six-acre lake in the back with the courthouse square in the front, and it was built in 1905 by a local pharmacist. Bess and Les worked for six months restoring and decorating. "We take great pride in the fact that we did it all ourselves," Bess said. Three antique-filled guestrooms are available. Guests can feed the deer in the park across the street, bike, hike, antique and see spectacular fall colors in the north Wisconsin woods.

Cheese Lace Crackers

Ingredients:

1/2 pound sharp cheddar cheese, grated finely
1/2 cup unsalted butter, cold, cut into bits
1/2 cup flour
1 teaspoon Worchestershire sauce
1/2 teaspoon salt
1/4 teaspoon cayenne pepper

- In a food processor, using the steel cutting blade, blend cheese, butter, flour, Worchestershire, salt and cayenne until ingredients form a ball. (If you have no food processor, use your hands.)
- With the aid of waxed paper, form the mixture into two logs about 6 inches long.
- Chill, covered, at least 2 hours.
- Slice crackers 1/4-inch thick. Place on an cookie sheet sprayed with non-stick cooking spray.
- Bake in a preheated oven at 400 degrees until the crackers are golden brown, about 7 minutes.
- Transfer warm crackers carefully to a wire rack to cool.

Tester's Comments: These are like lace florentine cookies -- you need to find just the right cooking time for your oven and kind of cookie sheets. Underdone and they're rubbery; overdone and you chisel them off. Anyway, they're absolutely delicious. But I didn't dare remove crackers until they were almost completely cool.

Makes 48 crackers

from **Asa Parker House B&B**
17500 St. Croix Trail North
Marine on St. Croix, MN 54047
612-433-5248

Guests at Marjorie Bush's inn are treated to homemade hors d'oeuvres in the parlor of this 1856 home. After hors d'oeuvres, guests may enjoy dinner in nearby Stillwater, another historic St. Croix rivertown, or in the village of Marine, home to 601 residents. The inn is just up the hill from the village center, perfect for a long stroll on a summer evening.

At the inn, a stately Colonial home built by a lumber baron, they can expect picture-perfect decor, fluffy pillows and comforters, and peace and quiet. Guests in the four guestrooms gather in the mansion's dining room for a leisurely homemade breakfast. Marge, a former kindergarten teacher, retired early from teaching and entered the innkeeping profession. The dried Victorian flower arrangements are her own, and guests find special romantic touches throughout the common areas and bedrooms.

Other Asa Parker House recipes:
Marjorie's English Country Scones, page 62
Poached Apples in Vanilla Creme Sauce, page 129
Blueberry Grunt, page 208

Donna's Granola

Ingredients:

8 cups old-fashioned oatmeal
1 cup sesame seeds
1 cup shelled, salted and roasted sunflower seeds
1 cup coconut
1 cup cashews
1 cup chopped walnuts
1/2 cup vegetable oil
1/2 cup honey
1/2 cup peanut butter
1/2 cup apple cider
1 cup dried cranberries ("craisins")
1 cup dried pineapple

- In the largest bowl or kettle in the house, mix the oatmeal, seeds, coconut and nuts.
- In a glass bowl, mix oil, honey, peanut butter and cider. Heat the ingredients in the microwave on high for 5 to 7 minutes or until peanut butter liquefies. Then mix well.
- Pour peanut butter mixture over the dry ingredients. Stir until all ingredients are moist.
- Pour granola into a 9 x 13-inch glass baking dish sprayed with non-stick cooking spray.
- Bake in a preheated oven at 200 degrees for 2 to 2-1/2 hours, depending on the crunchiness desired. Cool. Mix in dried fruit. Store in a covered container.

Makes 3-3/4 quarts

from **Just-N-Trails**
Route 1, Box 274
Sparta, WI 54656
608-269-4522 or 800-488-4521

This recipe is a hybrid of other granola recipes Innkeeper Donna Justin collected. "Recipes that need to be stirred every 10 minutes when baked at 350 degrees resulted in several batches of burnt granola," she said. Guests can mix it with yogurt or homemade applesauce or mixed fruit. "For variety, change the nuts and dried fruits, keeping the same measurements."

Donna has been operating a B&B in the 1920 farmhouse since 1986. She and husband Don bought the neat-as-a-pin dairy farm from his family in 1970; his grandfather had the house built. Over the years, the B&B has grown to five guestrooms in the main house, plus three cottages on the property, one in the former granary. Donna, a former teacher, got into innkeeping after the farm's 130 hilly and wooded untillable acres were opened for cross-country skiing and snow tubing. Soon guests wanted to stay overnight. And they always want to see the cows being milked -- or try it themselves -- and pet the calves. The Elroy-Sparta Bike Trail brings bikers who also want lodging.

Great Pie Crust

<u>*Ingredients:*</u>

2 cups flour
2 cups whole wheat blend flour (part whole wheat, part unbleached white)
1 teaspoon salt
1-3/4 cups vegetable shortening
1 tablespoon cider vinegar
1 egg
1/2 cup cold water

- Mix flours, salt and shortening with a pastry cutter or fork until crumbs are the size of peas.
- In a separate bowl, beat vinegar, egg and water.
- Pour egg mixture into flour, stirring until well-moistened.
- Form dough into a ball. Cover or wrap tightly and chill for at least an hour.
- Split dough into thirds. Roll each third out on a floured board, then place in a pie plate.

Tester's Comments: Rolls out easily. Great for making dough up, refrigerating, then rolling out the next day.

Makes 3 single crusts

from **Martin Oaks B&B**
107 First Street
P.O. Box 207
Dundas, MN 55019
507-645-4644

"This dough keeps well for a few days in the refrigerator and can be frozen for later use as well," said Innkeeper Marie Vogl Gery. She makes it a point to serve a dessert for breakfast, the finalé to a candlelit meal. Sometimes dessert is pie with this crust, which she swears by for any pie or quiche.

In 1990, Marie and spouse Frank bought this home, listed on the National Register of Historic Places and located on the Cannon River. The first portion of Sara Etta Archibald Martin's home was built in 1869, just a few years after Dundas was founded by her brothers and cousin; the "addition," where the three guestrooms are located, was constructed in 1876. At that time, the Dundas mills, where Sara's family patented their milling process, were quite successful. The old mill site, also on the National Register and just across the river from the B&B, burned in 1892, and the patents were sold to a company that is now General Mills.

Marie and Frank encourage guests to take the historic walking tour through this town of 422 or relax on their veranda or in the parlor. Marie, a professional storyteller, can fill them in on both past and present.

Another Martin Oaks recipe:
Lemon Poppyseed Muffins, page 60

229

Hearty Sausage with Apples

Ingredients:

1 pound "rope" sausage or sausage links
1 large Granny Smith or Cortland apple
2 tablespoons brown sugar, lightly packed
Dash of pepper

⚓ If "rope" sausage is used, cut the sausage into 2-inch pieces. In a non-stick skillet, brown the sausage and cook over medium to low heat until thoroughly cooked.

⚓ While the sausage is cooking, wash the apple. Core and slice it into wedges about 1/2-inch thick. "Leave the peeling on for color."

⚓ When the sausage is cooked, drain off all the grease. Place the apple slices in the bottom of the pan with the sausage.

⚓ Sprinkle the brown sugar and pepper over the msausage and apples.

⚓ Mix and cook over medium heat until the apples are browned, yet firm.

⚓ Serve as a side dish while still hot.

Tester's Comments: Apple easily can be doubled, and a tablespoon of maple syrup is a tasty addition.

Makes 4 servings

from **The Geiger House**
401 Denniston Street
Cassville, WI 53806
608-725-5419

"We serve this sausage side-dish with our Stuffed French Toast and fruit cup with honey-yogurt sauce," said Innkeeper Penny Neal. The local meat market makes a wonderful sausage which Penny and Marcus always have on hand.

The Neals have been serving guests since 1992, when they bought the Geiger House. Penny, originally from southern Wisconsin, and Marcus, a Phoenix native, were living a hectic life in St. Paul. "Our goals were to escape the 'big city,' live in a small quiet town, own an old house and have a job where one of us could stay at home." Many of their guests come to tiny Cassville seeking some of the same things, if only for a few days.

The Neals are happy to welcome guests to their 1855 home, which is decorated with primitive and country antiques that "give guests that cozy 'feather-bed' feeling," Penny said. The views from the four guestrooms are of the Mississippi River valley and the bluffs. The river is just steps away.

🏠*Other Geiger House recipes:*
Rhubarb Juice, page 28
Black Olive Quiche, page 137

Herbed Cheese Puffs

Ingredients:

    1 4-ounce package of Parmesan cheese, grated
    1 4-ounce package Romano cheese, grated
    1 cup mayonnaise
    1 teaspoon fresh basil
    1 teaspoon fresh oregano
    9 green onions
    3 cloves garlic
    1 package Pillsbury Tender Layer Buttermilk Biscuits, cocktail rye bread or puff pastry squares

- In a heavy-duty food processor, blend cheeses, mayonnaise, basil, oregano, onions and garlic.

- Separate each biscuit into 3 pieces. Spread mixture on each piece.

- Place on a greased cookie sheet. Bake in a preheated oven at 350 degrees until puffed and golden, about 20 minutes. Serve hot.

Tester's Comments: My husband thought this was one of the best things I've made in testing recipes for four cookbooks. I used 2 teaspoons each of dried herbs. I had trouble separating biscuits into 3 pieces (1 very thin layer was fine, 2 layers were too thick). Triscuits as a base were good. Adjust garlic for your own palate.

Makes about 3 dozen servings

from **Bluff Creek Inn**
1161 Bluff Creek Drive
Chaska, MN 55318
612-445-2735

These hot appetizers might be served to guests on the sideporch in the summer or by the fire in the parlor stove in the winter. Innkeeper Anne Delaney prefers using the biscuits, but notes the spread could top just about any "base" that creative, experimenting cooks want to try.

In addition to scrumptious snacks, Anne serves up a four-course breakfast that keeps guests coming back. She also puts her culinary skills to use in special dinners for small weddings or other events. And she enjoys cooking up romantic getaways. She's decorated the four guestrooms in this picturesque 1860 farmhouse in designer linens and family antiques.

This place must be good for romance. Anne is a newlywed herself, having met and courted Gary here. Since she never had weekends open, "I told him, 'If you want to see me, you'll have to come here to help!'" The innkeeping lifestyle agreed with him. Together they added a separate guest cottage to the property, which was originally deeded by President Abraham Lincoln.

Other Bluff Creek Inn recipes:
Apricot Baked French Toast, page 154
Bubbly Holiday Punch, page 186

Leonard Date Cookies

Ingredients:

1 cup butter
2 cups brown sugar, packed
2 eggs
1 teaspoon vanilla extract
3-1/2 cups flour
1 teaspoon salt
1 teaspoon baking soda
1 cup chopped dates
1 cup finely chopped nuts

- Cream butter and brown sugar together until fluffy.
- Beat in eggs and vanilla.
- In a separate bowl, combine flour, salt and baking soda. Mix into butter mixture.
- Stir in dates and nuts.
- Shape into rolls. Wrap in waxed paper. Place in freezer to firm dough before slicing.
- Slice cold dough about 1/4-inch thick and place on greased cookie sheets.
- Bake in a preheated oven for 375 degrees for 8 to 10 minutes. Remove from cookie sheets and cool.

Tester's Comments: Even folks who aren't fond of dates will enjoy these.

Makes 4 dozen cookies

from **Bed & Breakfast at The Pines**
327 Ardussi Street
Frankenmuth, MI 48734
517-652-9019

"When my parents got their first electric refrigerator, it was a Leonard, and a little cookbook came with the appliance," said Innkeeper Donna Hodge. "It seems the only thing that survived was this cookie recipe. I try to always have several rolls of cookie dough in the freezer, so I can bake them for guests at any time. My kids almost preferred the raw cookies to the baked ones!"

Donna and Richard's kids are grown and married now, but their bedrooms have been converted to three guestrooms at this B&B. Hodges had traveled in B&Bs in Scotland and Ontario, and they liked the concept. Their home is a traditional ranch-style, built in 1959, in a quiet neighborhood. Their large yards with evergreens and perennials also grows roses for guestrooms. Frankenmuth's Bavarian Inn and Zehnder's family-style dinners, Bronner's Christmas store and Birch Run's outlet mall shopping are all nearby.

Another Bed & Breakfast at The Pines recipe:
Golden Squash Raisin Bread, page 85

Oatmeal Raisin Cookies

Ingredients:

1/2 cup golden raisins
3/4 cup orange juice
2 eggs
1 cup sugar
1 cup brown sugar, packed
3/4 cup canola oil
2 cups flour
2 cups corn flakes
1 cup quick-cooking oatmeal
1 cup coconut
1 teaspoon salt
1 teaspoon baking soda
1/2 teaspoon baking powder
1 vanilla bean, split and seeds removed

☛ In a small saucepan, "plump" the raisins in the orange juice, simmering over low heat for about 15 minutes. When raisins are plump, remove from heat and drain off remaining juice.

☛ In a large mixing bowl, combine eggs, sugar, brown sugar and oil.

☛ Mix in flour, corn flakes, oatmeal, coconut, salt, soda, baking powder and vanilla bean. Mix well. Then mix in the drained raisins.

☛ Lightly spray cookie sheets with cooking oil spray. Drop the dough by teaspoonfuls onto the baking sheet, leaving room for cookies to spread.

☛ Bake in a preheated oven at 350 degrees for 10 to 12 minutes or until golden brown.

Tester's Comments: Great for a breakfast cookie on busy mornings. The corn flakes manage to stay crunchy.

Makes 100 2-inch cookies

from **Wickwood Country Inn**
510 Butler Street
P.O. Box 1019
Saugatuck, MI 49453
616-857-1465 or FAX 616-857-4168

"This was my Grandmother's recipe and we ate mountains of them," said Julee Rosso Miller. "Hers had lots of butter, but this version still disappears."

Cookies or another bedtime snack appear in each of the 11 guestrooms, and the aroma of baking wafts through the inn daily. Guests also are treated to hors d'oeurves and breakfasts of Silver Palate fame (Julee co-founded the store). The inn uses local farmer's market produce as much as possible.

🏠*Other Wickwood Inn recipes:*
Blueberry Cake, page 36
Sunday Pecan Coffeecake, page 45
Spicy Artichoke Dip, page 238

Oven-Roasted New Potatoes

Ingredients:

    5 pounds red new potatoes per person
    1/2 cup olive oil
    2 teaspoons dried or 1/4 cup fresh basil, chopped
    1 tablespoon dried rosemary
    1 teaspoon salt
    1 teaspoon pepper

- Wash potatoes and cut into quarters.
- Place in a large bowl. Add oil and toss to coat thoroughly.
- Then add rosemary, basil, salt and pepper and toss.
- Place potatoes in baking pans coated with non-stick cooking spray. Spread out so potatoes are in one or two layers only.
- Bake in a preheated oven at 375 degrees for 1 hour or until potatoes are slightly browned on edges.
- Turn oven down to 140 to 170 degrees to keep warm for serving.

Tester's Comments: Garlic powder and Parmesan cheese are good additions, especially for later in the day. I used 4 to 5 potatoes per person for a family-sized recipe.

Makes 15 servings

from **The Inn at Union Pier**
9708 Berrien Street
P.O. Box 222
Union Pier, MI 49129
616-469-4700 or FAX 616-469-4720

A side-dish like these potatoes often is part of the hearty breakfasts served in the dining room here. Innkeepers Joyce Erickson Pitts and Mark Pitts like to serve Michigan fruits, vegetables and locally-made dairy and meat products as often as possible. Breakfast might start with a fruit dish and freshly baked muffins, followed by a gourmet entree.

The Inn, close to Lake Michigan, draws guests year 'round. Summer guests are invited to bring their swimsuits, and the inn provides beach towels. In the cooler months, guests enjoy the Kakelugn (Swedish ceramic fireplaces) in many of the guestrooms and dining room.

Joyce and Mark bought this inn in 1993 after a long search for the right place. They left fast-paced careers in Chicago for "the slow lane" in Union Pier.

Other Inn at Union Pier recipes:
Amaretto Sour Cream Sauce, page 102
Mexican Mini Frittatas, page 145

Pecan Crescent Cookies

Ingredients:

1 cup butter
1/2 cup sugar (plus extra for decoration)
1 teaspoon vanilla extract
1 tablespoon water
2 cups flour
2 cups chopped pecans
1/8 teaspoon salt

- Using an electric mixer, cream butter, sugar and vanilla.
- Add water, flour, pecans and salt. Mix thoroughly.
- Using about 1 large teaspoonful of dough, roll dough into crescent shape.
- Place crescents on an ungreased cookie sheet at least an inch apart from each other.
- Bake in a preheated oven at 325 degrees for 10 to 15 minutes, until just slightly brown.
- Cool cookies, then roll in extra sugar.

Tester's Comments: These are rich and sugary, almost like shortbread. Using ground pecans makes rolling easier.

Makes 3 dozen cookies

from **Heirloom Inn B&B**
1103 South Third Street
Stillwater, MN 55082
612-430-2289

"These are wonderful with afternoon tea, cocoa or cider," said Sandie Brown. "We often keep these in the cookie jar for guests to help themselves." She and Mark obtained the recipe from friends in Maine. "We have fond memories of eating these with cider in the fall, sitting with friends around their fireplace."

Guests at the Brown's inn may enjoy these by the fire, too, sitting on red velvet Victorian settees and chairs, or, in warm weather, out on the wicker-filled screened porch. Their home, built after the Civil War, is a lovely example of Italianate architecture. Their four-year restoration process is an example of how lovely an historic home can again become. Everywhere, there is rich wood, from the high headboards on the antique beds to the inlaid parquet flooring in the parlors. The Browns have rebuilt porches, reroofed and had the exterior painted four colors, as well as other major projects.

"We have been staying at B&Bs throughout the country and Canada for more than 13 years," Sandie said about their interest in innkeeping. "We enjoy the lifestyle, antiques, good food and meeting new people."

Another Heirloom Inn recipe:
German Coffeecake, page 40

Sari's Taco Roll-Ups

Ingredients:

16 ounces "lite" cream cheese
16 ounces "lite" sour cream
1 4-ounce can chopped green chiles
1 bunch green onions, chopped
2 cups shredded cheese, Cheddar, hot pepper or taco-flavored
1 package taco seasoning mix
1 package 8-inch tortillas

Also:

Favorite salsa

- In a large bowl, blend cream cheese, sour cream, chiles, green onions, cheese and seasoning mix.
- Spread the mixture on tortillas.
- Roll up the tortillas into miniature jelly-rolls. Cover and chill.
- Cut each rolled tortilla into 1- to 1-1/2-inch pieces. Serve with salsa on the side for dipping.

Tester's Comments: Adding chopped ripe olives is good, too. Pack a whole tortilla (uncut) for a veggie lunch.

Makes about 70 bite-sized pieces

from **The American House**
410 East Third Street
Morris, MN 56267
612-589-4054

These hors d'oeuvres easily can be made ahead and "they are nice to keep on hand for guests who arrive after a long drive and haven't had a chance to stop for dinner yet," said Innkeeper Karen Berget.

Karen and husband Kyle opened their home as a B&B in 1984 after six months work. Built in 1901, the house had 11 previous owners, one of whom was a wealthy farmer and judge who moved into town for the winter so his children could attend school. The home was a duplex when the Bergets bought it.

But Karen, who grew up in Stillwater, the St. Croix River town with many restored mansions, knew what potential it had. They moved walls, replastered, soundproofed and did other restoration. They found a walnut and oak "picture frame" parquet floor and hand-stenciled walls in the dining room. Karen has stenciled the walls in the three guestrooms. The rooms are named after their grandparents and furnished with antiques.

The Bergets named their B&B after Morris' first hotel, built in 1875. The University of Minnesota-Morris is two blocks away, and guests can use the tandem bike to get there or anywhere else nearby they want to go.

Scottish Shortbread

Ingredients:

1/2 cup butter, at room temperature
1/3 cup powdered sugar, unsifted
1/4 teaspoon vanilla extract
7/8 cup flour, unsifted
2 tablespoons cornstarch

Also:

Powdered sugar

- Using a spoon, cream butter until light and fluffy.
- Blend in powdered sugar, then vanilla.
- On an unfloured board, work in flour and cornstarch by hand. Knead until smooth.
- Spray or grease a shortbread pan or 8- or 9-inch pan. Press shortbread dough into the pan. Prick entire surface with a fork.
- Bake at 325 degrees for 30 to 35 minutes, until lightly browned. Remove from oven and cut into pie-shaped wedges or squares while still warm. Let cool for almost completely before removing from the pan. Sprinkle with powdered sugar. Store in a covered container.

Tester's Comments: Incredibly rich, and the chocolate glaze I drizzled on wasn't necessary. A perfect recipe for a 3-year-old assistant (mine loved the kneading and patting). Shortbread crumbles easily when warm.

Makes 8 wedges or 9 squares

from **Quill & Quilt**
615 West Hoffman Street
Cannon Falls, MN 55009
507-263-5507 or 800-488-3849

"This is my combination of a lot of different shortbread recipes, none of which I liked as well as this one," said Innkeeper Denise Anderson. "We took a sailing vacation off the coast of Maine a number of years ago and the cook on board made shortbread on a woodburning stove. It was great! I kept trying until I could recreate it -- minus the woodstove, of course!"

In June 1994, Marcia and Dennis Flom bought the inn. Guests at the four-guestroom inn, built in 1897, might enjoy treats in front of the fireplace or out on the porch swing, depending on the season. They have probably finished off a perfect day, biking the Cannon Valley Bike Trail, tubing or canoeing the Cannon River, antiquing, or perhaps driving up to explore the gigantic Mall of America in Bloomington. Cannon Falls provides small town ambiance only about 40 minutes from the downtowns of Minneapolis or St. Paul.

Another Quill & Quilt recipe:
Cranberry Holiday Punch, page 189

Spicy Artichoke Dip

Ingredients:

2 cups (2 cans) artichoke hearts (not marinated), drained
1/4 cup fresh dill, washed
1 cup mayonnaise
1 cup grated Parmesan cheese
1-1/2 teaspoons freshly-squeezed lemon juice
1 teaspoon garlic salt

- Chop the artichokes and mince the dill. Set aside.
- Combine mayonnaise, Parmesan, lemon juice and garlic salt. Stir in the artichokes and dill.
- Put the mixture into a 1-quart or bigger casserole. Bake in a preheated oven at 350 degrees for 35 to 40 minutes.
- Serve hot with crackers.

Makes 4 cups

from **Wickwood Country Inn**
510 Butler Street
P.O. Box 1019
Saugatuck, MI 49453
616-857-1465 or FAX 616-857-4168

Every evening, Wickwood guests are treated to "appetite-teasers and nibbles" in the Library, one of the inn's four common rooms, or perhaps out on the screened gazebo or porch in the summertime. Guests can relax and chat a bit before heading off to one of Saugatuck's varied restaurants, a chamber music or jazz concert or theater -- or to a Lake Michigan beach to watch the sunset.

Whatever season draws guests to the Victorian resort town -- and there's plenty to do all year -- Wickwood is open and ready to welcome them. In the summer, wicker on the porch beckons travelers to slow down and "set a spell." For the holidays, each of the 11 guestrooms has a Christmas tree.

Breakfasts, all year 'round, are nothing less than guests would expect from the co-author of the Silver Palate cookbook series, Julee Rosso Miller, who owns the inn with husband Bill Miller. But it's as much the little things -- a fire in the fireplace, bedtime snacks, the morning newspaper at your door, breakfast served at your preferred time -- that the innkeepers insist on for traditional country inn hospitality.

Other Wickwood Inn recipes:
Blueberry Cake page 36
Sunday Pecan Coffeecake, page 45
Oatmeal Raisin Cookies, page 233

To-Die-For Chocolate Chip Cookies

Ingredients:

1 cup butter or margarine
1 cup sugar
1 cup brown sugar, packed
2 eggs
1 teaspoon vanilla extract
2-1/2 cups oatmeal, quick-cooking or old-fashioned
2 cups flour
4 ounces grated plain milk chocolate bar, like Ghiradelli
1 teaspoon baking soda
1 teaspoon baking powder
1/2 teaspoon salt
12 ounces semi-sweet chocolate chips

- In a large bowl, cream butter and sugars. Add eggs and vanilla and beat until fluffy and light.
- Pulverize or grind the oatmeal in a blender or food processor so it resembles flour.
- In a separate bowl, mix pulverized oatmeal, flour, grated chocolate bar, baking soda, baking powder and salt.
- Slowly add the flour mixture to the egg mixture. Beat until well combined. Dough will be thick.
- Stir in the chocolate chips by hand. Mix well.
- Drop dough in golf-ball-sized spoonfuls on an ungreased insulated cookie sheet.
- Bake in a preheated oven at 375 degrees for 10 to 12 minutes. Cool cookies on the sheet for 2 or 3 minutes before removing to a rack or shelf.

Tester's Comments: After trying these, my sister, a fellow chocoholic, says no more "regular" chocolate chip cookies for her. The cookies are moist and rich.

Makes about 2 dozen large cookies

from **Oakhurst Inn B&B**
212 8th Avenue South
Princeton, MN 55371
612-389-3553 or 800-443-2258

Every evening at this B&B, these cookies can be found on the bedside table or tucked in a goodie basket delivered to the room. They are the inn's signature treat, said Innkeepers Suzie and Dave Spain. Oakhurst Inn was named for the white oaks surrounding it. Built by a local banker in 1906, the home needed two years of renovation before the Spains could open in 1991 with three guestrooms. The wrap-around porch invites sitting in the summer, and the front parlor has a fireplace glowing in cooler seasons. Princeton is in central Minnesota, about an hour from the Twin Cities. Guests are welcome to use the inn's bikes and horseshoe pit.

Index

Contents by Inn

Traveling to these B&Bs?

The B&Bs featured in this book were members of one or more of the three state B&B associations at the time they were selected for inclusion. The Michigan and Wisconsin associations have adopted standards and require inspections of member inns, and they publish an annual directory.

In addition to contacting the state travel offices listed below for information, check your bookstore's regional section for B&B guidebooks which do not charge B&Bs to be included. Also, visitor bureaus or chambers of commerce in cities or towns you wish to visit can provide information about their member inns.

This information is provided only as a service to readers looking for more information; none of the associations or bureaus listed below have paid to be mentioned here.

Michigan:

🏠 **Lake to Lake B&B Association of Michigan**
7900 S. Lakeshore Dr.
Cedar, MI 49621
For the annual Michigan B&B Directory, send $3 per directory to B&B Directory, P.O. Box 428, Saugatuck, MI 49453, or call 1-800-83-BOOKS (832-6657) with a Visa/MasterCard (answered by voice mail only).

Michigan Travel Bureau
Department of Commerce
P.O. Box 3393
Livonia, MI 48151-3393
1-800-5432-YES (937)

Minnesota:

🏠 **Minnesota B&B Guild**
c/o Gary Delaney
Bluff Creek Inn
1161 Bluff Creek Dr.
Chaska, MN 55318

Minnesota Office of Tourism
100 Metro Square Building,
121 Seventh Place East
St. Paul, MN 55101-2112
612-296-5029 or 800-657-3700

Wisconsin:

🏠 **Wisconsin B&B Homes and Historic Inns Assoc.**
c/o Jim Stahlman
Yankee Hill B&B Inn
405 Collins Street
Plymouth, WI 53073

Wisconsin Division of Tourism
123 W. Washington Ave.
P.O. Box 7970
Madison, WI 53707
1-800-ESCAPES (372-2737)
Distributes the free directory published by WBBHHIA.

Ordering Information

☛ *WAKE UP & SMELL THE COFFEE - Lake States Edition* makes a great gift for cookbook collectors, B&B lovers, armchair travelers and breakfast eaters everywhere.

      Cost: $15.95 plus $2.00 postage and handling = $17.95 per book
      Books are sent special fourth class rate. Please allow several weeks for delivery.
      For UPS ground service delivery, please add $4.00 = $19.95 per book

COMPLETE YOUR COLLECTION!

If you enjoyed this book, you'll love *WAKE UP & SMELL THE COFFEE - Upper Midwest Edition, Southwest Edition* and *Pacific Northwest Edition.*

      ☛ **Upper Midwest** Edition has 180+ great breakfast, brunch and other favorite recipes from 86 inns in Wisconsin, Minnesota, Michigan, Illinois and Iowa. The format is the same as this book.

      Cost: $14.95 plus $2.00 postage and handling = $16.95 per book
      UPS ground service delivery, please add $4.00 = $18.95 per book

      ☛ **Southwest** Edition boasts more than 170 recipes from 65 B&Bs in Texas, Arizona and New Mexico, along with the helpful cooking hints and interesting details on each inn.

      Cost: $14.95 plus $2.00 postage and handling = $16.95 per book
      UPS ground service delivery, please add $4.00 = $18.95 per book

      ☛ **Pacific Northwest** Edition features more than 130 of innkeepers' best recipes from 58 B&Bs in Washington and Oregon. Information on each B&B is included in this edition, too.

      Cost: $11.95 plus $2.00 postage and handling = $13.95 per book
      UPS ground service delivery, please add $4.00 = $15.95 per book

TO ORDER BY PHONE using a credit card, call Voyageur Press in Stillwater, Minn., 1-800-888-9653 toll-free. (Shipping charges may vary from those listed above.)

TO ORDER BY MAIL, send a check to Down to Earth Publications, 1032 W. Montana, St. Paul, MN 55117. Make checks payable to Down to Earth Publications. MN residents please add 7% sales tax.

Mail to: Down to Earth Publications
             1032 W. Montana
             St. Paul, MN 55117

Please send me

      ____ "WAKE UP & SMELL THE COFFEE - *Lake States* Edition" at $17.95 each by 4th class mail ($19.95 each sent UPS ground service)
      ____ "WAKE UP & SMELL THE COFFEE - *Upper Midwest* Edition" at $16.95 each by 4th class mail ($18.95 each sent UPS ground service)
      ____ "WAKE UP & SMELL THE COFFEE - *Southwest* Edition" at $16.95 each by 4th class mail ($18.95 each sent UPS ground service)
      ____ "WAKE UP & SMELL THE COFFEE - *Pacific Northwest* Edition" at $13.95 each by 4th class mail ($15.95 each sent UPS ground service)

I have enclosed $_____ for _____ book(s). Send it/them to:

Name: _____

Street: _____ Apt. No. _____

City: _____ State: _____ Zip: _____
      (Please note: No P.O. Boxes for UPS delivery)

About the author

Laura Zahn discovered the wonderful "Breakfast" part of "Bed & Breakfast" while traveling the backroads of Minnesota, Wisconsin and Illinois to write her "Room at the Inn/Minnesota," "Room at the Inn/Wisconsin" and "Room at the Inn/Galena Area" guidebooks to historic B&Bs and country inns.

In St. Paul, Minn., she is president of Down to Earth Publications, a writing, publishing and public relations firm specializing in travel. Her travelwriting has appeared in many U.S. newspapers and magazines. Zahn has worked in public relations in Minnesota and as a reporter and editor on newspapers in Alaska and Minnesota.

"Wake Up and Smell the Coffee - Lakes States Edition" is her ninth book. It is the fourth in the "Wake Up & Smell the Coffee" series of regional books, following the Upper Midwest, Pacific Northwest and Southwest Editions. In addition to her three "Room at the Inn" guides (now out of print) and "The Ride Guide to the Historic Alaska Railroad," which she co-authored, she is the author of the award-winning "Bringing Baby Home: An Owner's Manual for First-Time Parents."

A native of Saginaw, Michigan, she passed a written test to win the "Betty Crocker Homemaker of the Year" award in high school and says, "Now I've finally done something remotely related, besides tour the Betty Crocker kitchens." She graduated from Northern Michigan University in Marquette. She shares her St. Paul home with Jim Miller, her geologist husband; Jay Edward Miller, who helped test some of the recipes; and Kirby Puckett Zahn Miller, who was proudly adopted from the Humane Society of Ramsey County on the day the Minnesota Twins won the American League pennant in 1987.